CONTENTS

TABLE OF CASES

Cases reported under initial names only are listed under plaintiff's surname, followed by respondent's surname, e.g H. (I.) v. G. (M.)

Table of Cases

Table of Cases

Table of Cases

TABLE OF STATUTES

Table of Statutes

TABLE OF STATUTORY INSTRUMENTS

TABLE OF INTERNATIONAL CONVENTIONS

TABLE OF ARTICLES OF THE CONSTITUTION

CHAPTER ONE

THE FAMILY

The Scope of Family Law

Despite the various meanings given to the word 'family' in modern society, Irish family law is mainly concerned with the family unit of husband and wife and their children, if any. Family law embraces the rights and obligations which flow from marriage. The traditional importance attached to the institution of marriage is illustrated by the vast amount of rules that have been developed, both by the Courts and the legislature, to govern the formation, functioning and dissolution of marriage. Family law is also concerned with the transfer of a child from one family to another by means of adoption, and the acquisition of parental rights by persons outside the family by way of guardianship, custody and wardship. Other social issues, such as domestic violence, the so-called 'one parent family', children in need of care and protection and the rights of cohabitees, have come to be the concern of Courts administering family law.

The Family Defined

Despite the fact that 'the family' is referred to in Articles 41 and 42 of the Constitution, nowhere in these Articles is the term defined. Accordingly, it has been left to the Courts to come up with a definition. The decided cases on the matter, most notably the *State (Nicolaou) v. An Bord Uchtála* (1966), make it clear that 'the family' referred to is that based on marriage (the nuclear family). This definition excludes the natural family or the family outside marriage. Nicolaou, as the natural father of a non-marital child, had challenged the constitutionality of the Adoption Act 1952 which allowed for the adoption of his child without his consent. The Supreme Court rejected his claim on the basis that he had no constitutional rights to his child. Accordingly, a cohabiting couple and their children, if any, are not to be regarded as a family under Irish law. In *G. v. An Bord Uchtála* (1980), O'Higgins CJ stated that Article 41 'refers exclusively to the family founded and based on the institution of marriage'. More recently, in *W. O'R. v. E.H.* (1996), the Supreme Court restated this traditional view of the family, where Hamilton CJ stated that a *de facto* family is not recognised by the Constitution.

Despite the ruling of the European Court of Human Rights in *Keegan v. Ireland*

(1994), that the State was in breach of Article 8 of the European Convention on Human Rights and Fundamental Freedoms (which embraces both marital and non-marital families), in failing to protect an unmarried father's 'right to respect for his private and family life' by providing that he be consulted in the adoption process, the Supreme Court's definition of 'the family' in *Nicolaou* continues to be the law on the matter. It should be noted that the Adoption Act 1998 now provides for consultation with the natural father in certain circumstances. This topic is considered in detail in Chapter 13.

The Courts have interpreted Article 41 as conferring rights on the family as a unit and not on the individuals who make up that unit. In *Murray v. Ireland* (1985), Costello J said that the rights referred to in Article 41 'belong to the institution itself as distinct from the personal rights which each individual member might enjoy by virtue of membership of the family'. Similarly, in *L. v. L.* (1992), Finlay CJ emphasised that Article 41 does not 'grant to any individual member of the family rights . . . against other members of the family, but rather deals with the protection of the family from external forces'.

Constitutional Protection

Article 41 of the Constitution recognises the family 'as the natural primary fundamental unit group of society', and as a 'moral institution possessing certain inalienable and imprescriptible rights' which are 'antecedent and superior to all positive law'. In *Ryan v. Attorney General* (1965), Kenny J said that 'inalienable' meant 'that which cannot be transferred or given away' and that 'imprescriptible' meant 'that which cannot be lost by the passage of time'. In Article 41.1.2. the State guarantees to protect the family in its constitution and authority 'as the necessary basis of social order and as indispensable to the welfare of the Nation and State'. Article 42 acknowledges that 'the primary and natural educator of the child is the Family'.

In recent years, there has been a number of constitutional challenges to legislation on the grounds that certain provisions of the impugned legislation amounted to a failure by the State to honour its pledge in Article 41 to protect the family. In *Dennehy v. The Minister for Social Welfare* (1984), the High Court rejected the claim of a deserted husband that certain sections of the Social Welfare (Consolidation) Act 1981, which made provision for deserted wives but not for deserted husbands in similar circumstances, were unconstitutional. Barron J held that the more favourable treatment of deserted wives was justified both by the provisions of Article 41.2, which assigns to woman a special role as wife and homemaker, and Article 40.1, which recognises a difference in capacity and social function. The Supreme Court finally got an opportunity of addressing the issues which were raised in the *Dennehy* case in *Lowth v. The Minister for Social Welfare* (1998). The facts were similar and much the same legal submissions on the constitutionality of the Social Welfare (Consolidation) Act 1981 were made in both cases. The evidence presented in the High Court in *Lowth* showed clearly how women in employment at the material times mentioned in the case were at a financial disadvantage in comparison to men. The Supreme Court held that it is settled law that Article 40.1 does not require that all citizens be treated equally, and that there were ample grounds for the Oireachtas to conclude that deserted wives were, in general, likely to have greater needs than deserted husbands so as to justify providing social welfare payments to meet such needs. In *T.F. v. Ireland* (1995), the Supreme Court rejected the contention that section 2(1)(f) of the Judicial Separation and Family Law Reform Act 1989, which allowed for judicial separation on a no-fault basis, constituted an attack on the institution of marriage on which the family is based. See Chapter 6.

The effectiveness of the State's guarantee in Article 41 to protect the family based on marriage is aptly demonstrated by the Supreme Court decision in *Re Article 26 and the Matrimonial Home Bill 1993* (1994). The Court, on a referral to it by the President under Article 26, ruled that the Bill, which purported to give each spouse automatic joint ownership of the matrimonial home and the household effects, was repugnant to Article 41, as it was a disproportionate intervention by the State in the rights of the family and constituted a failure by the State to protect the authority of the family. The Court went on to stress that the right of a married couple to make a joint decision as to the ownership of the matrimonial home is a right possessed by the family and that the exercise of this right is an important part of the authority of the family.

The Marital Family

Although the Constitution guarantees the family's rights, it does not enumerate these rights. Again, it has been left to the Courts to spell out exactly what these rights are. Some examples are discussed here, but this should not be considered to be an exhaustive list — the rights of the family are constantly the subject of interpretation by the Courts.

Marital Privacy

The right to marital privacy was recognised in *McGee v. Attorney General* (1974). In that case, the Supreme Court upheld the plaintiff's claim that section 17(3) of the Criminal Law Amendment Act 1935, which prohibited the importation of artificial contraceptives, was repugnant to Article 41 as it interfered with the authority of the family, in this instance the right of the husband and wife to decide how many children, if any, they might have. In the course of his judgment, Walsh J said that a decision by a husband and wife to limit their family or to avoid having children by the use of contraceptives 'is a matter peculiarly within the joint decision of the husband and wife and one into which the State cannot intrude unless its intrusion can be justified by the exigencies of the common good'.

The Right to Procreate

The right of a married couple to procreate, a personal right protected by Article 40.3.1., was recognised in *Murray v. Attorney General* (1985). The plaintiffs in that case were both serving life sentences for the murder of a member of the Garda Síochána. They claimed that the prison authorities had a duty to allow them to consort together for the purposes of procreation. In rejecting their claim, the High Court held that the right to procreate could be suspended while they served their sentences, as constitutional rights in general were not absolute and could be suspended in the interests of the common good.

Income Tax

The right of a married couple to be treated no less favourably for income tax purposes than a cohabiting couple was recognised in *Murphy v. Attorney General* (1982). The Supreme Court held that the provisions of the Income Tax Act 1967, which provided for the aggregation for income tax purposes of the income of a married couple while not requiring aggregation in the case of a cohabiting couple, were repugnant to Article 41. Such treatment, the Court held, could be regarded as 'a breach of the pledge by the State to guard with special care the institution of marriage and to protect it against attack'.

Consortium

An important right possessed by a married couple, which is guaranteed by Article 41 of the Constitution, is the right to consortium. Consortium was described by Kingsmill Moore J in *O'Haran v. Devine* (1966) as 'the sum total of the benefits which a husband and wife may be expected to confer on each other, such as, help, comfort, companionship, services and all the amenities of family and marriage'. In that case, the Supreme Court held that a husband was entitled to damages for loss of consortium in respect of his separation from his wife for a period of forty two weeks while she recovered in hospital and recuperated from injuries sustained in a motor accident. In *McKinley v. Minister for Defence* (1992), the Supreme Court held that the common law right of a husband to sue for loss of consortium was, by virtue of the principle of equality enshrined in Article 40 of the Constitution and the special recognition afforded to marriage by Article 41 of the Constitution, extended to a wife. In *Coppinger v. Waterford County Council* (1996), the High Court awarded £60,000 to a wife for the loss of consortium of her husband as a result of serious injuries sustained by him in a motor accident.

Guardianship and Custody

The right to guardianship (parental rights and duties in relation to a child) and custody (the right to physical care and control of a child) of children is conferred jointly on married parents under section 6 of the Guardianship of Infants Act 1964, as amended. The Act merely gives legislative expression to the constitutional right to guardianship and custody enunciated in Articles 41 and 42. See Chapter 14.

Education

The right of the marital family to provide for the education of the children of their union is provided for in Article 42.1. of the Constitution as follows:

> The State acknowledges that the primary and natural educator of the child is the Family and guarantees to respect the inalienable right and duty of parents to provide, according to their means, for the religious and moral, intellectual, physical and social education of their children.

The Supreme Court held in *Re Article 26 and the School Attendance Bill 1942* (1943) that it is only where the parents fail in their duty towards their children that the State can intervene under Article 42.3.2 to ensure that the children receive a 'certain minimum education'. In *Director of Public Prosecutions v. Best* (1999), a case which involved the prosecution of a mother for not sending her children to school, the Supreme Court was called on to construe the meaning of the words 'suitable elementary education' as used in section 17 of the School Attendance Act 1926. The mother defended the case on the basis that she was exercising her constitutional right to educate the children at home under Article 42 by providing them with a 'certain minimum education'. Denham J, in her judgment, said that in her view the minimum standard of education required by the 1926 Act was not necessarily equivalent to the primary school curriculum, and that a District Judge hearing a case under the 1926 Act should have expert evidence as to what, in the circumstances of that particular case, amounted to a 'suitable elementary education' before deciding to acquit or convict.

The Non-Marital Family

Irish society has undergone some radical changes in modern times, of which the recent introduction of divorce is but one example. An increasing number of people choose to live together and have children outside the institution of marriage. What is the legal position of a man and woman who live together without marrying? If they live together ostensibly as 'husband and wife', the relationship is often referred to as a 'common law' marriage. This concept, however, is not recognised under Irish law, as is evident from the judgment of Henchy J in *Nicolaou* where he stated: ' I am satisfied that no union or grouping of people is entitled to be designated a family for the purposes of the Article if it is founded on any relationship other than that of marriage', and later where he added:

> For the State to award equal constitutional protection to the family founded on marriage and the 'family' founded on an extra-marital union would in effect be a disregard of the pledge which the State gives in Article 41.3.1. to guard with special care the institution of marriage.

In view of the fact that the non-marital family is not protected by Article 41, the natural father and natural mother and their children, if any, must look elsewhere for constitutional protection.

Natural Father and Child

It is clear from the judgment of Walsh J in *Nicolaou*, where he stated: ' It has not been shown to the satisfaction of this Court that the father of an illegitimate child has any natural right, as distinct from legal rights, to either the custody or society of that child', that the natural father has no constitutional rights to his child. In *J.K. v. V.W.* (1990), the Supreme Court repeated the position espoused in *Nicolaou* that the natural father did not have any constitutional rights to his child. While the Court recognised that there may be rights of interest or concern arising from the blood link between the father and the child, the father did not have a constitutional right to guardianship. Although the natural father does not have any constitutional right to his child, Walsh J stated in *G. v. An Bord Uchtála* (1980) that the child has a natural right to look to his natural father for support.

The natural father has a number of statutory rights regarding his child. He has a defeasible statutory right under section 6A of the Guardianship of Infants Act 1964 (which was inserted by section 12 of the Status of Children Act 1987) to apply to the Court to be appointed guardian of his child. In *W.O'R. v. E.H.* (1996), the Supreme Court endorsed the finding of the Court in *J.K. v. V.W.*, and held that the rights of interest or concern that existed between a natural father and his child were matters that could be taken into account in determining the welfare of the children when the father applied for guardianship, custody of or access to the children. Under section 4 of the Children Act 1997 the natural father may now become guardian by agreement with the mother. The Adoption Act 1998 provides that in certain circumstances the natural father must be consulted and afforded the opportunity of applying to the Court to be appointed guardian of his child. The natural father, who has not become guardian by Court order or agreement with the mother, may apply under section 10 of the Adoption Act 1991 to adopt his own child.

Natural Mother and Child

The position of the unmarried mother in relation to her child was considered by the Supreme Court in *G. v. An Bord Uchtála* (1980). In his judgment O'Higgins CJ said that the mother, who had sought the return of her child which she had placed for adoption, 'is not the mother of a family, in the sense in which that term is used in the Constitution', but acknowledged that she 'is a mother and, as such, she has rights which derive from the fact of motherhood and from nature itself'. The Chief Justice identified these rights as among her personal rights under Article 40.3.1 which the State is bound to respect, defend and vindicate, and acknowledged that the mother 'had a natural right to the custody of her child who was an infant'. Section 6(4) of the Guardianship of Infants Act 1964, as amended, provides that the mother of a non-marital child is its sole guardian, while section 10(2)(a) of the Act confirms her right to custody of her child.

The unmarried mother has a constitutional right to privacy, such a right being identified in *Kennedy v. Ireland* (1987) as one of the fundamental rights of the citizen. However, the right to privacy is not unqualified. Its exercise may be restricted by the constitutional rights of others and by the requirements of the common good. The right of a natural mother to privacy and confidentiality in circumstances where she gives her child to a voluntary agency for placement with foster parents, on the understanding that her identity would be kept confidential, was recognised by the Supreme Court in *I.O'T v. B.* (1998). The natural mother has a number of legal rights, most notably the right to consent, or withhold consent, to adoption. As will be seen, her consent can only be dispensed with by order of the High Court in the best interests of the child.

Non-Marital Children

The child of parents who have not married is not regarded as a member of a family under Article 41 of the Constitution and his father and mother are not regarded as 'parents'. However, such a child has a natural right to support from his mother under Article 40, as well as a guarantee as to his other personal rights, both specified and unspecified. These rights include the right to life, to be reared and educated, to liberty, to work, to rest and recreation, to the practice of religion, and freedom of conscience. Although, it was established in *Nicolaou* that a natural father does not have any natural right to the custody of his child, Walsh J in his judgment in that case said that a non-marital child 'has a natural right to look to his father for support'. The courts have emphasised on many occasions that children born outside marriage and children born to married parents have equal constitutional rights. Section 3 of the Status of Children Act 1987 established the principle of equal legal rights for all children whether born within or outside marriage. In *G. v. An Bord Uchtála* (1980), Walsh J said that the child born out of wedlock had 'the natural right to have its welfare and health guarded no less well than that of a child born in lawful wedlock'. In the same case, O'Higgins CJ referred to the obligation imposed on the State under Article 42.5 to provide for a child born into a family where the parents fail in their duty towards that child for physical or moral reasons, and stated:

> In the same way, in special circumstances the State may have an equal obligation in relation to a child born outside the family to protect that child, even against its mother, if her natural rights are used in such a way as to endanger the health or life of the child or to deprive him of his rights. In my view this obligation stems from the provisions of Article 40.3 of the Constitution.

That the non-marital child has the same 'natural and imprescriptible' rights to education under Article 42 as a child born in wedlock, is evident from the judgment of Gavan Duffy P *In Re M, an Infant* (1946) where he stated:

> Under Irish law, while I do not think that the constitutional guarantee for the family (Art. 41 of the Constitution) avails the mother of an illegitimate child, I regard the innocent little girl as having the same 'natural and imprescriptible rights' (under Art. 42) as a child born in wedlock to religious and moral, intellectual, physical and social education, and her care and upbringing during her coming, formative years must be the decisive consideration in our judgment.

In *I.O'T. v. B.* (1998), the Supreme Court held that a person has an unenumerated right by virtue of the provisions of Article 40.3.1 of the Constitution to know the identity of his natural mother. In the words of Hamilton CJ such a right 'is a basic right flowing from the natural and special relationship which exists between a mother and her child . . .'. It is not an absolute or unqualified right, and its exercise may be restricted by the constitutional rights of others and by the requirements of the common good. Its exercise is restricted in the case of children who have been lawfully adopted under adoption legislation. In addition, the constitutional right to know the identity of one's natural mother may be restricted by the constitutional right to privacy and confidentiality of the natural mother who, as in the present case, gave her child to the society for placement with foster parents on the understanding that her identity would be kept confidential and would not be disclosed without her express consent. Where there is a conflict between the constitutional rights of a child and its natural mother, the Court must attempt to harmonise such rights having regard to the provisions of the Constitution. If the Court cannot harmonise those conflicting rights, it has to determine which right is superior having regard to all the circumstances of the case. In reaching its decision, the Court should consider, *inter alia*, the circumstances giving rise to the natural mother relinquishing custody of her child, the present circumstances of the natural mother and the effect thereon (if any) of the disclosure of her identity to the child, the attitude of the natural mother to the disclosure, the respective ages of the natural mother and her child, the reasons why the child wants to know the identity of the natural mother and to meet her, the present circumstances of the child, and the views of the foster parents, if alive.

Limited Legal Recognition for Extra-Marital Relationships

An increasing number of couples choose to live together and have children outside marriage. While such extra-marital relationships do not qualify for constitutional recognition, increasingly, as a matter of policy, the law has had to recognise that it would be unfair to treat a cohabiting couple as though they were strangers to each other. As a result, some of the benefits and obligations of matrimony have been extended to them. For example, a party to a *de facto* marriage may, in certain specified circumstances, invoke the protection of the Domestic Violence Act 1996, and child benefit is payable to an unmarried mother on the same conditions under which payment is made to a married parent. On the other hand, a party to a *de facto* marriage may not claim an interest in property under section 36 of the Family Law Act 1995. The Family Home Protection Act 1976, which prevents a spouse disposing of an interest in the family home without the prior written consent of the other spouse, cannot be invoked by cohabitees.

Proposals for Reform

A number of important developments have emerged in recent years which suggest that the time might be right for a fundamental review of existing attitudes to the family. The decision of the European Court of Human Rights in the *Keegan* case, to the effect that the notion of 'family' as expressed in Article 8 of the European Convention on Human Rights is not confined to marriage-based relationships, leaves the way open for change that might more accurately reflect the position currently prevailing in Irish society, where many couples are content to form stable relationships not based on marriage.

Constitution Review Group Report

The *Keegan* case received detailed consideration in the chapter on the family in the report of the Constitution Review Group in 1996. Acknowledging that the *Keegan* case does not require the State to confer constitutional rights on natural fathers, the Review Group noted that there had been much criticism of the continued 'constitutional ostracism' of natural fathers. While this criticism was understandable in the case of natural fathers living in a stable relationship with the natural mother or who have established a relationship with the child, the Review Group said that there did not appear to be any justification for conferring constitutional rights on every natural father 'simply by reason of biological links and thus include fatherhood resulting from rape, incest or sperm donorship'. The Review Group concluded that if an amendment were made to the Constitution to cater for relationships not based on marriage, the proper approach was to embody the provisions of Article 8 of the European Convention on Human Rights in any such amendment, and leave it to the judiciary on a case-by-case basis to define the type of unit that constitutes a family. As a possible solution to the problem, one of the recommendations made by the Review Group as a means of conferring constitutional rights on those natural fathers who are living in a stable relationship with the mother of the child, thereby establishing 'family ties', is the inclusion in the Constitution of a revised Article 41 which would continue to protect the family based on marriage and contain 'a guarantee to all individuals of respect for their family life whether based on marriage or not'.

The Review Group pointed out that Articles 41 and 42 as presently framed place too much emphasis on 'the rights of the family as a unit' as compared with 'the rights of the individuals within that unit', in some instances to the detriment of individual members. It recommended that a revised Article 41 should contain a recognition by the State of the family as the primary and fundamental unit of society, but that the rights which derive from marriage, family, parenthood or childhood are guaranteed to, or imposed on, individuals.

The Review Group considered a number of Articles of the United Nations Convention on the Rights of the Child, which was ratified by Ireland in 1992, namely Article 7, (which confers on the child the right to a birth name, the right to acquire nationality and, as far as possible, the right to know and be cared for by his or her parents), and Articles 3, 9 and 18, all of which make reference to the concept of 'the best interests of the child'. As a result, the Review Group recommended that the rights mentioned in Article 7 of the Convention, and an express requirement that 'the best interests of the child be the paramount consideration', be inserted in a revised Article 41 of the Constitution.

Noting that the rights of natural mothers are unenumerated personal rights under Article 40 of the Constitution, the Review Group recommended that those rights should be enumerated, and that it would be appropriate to specify them in Articles 41 and 42. If, as suggested by the Review Group, a new section were inserted in a revised Article 41 giving every individual a right to respect for their family life, this would clearly include the rights of a natural mother in relation to her child.

Commission on the Family Report

The Commission on the Family, in its final report presented to the Government in May 1998, recommended that marriage as an institution should be supported by public policy. The Commission favoured marriage as having clear advantages in promoting security and continuity in family life. However, the report also recommended that protection for non-marital families should be enshrined in the Constitution, pointing out that the constitutional pledge in Article 41 to protect marriage should not prevent the Oireachtas from legislating for families not based on marriage.

Further Reading

Shatter, *Family Law*, 4th. Ed. Dublin: Butterworths 1997.
Casey, *Constitutional Law in Ireland*, 2nd. Ed. London: Sweet & Maxwell 1992.
Constitution Review Group Report. Dublin: Stationery Office,1996.
Commission on the Family Report. Dublin: Stationery Office,1998.
Ward, 'The Irish Family Outside Marriage and the European Convention on Human Rights — Keegan v. Ireland', (1994) 7 ILT 168.
Staines, 'The Concept of the Family under the Irish Constitution', (1976) 11 Ir Jur (n.s.)168.

CHAPTER TWO

MARRIAGE

The Nature of Marriage

Marriage was defined by Penzance LJ in *Hyde v. Hyde* (1866) as 'the voluntary union for life of one man and one woman to the exclusion of all others'. This definition is now generally accepted in Irish law and was cited with approval in *Griffith v. Griffith* (1944). More recently in *B. v. R.* (1995), Costello P observed that 'marriage was and is regarded as the voluntary and permanent union of one man and one woman to the exclusion of all others for life'. According to the definition, a marriage must be between persons of the opposite sex; it must be monogamous, intended to be for life and voluntarily contracted by parties having the capacity to contract. In addition, certain formalities, either civil or religious, must be complied with.

Whereas marriage is essentially a contract, it is also a relationship, in that it confers a status on the parties. In *Ussher v. Ussher* (1912) Pallas CB stated that marriage 'confers a status, through which unborn children obtain a title; and it is not revocable by the consent of even both parties'. In *N.(orse K.) v. K.* (1986) McCarthy J described marriage as 'a civil contract which creates reciprocating rights and duties between the parties but, further, establishes a status which affects both the parties to the contract and the community as a whole.'

Marriage under the Constitution

In *Ryan v. Attorney General* (1965), Kenny J held that the right to marry is one of the unspecified personal rights protected by Article 40 of the Constitution. However, this right, like personal rights generally, is not absolute. In fulfilling its duty to promote the common good, the State may place restrictions on the right to marry. It does this by regulating the minimum age for marriage and by prohibiting marriage between persons who are within the forbidden degrees of relationship.

Marriage has been given an elevated status under Irish constitutional law. In Article 41.3.1 of the Constitution, the State pledges itself 'to guard with special care the institution of marriage, on which the family is founded, and to protect it against attack'. That this constitutional provision is not just an empty formula is evident from a number of decisions of the Supreme Court which illustrate that the law can be effectively used to support the institution of marriage and thereby discourage other forms of cohabitation. In *Murphy v. Attorney General* (1982), the fact that a working married couple was more heavily taxed than a cohabiting couple was held by the Supreme Court to be a failure by the State to honour its pledge under Article 41. The Supreme Court again found that the State had failed to protect the institution of marriage in *Hyland v. Minister for Social Welfare* (1990). The Court ruled that certain sections of the Social Welfare (No. 2) Act 1985, under which a married couple received less in payments than a cohabiting couple, were repugnant to Article 41.

More recently, in *T.F. v. Ireland* (1995), a case that is dealt with in more detail in Chapter 6, the Supreme Court had an opportunity of considering the position enjoyed by the institution of marriage under the Constitution. The case came before the Court by way of appeal from a decision of the High Court rejecting the plaintiff's claim, among other things, that section 2(1)(f) of the Judicial Separation and Family Law Reform Act 1989 was contrary to Article 41.3.1. Section 2(1)(f) provides that an application for a decree of judicial separation may be made on the grounds that 'the marriage has broken down to the extent that the 'court is satisfied in all the circumstances that a normal marital relationship has not existed between the spouses for a period of at least one year immediately preceding the date of the application'. In dismissing the plaintiff's appeal, the Court conducted a wide-ranging review of the relevant authorities. The Court held that the extension of grounds for judicial separation by the 1989 Act may interfere with the parties personal and constitutional rights, but that such rights are not unlimited and their exercise may be regulated when the common good requires this to be done. A decree of judicial separation in respect of the spouses concerned does not and could not affect the bond of marriage. The provision of grounds for judicial separation does not, *per se*, constitute a failure to guard the institution of marriage with special care or a failure to protect it against attack.

A further example of how Irish law discourages cohabitation in favour of marriage can be found in the judgment of Kelly J in *Ennis v. Butterly* (1997), where he stated:

> Given the special place of marriage and the family under the Irish Constitution, it appears to me that the public policy of this State ordains that non-marital cohabitation does not and cannot have the same constitutional status as marriage.

The Agreement to Marry

Abolition of Action for Breach of Promise

An agreement to marry (an 'engagement') at one time gave rise to a binding contract which, if broken without lawful justification, could give rise to a claim for damages for what was known as 'breach of promise'. Section 2 of the Family Law Act 1981 effectively abolished actions for 'breach of promise' by providing that engagements to marry are not enforceable at law. The High Court case of *Ennis v. Butterly* (1997) involved a claim by the plaintiff for damages for breach of contract, negligent misrepresentation and fraudulent misrepresentation in respect of an alleged breach of promise to marry and breach of an agreement to cohabit. The parties, who were both married but not to each other, had lived together as man and wife, with an interruption of one year, between September 1985 and May 1994. Initially, the dwellinghouse in which the parties lived had been purchased in their joint names, but later the defendant transferred his share in the premises to the plaintiff. During their cohabitation the parties agreed to marry once divorce became available in this jurisdiction, when they could seek dissolution of their respective marriages. The defendant had even purchased an engagement ring for the plaintiff. Kelly J held that the plaintiff's claim, arising from the breach by the defendant of an agreement to marry, must fail by reason of section 2 of the Family Law Act 1981. He stated that even before the enactment of the 1981 Act the common law regarded a promise by a married person to marry a person whom he knew to be already married as contrary to public policy.

Cohabitation Agreements

Ennis v. Butterly (1997) is also significant in that it gave the Court an opportunity to consider a claim to enforce an agreement to cohabit, in effect a claim for 'palimony'. The Oxford English Dictionary defines 'palimony' as a slang American word meaning 'compensation claimed by the deserted party after the separation of a couple living together out of wedlock'. Kelly J pointed out that agreements by persons to cohabit were unenforceable at common law as being injurious to morality and marriage. Considering the special position of marriage under the Constitution, Irish law would lean very strongly against such agreements. He rejected the plaintiff's claim saying that: 'To permit an express cohabitation contract (such as is pleaded here) to be enforced would give it a similar status in law as a marriage contract'.

Gifts between Engaged Couples

The fact that an agreement to marry is no longer enforceable as a contract does not mean that such an agreement is devoid of any legal consequences. The Family Law Act 1981 makes special provision concerning the property relationships of couples where an engagement is terminated. Section 3 of the 1981 Act provides that where a wedding gift is made to an engaged couple, or to either of them, by a third party, it shall be presumed, in the absence of evidence to the contrary, that it was a gift to both of them as joint owners and subject to the condition that it shall be returned to the donor, or his personal representative, if the marriage, for whatever reason, does not take place. Gifts between engaged couples (including engagement rings) are dealt with in section

4. There is a presumption that a gift is conditional, in the sense that it be returned to the donor, if the engagement is terminated for any reason other than by the death of the donor. Where the death of the donor terminates the engagement, it is presumed that the gift was unconditional. Both presumptions may be rebutted by evidence to the contrary.

Gifts from Third Parties

The 1981 Act also allows third parties to claim compensation in respect of substantial expenditure incurred by them on behalf of one of the parties to the engagement. Where a party to a broken engagement has received a substantial benefit (other than a wedding gift) from a third party in consequence of an engagement, section 6 enables the Court, on the application of the third party, to make such order (including a compensation order) as appears just and equitable in the circumstances. There is no indication in the section as to what a substantial benefit might consist of. For example, where a family member of one of the parties has carried out substantial work in the improvement of property intended to be used by the couple as a family home, that person should be able to avail of the section to receive compensation for the expense involved.

Property Disputes between Engaged Couples

Section 5 of the 1981 Act deals with property disputes between ex-fiancées. The section recognises the fact that a special relationship exists between the parties to an engagement. This may lead them to enter into informal transactions for the acquisition or improvement of property which may be owned or purchased by one or both of them. Section 44 of the Family Law (Divorce) Act 1996 provides that where an agreement to marry is terminated, section 36 of the Family Law Act 1995 shall apply, as if the parties to the agreement were married to each other, to any dispute between them, or claim by one of them, in relation to property in which either or both of them had a beneficial interest while the agreement was in force.

Expenditure on Preparations for Marriage

Section 7 of the 1981 Act affords a legal remedy to a fiancée if he or she has spent money in preparation for the wedding or marriage which is wasted when the engagement breaks down. The remedy is also available to another person who has spent money on behalf of a fiancée in preparation for the big event. The section enables the Court, on the application of a fiancée or the other person who has incurred substantial expenditure and has not benefited from the expenditure, to make such order (including an order for the recovery of the expenditure) as appears to it to be just and equitable in the circumstances. Accordingly, compensation could be obtained for wasted money spent on booking the wedding reception or any other expense usually associated with marriage.

Section 9 provides that proceedings under the 1981 Act must be commenced within three years of the termination of the engagement.

Capacity to Marry

Capacity to marry is generally governed by the law of the country in which the parties are domiciled at the time of their marriage, i.e. the *lex domicilii*. To contract a valid marriage according to Irish law, the parties must be:

(a) Over 18 years of age

Section 31 of the Family Law Act 1995 provides that a marriage solemnised between persons either of whom is under 18 is void. Where a person requested to solemnise a marriage sees fit to do so, he may request evidence of age with respect to either or both parties. It is an offence, punishable with a fine of up to £500 on summary conviction, to knowingly solemnise a marriage between parties either or both of whom are under age, or to be knowingly a party to such a marriage. An application may be made to the Court under section 33 of the 1995 Act to exempt the marriage from the minimum age requirements. The Court may grant an exemption where it is satisfied that there are serious reasons to justify it and that the exemption is in the best interests of the parties.

(b) Of opposite sex

A valid marriage cannot be contracted by persons of the same sex. Whether or not a person is male or female will depend on medical evidence. However, a potential problem may arise where a person who was born a male becomes a female (or *vice versa*) as a result of a sex change operation. Since the issue has never come before the Courts here, the only guideline that exists is the decision in the English case of *Corbett v. Corbett* (1970), where it was held that a man who had undergone a sex change operation and then lived as a woman was not a woman biologically, since sex was determined once and for all at birth. Therefore, he was incapable of contracting a valid marriage with a man.

(c) Free to marry

Marriage, according to Irish law, must be monogamous. Accordingly, a so-called second 'marriage' contracted with a third party while a first marriage validly exists, is void. A party is only permitted to remarry a third party after the death of a spouse or on obtaining a decree of divorce or nullity. It should be emphasised that it is only necessary to obtain a nullity decree where a marriage is voidable. In theory, a party to a void marriage is free to remarry without the necessity of obtaining a nullity decree. Where a party to a subsisting marriage that is valid marries a third party he may commit the crime of bigamy. See the case of the *People v. Ballins* (1964) discussed below. However, the judgment of Costello P in *B. v. R.* (1995), establishes the principle that no crime is committed if a husband and wife, being validly married, marry each other a second time. The parties married each other in a civil ceremony in the USA. Subsequently, they married each other in Ireland in a full religious ceremony according to the rites of the Roman Catholic Church. They lived together in the USA until the marriage broke up. The husband obtained a divorce in the US State where the first marriage had taken place, based on the wife's desertion. The wife sought, *inter alia*, a declaration that the marriage celebrated in Ireland was void by reason of their prior subsisting marriage.

The present confused state of the law of bigamy in this country was highlighted in the High Court case of *O.B. v. R.* (1999). The Court annulled a marriage on the ground that the wife at the time of the marriage was incapable of giving a full, free and informed consent. The wife had obtained a Catholic church annulment some twenty years previously, on the basis of which she went through a ceremony of marriage with another man. Because of the confused state of the law on bigamy, coupled with the fact that most people regarded bigamy as a medieval crime no longer committed, Kinlen J suggested that 'the legislature should consider seriously the abolition or restructuring of the crime of bigamy'.

(d) Outside the prohibited degrees of relationship

Persons within the prohibited degrees of consanguinity (blood relationship) and affinity (relationship by marriage) are not free to contract a valid marriage. Without going into detail as to the categories of persons whose marriage is forbidden, suffice it to say that the prohibited degrees include both marital and non-marital issue and half- or full-blood relatives. An adopted child is within the prohibited degrees in relation to its natural family and adoptive parents. It would appear, however, that there is nothing to prevent an adopted child marrying a child of his adoptive parents.

Formal Validity

The only formality required by the common law for the celebration of a valid marriage was that the parties intending to get married exchanged their mutual consent in the presence of a priest in holy orders. At present, as a general rule, the law of the country where the marriage is celebrated (the *lex loci celebrationes*) dictates the formalities that must be complied with. The formalities required for the solemnisation of marriage under Irish law are a mixture of ecclesiastical and civil rules. The present law is complex and is set out in legislation dating from the Marriages (Ireland) Act 1844 right up to the Family Law (Miscellaneous Provisions) Act 1997. While individual churches are permitted to regulate marriages for their own purposes, church marriages must comply with the civil law. Experience has shown, however, that it is only on rare occasions that the operation of internal church laws produces conflict with the civil law. This is probably due to the fact that the civil law recognises, with minimal conditions, the validity of marriages celebrated according to the internal rules of the various churches recognised by the State. Where conflict does arise, the civil law will prevail. A conflict between canon law and civil law arose in the *People v. Ballins* (1964). The accused had gone through a ceremony of marriage with one William Ballins in 1954 in a Registry Office in England and, while the said William Ballins was still alive, she went through another marriage ceremony with one John Kenny in a Catholic Church in Limerick in 1960. This unfortunate state of affairs was allowed to occur as a result of the fact that the Roman Catholic Church does not recognise civil marriages between Roman Catholics, wherever celebrated. The Court held that the accused had committed bigamy. Because of certain mitigating circumstances, including the fact that the accused had been advised by a priest in England that she could remarry in a Catholic church in Ireland without committing bigamy, the accused was given a conditional discharge.

Church Marriages

For the purposes of marriages celebrated according to internal church rules, the law regulates marriages for the following religious denominations: Roman Catholic, Church of Ireland, Presbyterian, other Christians, Society of Friends, and Jews. It is not proposed to examine the requirements of each denomination in detail. Parties contemplating marriage according to the rites of a particular religion can obtain complete details from an individual member of the clergy or their local Registrar of Marriages.

Civil Marriages

Marriage by civil contract may be solemnised on the parties obtaining a Registrar's certificate or licence. To obtain a certificate or licence, notice must be given to the District Registrar of the district where the parties have resided. If they reside in different districts, notice must be given to both District Registrars. The notice must state the parties' names, addresses and occupations, their status, i.e. whether single, divorced, widow or widower, whether they are of full age to marry, their usual place or places of worship, the place where the marriage is to be solemnised, and whether the marriage is to be celebrated by certificate or licence. The notice to the District Registrar must be accompanied by a solemn declaration by the party giving notice that there is believed to be no impediment to the marriage, that the residential conditions are satisfied and that any necessary consents have been given or dispensed with.

On receipt of the notice, the District Registrar must enter it in the marriage notice book. He must send a copy of the notice on the day it is received, or on the next day, by registered post to the clergyman of the place of worship where the marriage is to be solemnised and the clergyman of the place of worship where the parties or either of them usually attend. Where the marriage is to take place in the District Registrar's office, the notice must be displayed in a prominent place in his office for 21 days in the case of a marriage by certificate and seven days in the case of a marriage by licence. Where the parties have no usual place of worship, the Registrar, at the parties' expense, must publish a copy of the notice once on two consecutive weeks at least in a newspaper circulating in the district in which the marriage is to be solemnised.

Where the marriage is by Registrar's certificate, the parties must establish that each of them has resided within the District Registrar's district for at least seven days preceding the giving of notice. The Registrar may issue his certificate and the marriage may proceed after the expiration of 21 days from entering the notice in the marriage notice book. In the case of a marriage by licence, where the parties reside in the same district, one party must establish 15 days' residence in that district and the other at least seven days. Where they reside in different districts each must establish 15 days' residence in their respective districts. The Registrar may issue his licence on the expiration of seven days following the giving of notice and the marriage may take place. Where one of the parties is certified by a doctor to be seriously ill and unable to attend at a registry office, the Registrar General can issue a special licence to marry under section 16 of the Marriages Act 1972.

Notification of Intention to Marry

Section 32 of the Family Law Act 1995 provides that a marriage solemnised after the commencement of the section (1 August 1996) shall not be valid unless the parties concerned notify the registrar in writing of their intention to marry not less than three months prior to the date on which the marriage is to take place, or that an exemption from the section was obtained under section 33, prior to the marriage. An exemption may be granted by the Court on the application of both parties. Section 3 of the Family Law (Miscellaneous Provisions) Act 1997 provides for the retrospective validation of marriages where notification is or was given in error to the wrong Registrar of Marriages.

Failure to Comply with Formalities

As we have seen, failure to comply with the notification requirements of section 32 of the 1995 Act will render the marriage void. Non-compliance with the formalities relating to marriage by certificate or licence, or the requirements that the marriage is celebrated in the right place and before the right celebrant, will only invalidate the marriage where the parties knowingly and wilfully failed to comply with them. It was held in *B. v. R.* (1995), that the legal formalities required for the celebration of a marriage according to the rites of the Catholic Church in Ireland under the Registration of Marriages (Ireland) Act 1866 were not properly complied with, in that the marriage certificate contained a false statement to the effect that the parties were a 'spinster' and 'bachelor' respectively. The wife's mother had made the arrangements and she was not aware of the previous civil ceremony in the USA. The parties had signed the certificate which was prepared in good faith, without adverting to the fact that it contained incorrect information. Costello P held that non-compliance with the formalities did not invalidate the marriage ceremony itself.

The Presumption of Marriage

Where it is proved that a marriage ceremony took place, there is a presumption that the formalities have been complied with. It is also presumed that the parties had the capacity to marry and genuinely consented to the marriage. In *Mulhearn v. Cleary* (1930) it was held that once it was proved that the parties went through a ceremony of marriage there was a presumption in favour of its validity. Kenny J held in *S. v. S.* (1976) that this presumption can only be rebutted by proof beyond reasonable doubt, or by establishing with a high degree of probability, that the marriage was invalid. Where the parties have lived together as husband and wife, it is presumed that they did so in consequence of a valid marriage. Again, this presumption may be rebutted where it is proved beyond reasonable doubt that the parties did not go through a formal ceremony of marriage.

Declarations as to Marital Status

Section 29 of the Family Law Act 1995 Act enables the Court to make the following declarations as to marital status:

(a) a declaration that a marriage was valid at its inception
(b) a declaration that a marriage subsisted on a specified date
(c) a declaration that a marriage did not subsist on a specified date
(d) a declaration that the validity of a foreign divorce, annulment or legal separation is entitled to recognition in the State
(e) a declaration that the validity of a foreign divorce, annulment or legal separation is not entitled to recognition in the State.

An application to the Court for a declaration as to marital status may be made by either spouse or by any other person with a sufficient interest in the matter. Before the Court can make an order under the section it must be satisfied that either of the spouses is domiciled in the State at the date of the application, or has been ordinarily resident in the State throughout the year ending on the date of the application. Where either spouse has died before the date of the application, the Court must be satisfied that spouse was so domiciled or ordinarily resident at that date. The other spouse or the spouses concerned, or the personal representatives of the spouse or each spouse, must be joined in the proceedings. Provision is made for notice of the proceedings to be served on the Attorney General or any other person and for relevant documents to be supplied to the Attorney General. The Attorney General can apply to be added as a party to the proceedings. The Court can order that the Attorney General or any person served with notice be added to the proceedings.

The procedure available under the section will prove attractive in practice to spouses who want to have their marital status clarified. Where a foreign divorce has been obtained based on the domicile of either or both of the parties, an application can be made to the Court under the section for a declaration that the divorce is valid under Irish law. In *G.McG. v. D.W.* (1999) the parties agreed that the Court should treat proceedings, which started out as a petition for nullity by reason of the petitioner's prior subsisting marriage to another person, as if it were an application for a declaration pursuant to section 29 of the 1995 Act that a foreign divorce was valid. The significance of the case as it relates to the recognition of foreign divorces is discussed in Chapter 6. Subsequently, Mc Guinness J rejected an attempt by the Attorney General to reopen her decision in *G.McG. v. D.W.* declaring a foreign divorce valid. The Attorney General had not been aware of the original proceedings, and argued that it was not open to the Court to make the declaration under section 29 where there was no proper contradictor to oppose the declaration. McGuinness J accepted that while the declaration was binding on the parties to the original proceedings, it was not binding on the State. However, having reviewed both Irish and English authorities on the matter, the learned judge said that the Court did have the power to make the declaration in question in the absence of a party making the opposing arguments, and added that 'it would be a manifest and striking injustice to the parties to reopen a decision of such practical importance to their ordinary lives and in reliance upon which they have already acted'.

Further Reading

Shatter, *Family Law*, 4th. Ed. Dublin: Butterworths 1997.
Binchy, *A Casebook on Irish Family Law*. Abingdon: Professional Books 1984.
Duncan, 'Supporting the Institution of Marriage in Ireland', (1978) 13 Ir Jur (n.s.) 215.
O'Reilly, 'Marital Privacy and Family Law', (1977) 65 Studies 8.

CHAPTER THREE

NULLITY

A decree of nullity declares a marriage to be null and void — this is different to divorce which terminates a marriage that was valid in all respects. Nevertheless, a decree of nullity ends the marriage in the same way as divorce, in that the parties are free to marry again. Nullity is concerned with conduct before and at the time of the marriage while divorce is solely concerned with conduct after the marriage.

As there is a presumption that a marriage is valid, the authorities make it clear that the onus of proof is on the petitioner to establish, on the balance of probabilities, that the marriage is invalid. According to McCarthy J in *N (orse. K.) v. K.* (1986) 'A petitioner must establish the case upon the balance of probabilities standard but this must take into account the frequent absence of opposition, the possibility of collusion, and so forth'. In *S. v. K.* (1993), Denham J stated that: 'In view of the constitutional protection of the institution of marriage, it is quite clear that there is a heavy burden of proof on the petitioner. There is a severe and heavy burden on the petitioner of a quasi-criminal trial nature'.

Although the parties may have gone through a ceremony of marriage and cohabited as man and wife, certain defects may exist which render that marriage void or voidable. The distinction between a void and voidable marriage is vital to an understanding of the law of nullity. A void marriage is really a contradiction in terms, as such a marriage has, from its beginning, no existence or validity whatsoever in the eyes of the law. A voidable marriage, on the other hand, is and remains a valid marriage until a decree of nullity is granted on the application of either party to the marriage. The distinction was described by Greene LJ in *De Renville's case* (1948) as follows:

> A void marriage is one that will be regarded by every court in any case in which the existence of the marriage is an issue as never having taken place and can be so treated by both parties to it without the necessity of any decree annulling it; a voidable marriage is one that will be regarded by every court as a valid subsisting marriage until a decree annulling it has been pronounced by a court of competent jurisdiction.

Although strictly speaking, there is no need to seek a decree of nullity in the case of a void marriage, as such a marriage has no legal effect, a formal declaration of nullity is usually sought for record purposes as the best possible evidence that the marriage in question is void. The parties are free to remarry, but where no decree exists the possibility of a prosecution for bigamy arises. Of course, in the event of such a prosecution, the fact that the marriage is void could be successfully pleaded by way of defence. In any event, for all concerned, a decree of nullity is the best possible evidence that the marriage in question is void. Only the spouses can challenge the validity of a voidable marriage, and then only during their joint lives. Where the marriage is void, the parties themselves and any interested third party may question the validity of the marriage, even after the death of the parties themselves.

The consequences of a decree of nullity are pretty drastic as far as the spouses are concerned. As a void marriage is deemed in law never to have existed, the parties have no succession rights to one another nor do they have any obligations of maintenance or support towards one another. Where a voidable marriage is annulled, the decree retrospectively invalidates the marriage and the legal position of the parties is the same as if the marriage were void. Any children born to a couple whose marriage has been annulled are regarded as non-marital. At common law, where a marriage was void or where a voidable marriage was annulled, the mother was regarded as sole guardian of any child born to the parties. The position of the natural father has been greatly improved by section 2 of the Guardianship of Infants Act 1964 (inserted by section 9 of the Status of Children Act 1987), which provides that where a void marriage is celebrated which the father reasonably believed resulted in a valid marriage, the father will be regarded as joint guardian of his child without having to apply to the Court: (i) where the ceremony occurred before the birth of the child, or, at some time during the period of ten months before that birth, or (ii) where the ceremony occurred after the birth of the child, at the time of that ceremony. Where a voidable marriage is annulled, the father remains a joint guardian with the mother of any child born to them before or within ten months of the granting of the nullity decree.

By virtue of section 36 of the Family Law Act 1995, where a marriage has been annulled under the law of the State, or in the case of a foreign annulment that is recognised in the State, either of the parties may apply to the Court within three years of the date of the annulment to determine any question arising between them as to the title to or possession of any property. In the case of a void marriage that has not been annulled, an application under section 36 must be made within three years of the parties ceasing to live together. Section 46 of the Family Law Act 1995 enables the Court granting a decree of nullity to declare that either of the spouses is unfit to have custody of dependent children and shall not be entitled to custody on the death of the other spouse.

Void Marriages

A marriage is void under Irish law due to: (1) lack of capacity, (2) failure to comply with formalities and, (3) lack of valid consent.

Lack of Capacity

This may arise in the following ways:

a) Where either party is under the age of eighteen, by virtue of section 31 of the Family Law Act 1995. However, section 33 allows the Court, on an application by both of the parties to an intended marriage, to exempt the marriage from the application of section 31.

b) Where either party is at the time of the marriage validly married to another person.

c) Where the parties are not respectively male and female.

d) Where the marriage is between parties who are within the forbidden degrees of relationship. These relationships may arise either from consanguinity (blood) or affinity (marriage).

Failure to Comply with Formalities

A marriage is void if it was knowingly celebrated without some of the essential formalities. The matter is now regulated by Part V of the Family Law Act 1995. See Chapter 2.

Lack of Valid Consent

The definition of marriage by Penzance LJ in *Hyde v. Hyde* (1866) as 'the voluntary union for life of one man and one woman to the exclusion of all others', implies that the full and free consent of both parties is a fundamental requirement for a valid marriage. The Courts now tend to view the marriage contract as to its validity in the same way as a commercial contract, and require that there be true consensus ('the meeting of minds') between the parties at the time of the marriage ceremony. Any of the invalidating elements which render an ordinary contract void, such as duress, undue influence, fraud, mistake or mental incapacity, will prevent the true meeting of minds. In addition to the traditional invalidating elements, the Supreme Court held in *M.O'M. (orse. O'C.) v. B.O'C.* (1996) that there can be no informed consent in the absence of adequate knowledge of a 'circumstance of substance'.

Duress

Duress will negate the consent of either party to the marriage. Traditionally, the Courts emphasised that there must exist a reasonably entertained fear of a threat to life, limb or liberty. In the English case of *Szechter v. Szechter* (1970), the petitioner, who had been a political prisoner in Poland, had married the respondent solely in order to be allowed to leave the country. The Court held that the marriage was a nullity because of the duress emanating from the Polish authorities. Simon P stated that for duress to invalidate a marriage it must be proved that:

> the will of one of the parties thereto has been overborne by genuine and reasonably held fear caused by threat of immediate danger (for which the party is not himself responsible) to life, limb or liberty, so that the constraint destroys the reality of consent to ordinary wedlock.

Griffith v. Griffith (1944) is a typical example of the strict view of duress, dictated by the public policy of the time that it should be difficult to opt out of marriage, which required that there be a threat to life, limb or liberty for a petition to succeed. The petitioner, a 19 year old apprentice, was accused of having unlawful carnal knowledge of the respondent who was under the age of 17 years, causing her to become pregnant. The respondent and her mother threatened to report the matter to the police and the petitioner married the respondent because he feared possible prosecution and imprisonment. It subsequently transpired that sexual intercourse had not taken place between the parties and that the allegation that the petitioner had made the respondent pregnant was false. The High Court granted a decree of nullity based on duress. In his judgment, Haugh J said that the petitioner's consent to marry resulted from 'a real and grave fear inspired by an unjust and fraudulent misrepresentation of a very grave and vital matter going to the root of his consent; and it was this fear, so unjustly imposed, that led to the marriage now impugned'. He went on to hold that a consent obtained by a combination of fraud and fear was not a consent that bound the petitioner.

Ever since the decision in *B. v. D.* (1973), the Courts have departed from the strict view of duress as outlined in the *Griffith* case and taken a broader view of duress. In taking a more enlightened view, the Courts are trying to ensure that before parties commit themselves for life they are fully aware of all the issues involved and give a full, free and informed consent. What constitutes duress is a question of degree in any particular case. In *B. v. D.* the petitioner, who was 27 at the date of the marriage, informed her sister a week before the ceremony that she did not want to marry the respondent. Their courtship had been devoid of any real affection. The respondent, then aged 34, was domineering in most respects. He frequently used the petitioner's car as if it were his own and even demanded money of her on occasion. However, she went through the ceremony rather than go to the trouble of calling it off. The High Court granted a decree of nullity on the basis that the conduct of the respondent amounted to duress. Murnaghan J described the relationship that existed between the parties as follows:

I have very little doubt but that gradually, from the first time they met, the petitioner found herself in her relationship with the respondent in a groove, which as time went on got deeper and deeper, and out of which she was constitutionally unable to extract herself, and in which perhaps she was prepared in the circumstances, if not content, to remain.

The decision of the High Court in *S. v. O'S.* (1978) represents a further departure from the narrow view of duress and a broadening of its scope. In that case, the petitioner married the respondent who at the time of the ceremony was suffering from a form of mental illness known as Munchausen syndrome, a condition by which he could feign serious illness. The respondent had persuaded the petitioner to marry him, stating that if she did not do so she would be responsible for the breakdown of his health or even for his suicide. The High Court annulled the marriage. In delivering the judgment of the Court, Finlay P stated:

Essentially, it seems to me that the freedom of will necessary to enter into a valid contract of marriage is one particularly associated with emotion and that a person in the emotional bondage of another person couldn`t consciously have the freedom of will.

The 'freedom of will', as Finlay P described it in *S. v. O'S.*, that is essential if there is to be genuine consent was also absent in *P.W. v. A.O'C. (orse. W.)* (1992) where the High Court held that the respondent's threat to commit suicide constituted duress which had prevented the petitioner's consent being a fully free exercise of an independent will. Blaney J accepted that the petitioner was a compliant and co-operative person and was dominated by the respondent who was used to having her own way. He stated that the effect of the respondent's threat 'was to deprive the petitioner's consent of the necessary element of freedom required of a consent to marriage'.

The present law on duress is encapsulated in that part of the judgment of Finlay CJ in *N. (orse. K.) v. K.* (1986) where he stated:

If the apparent decision to marry has been caused to such an extent by external pressure or influence, whether falsely or honestly applied, as to lose the character of a full free act of that person's will, no valid marriage has occurred.

The case involved a young couple who had a short and casual relationship prior to their marriage, as a result of which the petitioner became pregnant. The petitioner was aged 19 and the respondent was aged 20 at the date of the marriage. The evidence showed that the petitioner was a reserved and obedient person. Both sets of parents had suggested that the parties should marry, as the proper course to take, and the respondent agreed when approached. The parties showed little interest in one another and married following a courtship in which they rarely socialised together. They lived together for a while in the home of the respondent's parents. After a short time the petitioner returned to her parents' home. The parties separated after the birth of the baby. The High Court refused to annul the marriage on the grounds that the parties had decided to marry in any event. The Supreme Court overturned the decision of the High Court and granted a decree based on duress. The decision of the Court establishes the principle that pressure of events, in this case the petitioner's unwanted pregnancy, may be sufficient to overbear the will and prevent a party from giving a true consent to marriage. The mere fact that the petitioner was pregnant implies pressure and a risk of lack of real consent.

The petitioner in *N. (orse. K.) v. K.* had alleged that her father's reaction on learning that she was pregnant was to suggest that she should marry or have an abortion. The father denied this and the Court accepted his word. Of course, had the Court accepted the petitioner's version of events, it would have deemed this to amount to pressure from a person sufficient to overbear the will of the petitioner, thereby negating consent. In the event, the Court was prepared to accept that pressure of events, in this case the pregnancy of the petitioner, may amount to duress. The facts of *B. (orse. O'R.) v. O'R.* (1991) were somewhat similar to those of *N. (orse. K.) v. K.*, in that both cases involved a young girl becoming pregnant, parental disapproval, a rushed marriage and eventual marriage breakdown. In *B. (orse. O'R.) v. O'R.* the petitioner sought a decree of nullity on the ground that she did not give a true consent, as her mind was overborne by the fact that she was pregnant. Carroll J refused to grant a decree on the basis that 'events alone cannot constitute duress or unreasonable influence.' The learned judge's insistence that pressure to overbear free will must come from a person and not events is consistent with the approach she took in *P.C. (orse. O'B.) v. O'B.* (1985) that 'self-imposed duress' is not sufficient to justify a decree of nullity being granted. On appeal, the Supreme Court overruled the decision of Carroll J and reaffirmed the decision in *N. (orse. K.) v. K.* that a person's will does not have to be overborne by pressure from a person, but may in fact be overborne by pressure of events.

There have been a number of cases in recent years where a decree of nullity was sought where an unexpected pregnancy resulted in allegations of parental or external pressure exerted on one or more of the parties to get married. In *W. (orse.C.) v. C.* (1989) the petitioner became pregnant after being forced into sexual intercourse by the respondent. Prior to that, the respondent had insulted her regularly and she had tried unsuccessfully to end the relationship. Her father's attitude when she told him she was pregnant was that she would have to marry the respondent. The principal of the school where she taught told her that she had no future in teaching unless she got married. She decided to marry and the respondent agreed. The marriage was a complete failure. The respondent was cruel and sadistic to her and she left him after two years. The High Court granted a decree of nullity on the ground that the petitioner had not given a true consent to the marriage. Barron J accepted that the petitioner was completely obsessed by the pregnancy and that her decision to marry was 'brought about by the strain of her circumstances and the lack of ability for normal thought which she was manifesting at that time'. In *A.C. (orse. J.) v. P.J.* (1995) the High Court annulled the marriage of a 21 year old girl from rural Ireland who had been brought up in a strict religious environment. She had become pregnant by the respondent while living in Dublin. She was so afraid of telling her parents that she developed a psychiatric condition, for which she had to be hospitalised. The Court ruled that her consent to marriage was not the exercise by her of a full and free independent will.

More recently, in *D.C. v. N.M. (orse. N.C.)* (1997) the High Court refused to accept that pressure of events, in the form of the respondent's pregnancy, had forced the petitioner to enter into the marriage. The petitioner based his petition on the ground, *inter alia*, that his consent to the marriage was obtained by undue influence and/or duress exerted upon him by the respondent by reason of her alleged pregnancy by him. In refusing to annul the marriage on this ground, Geoghegan J referred to a number of cases (without mentioning them by name) where a decree of nullity was granted where a young girl became unexpectedly pregnant and there was parental or external pressure exerted on one or more of the parties to get married. He said that there was no evidence of such pressure being applied in this case. There had been a long-term plan to get married and each party wanted this. The decision to get married was related to the pregnancy, as each party felt a sense of duty to the other. However, the couple were not particularly young — he was 21 and she was a mature 19 at the date of the marriage. This was not a case where there was external pressure which a young immature person was unable to withstand. However, in *W.D. v. C.D.* (1998), the High Court decided that the decision of the parties to marry had been caused to such an extent by external pressures from both families as to lose the character of a fully free act on each party's behalf. In the circumstances, no valid marriage had taken place. The evidence revealed that the respondent became pregnant as a result of a casual relationship with the petitioner. The petitioner did not want to marry but had been forced to do so by extreme pressure brought to bear on him by the parents of both parties.

The mere fact that prior to marriage a petitioner had expressed misgivings or second thoughts about proceeding with the ceremony does not mean that he married under pressure amounting to duress. In *O'S. v. W. (orse. O'S.)* (1989) the petitioner had doubts about the wisdom of the marriage and expressed them to the respondent. Two months before the wedding he told the respondent he wanted to call it off. She was very upset and threatened to consult a solicitor if he did not go ahead with the wedding. The petitioner sought the advice of a solicitor who told him the respondent might have a claim against him. He told his future brother-in-law that he no longer loved the respondent and did not want to marry her. However, he reluctantly decided to proceed with the marriage, which was a complete failure and only lasted about eleven months. The basis for his petition was that he had not given a real consent. The Court rejected his petition as the evidence did not establish that he was under duress when he married. As regards the threat of legal proceedings, Costello J felt that such a threat did not overbear the will of the petitioner to such an extent as to vitiate his consent.

Mistake

Mistake will rarely make a marriage void. To do so the mistake must be fundamental, to the extent that the petitioner is mistaken either as to the nature of the ceremony or the identity of the other party. A mistake as to some attribute of the respondent, such as his wealth or health, is not enough. In *Valier v. Valier* (1925) the petitioner, an Italian with very little understanding of the English language, went through a marriage ceremony, arranged by the respondent, in a registry office in the belief that it was a ceremony of betrothal. The Court annulled the marriage on the basis that the mistake as to the nature of the ceremony negated the petitioner's consent. A mistake as to the effect of the marriage or the status or quality of the other spouse does not negate consent. Thus, in *Moss v. Moss* (1897) the husband's mistaken belief that he had married a virgin, when in fact she was pregnant by another man, was held to have no effect.

Mental Incapacity

The common law position, which provides that a marriage is void where either party lacks the mental capacity to understand the nature of the marriage contract and its resultant responsibilities, was considered in *Park v Park* (1953). The test to be applied was laid down as follows:

> Was the (person) capable of understanding the nature of the contract into which he was entering, or was his mental condition such that he was incapable of understanding it? In order to ascertain the nature of the contract of marriage a man must be mentally capable of appreciating that it involves the responsibilities normally attaching to marriage. Without that degree of mentality it cannot be said that he understands the nature of the contract.

A person who has been certified as insane is deemed by the Marriage of Lunatics Act 1811 to be incapable of contracting a valid marriage while he remains insane. Persons who have not been certified as insane, but who are suffering from mental illness, emotional immaturity or drug or alcohol addiction at the time of the marriage, may be incapable of understanding the nature of marriage and of giving a full, free and informed consent. Of course, where genuine consent is absent, the marriage will be declared null and void. On the other hand, where a person is capable of consenting to marriage, but is incapable of entering into and sustaining a normal marital relationship, the marriage is voidable. In some cases, the same factor, for example mental illness, may render the person both incapable of consenting to marriage and unable to sustain a normal marital relationship. In such cases, the Court should first consider whether the marriage is void. Where the Court declares the marriage void, there is no need to consider whether it is also voidable.

Recent developments in psychiatry make it possible to more readily identify psychological and emotional factors which so affect a person as to make that person incapable of entering into a valid marriage. Persons suffering from psychotic disorders are prone to severely disturbed, bizarre and unpredictable behaviour which seriously affects their ability to make mature and informed decisions. Late onset psychosis (schizophrenia) and affective psychosis (manic depression) are the most common forms of mental illness encountered in the reported cases on nullity. In *M.E. v. A.E.* (1987) a decree of nullity was granted based in part on the fact that the respondent was suffering from a psychiatric disorder at the time of the marriage which prevented him from giving a full, free and informed consent. The evidence established that he suffered from paranoid schizophrenia. In *J.S. v. M.J.* (1997) the High Court declared the marriage void, having accepted the evidence of a psychiatrist that the respondent was suffering from a severe psychiatric illness, in the form of depression occurring as part of a schizo-affective illness, at the time of the marriage and was incapable of giving a true consent to the marriage.

Very often the incapacity to give a full, free and informed consent may result from a party's emotional immaturity, which may take the form of psychological disability or defective personality. In *O'R. v. B.* (1995) the parties went through a ceremony of marriage in 1981. The only child of the marriage was born in 1984. The petitioner claimed that the respective mental and psychological condition of the respondent and himself prevented them from entering into and sustaining a normal marriage relationship. He further claimed that he entered the marriage by reason of duress in that the respondent became distressed when he attempted to end the engagement. The respondent denied that they had lacked the capacity to enter into and sustain a normal marriage relationship and that they did not give a full, free and informed consent. She further denied that she had repudiated the marriage. The Court granted a decree of nullity on the ground that the petitioner was incapable of giving a full, free and informed consent to the marriage because of his immaturity, psychological disability and defective personality.

In *J.W.H. (orse. W.) v. G.W.* (1998) and *D.K. v. T.H. (orse. T.K.)* (1998) O'Higgins J reviewed the various authorities which establish that a marriage can be annulled on the basis of incapacity to enter into a marital relationship by virtue of lack of emotional maturity as well as incapacity by virtue of various psychological factors. In *J.W.H. (orse. W.) v. G.W.* he expressed the view 'that the emotional immaturity has to be such as would render the person quite incapable of forming and sustaining [a] marriage relationship.' In refusing a decree of nullity, he declined to accept the petitioner's claim that her parents had pressurised her into getting married and that, as a result, she had not given her free and informed consent to the marriage. There was evidence that her father did not like the respondent and was against her living with him unless they got married. However, the learned judge was satisfied that the petitioner married the respondent, by whom she had a child who was nine months old at the date of the ceremony, to get away from her father's influence and the strict home routine he imposed on her. She desired more freedom than she enjoyed at home. She wanted to set up home with the respondent and emulate the life-style of her friends. In *D.K. v. T.H. (orse. T.K.)* O'Higgins J expressed himself satisfied that there can be psychological and emotional factors which so affect a person as to make that person incapable of entering into a valid marriage. There was evidence from a psychiatrist that factors such as sexual abuse by a priest as a child, the death of his father when he was aged fourteen, the remarriage of his mother, disharmony between himself and his stepfather and damage done by drug taking when he was a teenager, and their combined effect on his psychological status, prevented the petitioner from understanding the nature and consequences of a long-term marriage relationship. On the basis of the report of the psychiatrist and the evidence of the petitioner, the judge granted a decree of nullity, stating that he had no doubt that the petitioner was 'in such an emotional and psychological state as to be quite incapable of entering into a marriage relationship' and annulled the marriage.

Emotional immaturity was also the basis of an application for a decree of nullity in *D.McC. v. E.C.* (1998). The evidence showed that the petitioner had been seriously sexually abused by his father from the age of six until he was fourteen years of age. His mother left home when he was fifteen because of physical abuse by the father. At seventeen shortly after leaving school, he left home and went to live with a girlfriend with whom he had a child. The relationship was stormy at times and he left her on many occasions. He became an alcoholic and received treatment for this condition in a psychiatric hospital. Some years later, he married the respondent. After several violent incidents, the marriage ended in failure. The Court was satisfied that the applicant was extremely immature when it came to entering close emotional relationships with other people. This was due to his appalling childhood, his alcoholism and his stormy relationship with his previous girlfriend. In declaring the marriage null and void, McCracken J stated that the applicant 'did not fully understand the nature of a proper marriage, and certainly was incapable of entering into or sustaining a normal marital relationship with the Respondent.'

Absence of Adequate Knowledge of a 'Circumstance of Substance'

The Supreme Court held in M.O'M. *(orse. O'C)* v. *B.O'C.* (1996) that there can be no informed consent in the absence of adequate knowledge of a 'circumstance of substance'. The net point at issue in the case was whether the consent to marriage given by the wife was an informed one. The wife contended that it was not an informed consent, because she had not been told by her husband prior to the marriage that he had attended a psychiatrist for about six years. She stated that she would not have married him had she known this beforehand. The High Court held that the wife's consent was a full, free and informed one. On appeal the Supreme Court referred to the decision in *N. (orse. K)* v. *K.* (1986), which established that for a marriage to be valid it is necessary that the consent of each spouse, in addition to being freely given, should be an informed consent. The Supreme Court, in allowing the appeal, accepted that the wife's lack of knowledge that her husband had attended a psychiatrist prior to the marriage meant that she did not have adequate knowledge of a 'circumstance of substance' and that, accordingly, the wife's consent was not an informed one. In his judgment Blaney J stated:

> What has to be determined, accordingly, is whether the consent of the wife was an informed consent, a consent based on adequate knowledge, and the test is a subjective one, that is to say, the test is whether this spouse, marrying this particular man, could be said to have had adequate knowledge of every circumstance relevant to the decision she was making, so that her consent could truly be said to be an informed one.

Absence of adequate knowledge of a circumstance of vital significance resulting in there being no informed consent was also in issue in *B.J.M.* v. *C.M.* (1996). The respondent had been badly burned as a small child, as a result of which she had extensive scarring over the whole front of her torso. As the parties had no sexual contact prior to the marriage, the petitioner was not aware of the respondent's condition until the honeymoon. In granting a decree of nullity, the High Court held that the consent of the petitioner was not a full, free and informed consent in the absence of adequate knowledge on his part of a circumstance of vital significance to him. Similarly, in *J.S.* v. *M.J.* (1997) it could be said that the petitioner, who was unaware prior to the marriage that the respondent suffered from a severe psychiatric illness in the form of depression occurring as part of a schizo-affective illness, did not have adequate knowledge of every circumstance relevant to the decision he was making. The High Court accepted the evidence of a psychiatrist to the effect that this illness rendered the respondent incapable of giving a true consent and declared the marriage void.

In *P.F.* v. *G.O'M. (orse. G.F.)* (1999) O'Higgins J distinguished the decision in *B.J.M.* v. *C.M.* (1996) from the case at hearing. The applicant husband sought to have the marriage annulled on the grounds that he had not given a full, free and informed consent, as he had not adequate knowledge of a circumstance of substance, namely, the relationship of his wife with another man at the time the parties became engaged. In *B.J.M.*, Flood J held that the undisclosed physical condition of the wife had prevented the husband giving a full, free and informed consent. However, in *P.F. v. G.O'M*, O'Higgins J refused to accept that the wife's undisclosed pre-marital relationship prevented the husband from giving a full, free and informed consent.

Voidable Marriages

There are two grounds on which a marriage may be declared voidable, namely, 1) impotence resulting in non-consummation, and, 2) lack of capacity to enter into and sustain a normal life-long functional marital relationship.

Impotence

Impotence means a party's inability to consummate the marriage. Consummation is achieved by one act of sexual intercourse after the marriage ceremony. The required act of sexual intercourse must be 'ordinary and complete and not partial and imperfect', so that a husband who can sustain an erection for only a very short period of time has been found incapable of consummating his marriage — *W. v. W.* (1967). However, the lack of ability to ejaculate does not prevent consummation — *R. v. R.* (1952). In *Baxter v. Baxter* (1948), the House of Lords held that a marriage had been consummated even though the husband, at the wife's insistence, had always worn a contraceptive sheath during sexual intercourse, thereby preventing the possibility of conception.

Where non-consummation is due to incapacity, it may be from physical or psychological reasons. It may be an inability to have sexual intercourse with all persons of the opposite sex (physical) or merely with the other party to the marriage (psychological). The incapacity must be incurable in the sense that there is no practical possibility of consummation at the time of the hearing of the petition for nullity. Incapacity will be regarded as incurable if the party suffering the incapacity refuses to undergo an operation to cure the defect, or it can be cured only by a dangerous operation or one that is unlikely to succeed.

In the case of psychological impotence, the spouse suffering the incapacity may be perfectly capable of having sexual intercourse with members of the opposite sex generally, but may be repulsed by the thought of having sexual intercourse with the other spouse. This was the position in *S. v. S.* (1976), where the husband was unaffectionate towards the wife and refused to have sexual intercourse with her following the marriage, so that the marriage was never consummated. When the marriage broke down both parties formed second relationships. The Supreme Court granted a decree of nullity on the basis of the husband's impotence. Similarly, in *R. (orse. W.) v. W.* (1980) the wife could not bring herself to having sexual intercourse with her husband after the marriage, resulting in its non-consummation, but formed a relationship with another man following the breakdown of the marriage, by whom she had a child. The High Court annulled the marriage. In *N.F. v. M.T.* (1982) the marriage was declared null and void by reason of the physical and psychological incapacity of the wife to consummate the marriage. O'Hanlon J accepted that the husband had at all times been willing to have sexual intercourse with the wife, but that she was incapable of consummation because of difficulties related to her physical make-up and by reason of psychological problems that affected her. She refused to submit to medical examination to establish whether the physical problem could be resolved by medical intervention. Even though the possibility remained that the wife could have normal marital relations with some other partner in the future, the learned judge found 'that there is and will remain a complete incapacity *qua* the petitioner'.

Psychological impotence should be distinguished from wilful refusal to consummate. Whereas, a spouse's inability to have sexual intercourse with the other spouse renders a marriage voidable, there is judicial support for the proposition that a decision by a spouse at the time of the ceremony not to consummate may vitiate consent and render the marriage void. Kenny J in his judgment in *S. v. S.* stated that:

> [T]he intention to have sexual intercourse is such a fundamental feature of the marriage contract that if at the time of the marriage either party has determined that there will not be any during the marriage and none takes place . . . a spouse who was not aware of the determination of the other is entitled to a declaration that the marriage was null.

A Petitioner's Own Impotence as the Basis of a Claim for Nullity

An impotent spouse may rely on his own impotence to support a petition for nullity where he or she can satisfy the Court that the other spouse has repudiated the marriage — *McM. v. McM. and McK. v. McK.* (1936). In *R. (orse. W.) v. W.* (1980) the petitioner successfully pleaded her own impotence because the respondent had repudiated the marriage by seeking a church annulment. Lynch J was of the view in *L.C. v. B.C. (orse. B.L.)* (1986) that a party can rely on his own impotence not only where the other party has repudiated the marriage, but also where that other party is impotent. The petitioner was successful in obtaining a decree based on her own impotence in *E.C. (orse. M.) v. K.M.* (1991). The fact that the respondent had supported the petitioner's application for a church annulment was deemed to be a repudiation by him of the marriage.

Lack of Capacity to Enter into and Sustain a Normal Life-Long Functional Marital Relationship

This ground for nullity renders a marriage voidable and was first recognised by Barrington J in *R.S.J. v. J.S.J.* (1982), where he stated:

> The law has always accepted impotence as a ground for avoiding a marriage. But in ways what is contended for here is a much more serious impediment to marriage. No doubt there have been happy marriages where one of the parties was impotent. But it is impossible to imagine any form of meaningful marriage where one of the parties lacks the capacity of entering into a caring, or even a considerate, relationship with the other.

Two years later in *D. v. C.* (1984) Costello J affirmed the judgment of Barrington J and emphasised 'that there is more to marriage than its physical consummation' and that marriage involves 'the creation of an emotional and psychological relationship between the spouses'. Costello J went on to recognise the developments that have taken place in psychiatry in recent times and stated that:

> It is now possible to identify psychiatric illnesses, such as for example manic-depressive illness, which in some cases may be so severe as to make it impossible for one of the partners to the marriage to enter into and sustain the relationship which should exist between married couples if a life-long union is to be possible.

This ground for nullity is concerned with the question of a person's capacity to perform the marriage contract and not with that person's capacity to understand the nature of the contract of marriage. The Supreme Court confirmed the existence of this new ground for nullity and broadened its scope in *F.(orse. C.) v. C.* (1991). In the course of his judgment, Finlay CJ approved of the principles established in *R.S.J. v. J.S.J.* and *D. v. C.*, and in particular the analogy drawn by Barrington J in *R.S.J. v. J.S.J.* between impotence and incapacity to enter into and sustain a proper marital relationship, and stated that the analogy was not confined to cases where the incapacity was caused by psychiatric or mental illness, but also applied 'in cases where it arose from some other inherent quality or characteristic of an individual's nature or personality which could not be said to be voluntary or self induced'. This landmark decision of the Supreme Court acknowledges that certain characteristics present in a person at the time of the marriage, such as mental illness, sexual orientation and emotional immaturity, may deprive that person of the ability to enter into and sustain a loving and considerate marital relationship. Each of these characteristics will be examined by reference to the many decisions that have been handed down by the Courts since *R.S.J. v. J.S.J.*.

Mental Illness

A person suffering from one of the psychotic disorders at the time of the marriage ceremony may be incapable of understanding the nature of marriage and of giving a full, free and informed consent, thereby rendering the marriage void. On the other hand, the degree of mental illness may not be such as to render the person incapable of consenting, but at the same time it may affect that person's capacity to sustain a normal marital relationship, thereby rendering the marriage voidable. The mere fact that a person is mentally ill does not mean that he is incapable of entering into and sustaining the life-long relationship that marriage involves, as was made clear by Costello J in *R. v. R.* (1984). All that is required is that a person about to get married is, at the date of the marriage, capable of appreciating the 'emotional and psychological relationship' that marriage entails. It is significant that in *R.S.J. v. J.S.J.* Barrington J, while accepting that the petitioner suffered from a form of schizophrenia, was not satisfied that this prevented the petitioner from sustaining a normal marital relationship. In *D. v. C.*, the petitioner obtained a decree on the basis that the respondent 'suffered from a manic depressive illness which was present throughout the duration of his relationship with the petitioner both before, at the time of, and after their marriage'.

The case of *R. v. R.* (1984) is significant in that it highlights the important part that medication can play in ameliorating the effects of the psychotic disorders. It is a generally accepted medical fact that many people recover from an attack of schizophrenia well enough to return to relatively normal life, and can avoid a recurrence of a bad attack with the aid of constant medication. Unfortunately, in this case the respondent, who had been diagnosed as a paranoid schizophrenic and hospitalised five years prior to the marriage (a fact unknown to the petitioner at the time of the marriage), had discontinued taking drugs prescribed for his condition shortly before the marriage. As a result, his condition deteriorated since the marriage and he had to be hospitalised again. Costello J concluded from the medical evidence that the respondent was not capable of entering into a meaningful and stable marital relationship, and that the marriage had made his condition worse.

This ground for nullity, as the result of one or other of the parties suffering from a form of mental illness, was successfully pleaded in *D.C. v. D.W.* (1987) (schizophrenia), *G.M. (orse. G.) v. T.G.* (1991) (severe psychotic endogenous depression), *P.K. v. M.B.M. (orse K.)* (1995) (paranoid psychosis) and *J.S. v. M.J.* (1997) (depression occurring as part of a schizo-affective illness).

Sexual Orientation

The judgment of Hamilton J in *McD. (orse O'R.) v. O'R.* (1984) established for the first time in this jurisdiction that homosexuality in itself does not constitute a ground for nullity. It is only where homosexuality prevents performance of the fundamental incidents of marriage that it can be relied upon to support a petition for nullity. The petitioner sought to have her marriage to the respondent annulled on the basis that he engaged in a homosexual relationship prior to his marriage. While accepting that the respondent did engage in such a relationship, Hamilton J was satisfied that the relationship had ended before the marriage ceremony. There was evidence that the parties had a normal sexual relationship for some time subsequent to the ceremony. Indeed, the petitioner had a number of miscarriages. The Court refused to annul the marriage.

In *F. v. F.* (1990) the petitioner became suspicious in the course of the parties' courtship that the respondent might have homosexual tendencies. When she confronted him on the matter, he assured her that he was not a homosexual, although he did admit that he had one encounter with a male which was based on tenderness rather than sexual. Within a few weeks of the parties' marriage, the respondent told the petitioner that he could not share his life with anyone, and the relationship came to an end. Two homosexuals gave evidence that the respondent had led a promiscuous homosexual lifestyle prior to the marriage, and a consultant psychiatrist stated that he considered the respondent to be severely psychologically disturbed and of a compulsive homosexual nature. Barron J granted a decree of nullity on the basis that the respondent 'was unable by virtue of psychiatric illness to maintain the life long relationship required of marriage'.

In *F. (orse. C.) v. C.* (1991) (also known as *U.F.(orse. U.C.) v. J.C.* (1991)) the Supreme Court accepted that the incapacity of one party to form and maintain a normal marital relationship with the other party is a ground for nullity, and in so doing extended the principles laid down by Barrington J in *R.S.J. v. J.S.J.* and Costello J in *D. v. C.* to cases where the alleged incapacity is due to a homosexual nature. The parties in *F. (orse. C.) v. C.* had married in 1981 and had a child the following year. Shortly afterwards, the petitioner discovered that the respondent was a practising homosexual and had been so at the time of the marriage. The Supreme Court annulled the marriage on the ground that the respondent was, by virtue of his homosexual nature at the time of the marriage, unable to form a normal marital relationship. In the course of his judgment, Finlay CJ said that developments in the law of nullity due to modern advances in psychiatric medicine should take account of widespread research in the area of sexual orientation and development of the individual, and that the existence in one party to a marriage of 'an inherent and unalterable homosexual nature may form a proper legal ground for annulling the marriage at the instance of the other party to the marriage in the case, at least, where that party has no knowledge of the existence of the homosexual nature'.

Emotional Immaturity

Emotional immaturity arising from psychiatric or personality disorder may negate consent to marriage or affect the capacity of a person to maintain a normal marital relationship. This ground for nullity was first recognised by Barrington J in *W. v. P.* (1984). The respondent in that case was very immature and on occasion, had to be managed like a child by the petitioner. The abnormal behaviour of the respondent, both before and after the marriage ceremony, included trying to cause himself physical injury by beating himself about the head and banging his head off the wall, trying to smother himself be holding his head under water, going on hunger strike when he believed that the petitioner was going to leave him, and trying to hang himself on one occasion. The psychiatric evidence showed that the respondent's 'degree of underdevelopment and immaturity of personality was such as markedly to impair his capacity to sustain a normal and viable marriage relationship'. Barrington J granted a decree of nullity on the ground that the respondent at the time of the marriage 'was suffering from such psychological or emotional disability or incapacity as made it impossible for him to enter into and sustain a normal marriage relationship with the petitioner'. Three years later in *B. v. M.* (1987) Barrington J granted a decree of nullity on the ground that the respondent was suffering from 'such a degree of emotional immaturity as to preclude the formation of a normal marital relationship'.

A number of decisions since *W. v. P.* emphasise that the emotional immaturity must exist in a person 'to an abnormal degree', as Carroll J put it in *P.C. (orse. O'B.) v. O'B.* (1985), before it will affect the ability of that person to sustain a normal marital relationship. The Supreme Court held in *H.S. v. J.S.* (1992) that it is only in cases where the immaturity or irresponsibility of a person negates that person's capacity to maintain a lasting marriage relationship that a marriage should be annulled on the ground of emotional immaturity. In *J.W.H. (orse. W.) v. G.W.* (1998) O'Higgins J said that 'the emotional immaturity has to be such as would render the person quite incapable of forming and sustaining [a] marriage relationship'. While accepting that the petitioner was emotionally immature, the learned judge could not find any evidence of any psychological abnormality or lack of intelligence in the petitioner and was not satisfied that the petitioner and the respondent lacked the capacity to enter into and sustain a normal life-long functional relationship with each other.

Emotional immaturity should be distinguished from temperamental incompatibility or mere inadequacy of emotional response. In *P.C. v. V.C.* (1990) O'Hanlon J emphasised that temperamental incompatibility is not a ground for nullity. However, he felt that the present case went beyond temperamental incompatibility and into the realm of emotional immaturity and psychiatric weakness, and found that the parties to the marriage were unable to enter into and sustain a normal marital relationship with each other 'by reason of incapacity deriving from lack of emotional maturity and psychological weakness and disturbance affecting both parties to a greater or lesser degree'. In *O'R. v. B.* (1995) Kinlen J found that the petitioner was so emotionally immature at the time of entering into the marriage as to be unable to enter into and sustain a normal marital relationship. However, the learned judge made it clear that temperamental incompatibility is not a ground for declaring a marriage null and void. In *K.T. v. D.T.* (1996) the Supreme Court held that the inadequacy of the emotional response of the parties to each other was not of such a degree as would justify granting a nullity decree.

A Petitioner's Own Inability as the Basis of a Claim for Nullity

On the basis of an analogy between this ground for nullity and impotence, Barrington J held in *R.S.J. v. J.S.J.* that a petitioner can only rely on his own inability to enter into and sustain a normal marital relationship where the respondent has repudiated the marriage. Blaney J adopted a similar approach in *D.C. v. D.W.* (1987), but allowed the wife's petition based on her own incapacity because the husband had repudiated the marriage.

However, the requirement that the respondent should have repudiated the marriage before the petitioner could rely on his own incapacity to ground a petition for nullity, was rejected by the Supreme Court in *P.C. v. V.C.* (1990). Finlay CJ was of the view that as both parties were unaware at the time of the marriage 'that factors connected with the personality and psychology of each partner' would make it impossible for them to maintain a normal marital relationship for any length of time, 'the petitioner should not be denied a decree of nullity because the respondent wishes to hold him to the marriage bond'. In *O'R. v. B.* (1995) Kinlen J expressed himself satisfied that the petitioner could rely on his own incapacity to support his petition, even though he accepted that the respondent had not repudiated the marriage.

More recently, in *D.McC. v. E.C.* (1998), McCracken J was of the view that the Supreme Court's approach in *P.C. v. V.C.* was the correct one. McCracken J stated that the earlier approach was based on the premise that marriage is a contract and should be treated like every other contract. However, he felt that as marriage involves complex human relationships, it should not be treated like an ordinary contract. The concept of nullity as developed by the Courts is not known to the ordinary law of contract. In the case of an ordinary contract, there may still be a valid contract even though one party is unable to perform it. However, the law of nullity operates on the basis that, although the contract was formally entered into, there may be circumstances in which it is void because of one party's inability to perform the contract at the time it was entered into. The learned judge went on to say:

> It is the whole essence of nullity that there never was a contract of marriage,

the parties were never married, and no obligations arise on either side. It is not a question of a breach of the contract of marriage, but of its existence, which is why the person whose marriage has been declared a nullity is free to marry.

Bars To a Nullity Decree

As a void marriage is one that never legally existed, there can be no bar or defence to a petition for nullity relating to a void marriage. In the case of a voidable marriage, there are a number of bars to relief, namely approbation, delay and collusion.

Approbation

The principle on which approbation operates was aptly stated by Watson LJ in the English case of *G. v. M.* (1885) as follows:

> In a suit for nullity of marriage there may be facts and circumstances provided which so plainly imply, on the part of the complaining spouse, a recognition of the existence and validity of the marriage, as to render it most inequitable and contrary to public policy that he or she should be permitted to go on to challenge it with effect.

Approbation is conduct which clearly shows that the petitioner has accepted the marriage as valid at a time when he knows that he has a right to have it set aside. Examples of conduct that amounted to approbation are to be found in the English cases of *W. v. W.* (1952) and *Slater v. Slater* (1953). In *W. v. W.* the Court refused to grant a decree of nullity to the husband who, before instituting proceedings, had jointly, with his impotent wife, adopted a child with full knowledge at the time of the adoption that he was entitled to have his marriage annulled. However, in *Slater v. Slater* the fact that the couple had adopted a child was not a bar to the wife's petition for nullity, as she was unaware at the time of the adoption of her right to seek a decree. Accordingly, where the respondent satisfies the Court that the petitioner by his conduct caused the respondent to believe that he would not petition for nullity, a petition must be refused. The respondent's belief must be reasonably held and the petitioner must have known that he had grounds on which to petition for nullity.

In *Pettit v. Pettit* (1962) Donovan LJ stated that 'knowledge of the facts and the law should be regarded as prerequisites of approbation', while in *D. v. C.* (1984) Costello J stated that approbation only occurred where 'the petitioner acted not only with knowledge of the facts which entitled her to a nullity decree but also with a knowledge that these facts would, as a matter of law, have entitled her to the right she now seeks'. In *N.F. v. M.T.* (1982) O'Hanlon J said that he was satisfied, on the basis of the principles established in *Pettit v. Pettit*, that there was no evidence of delay or other forms of approbation of the marriage as would operate as a bar to proceedings for nullity. O'Hanlon J accepted the evidence of the petitioner that his delay in presenting a petition for nullity based on the respondent's impotence was due to the fact that he had been wrongly legally advised at first that he had no real prospects of success. In *R.McG. v. K.N. (orse. McG.)* (1995) the High Court held that applications by the husband to the Court for maintenance, at a time when he had full knowledge of his right to petition for nullity, amounted to approbation on his part.

Delay

Mere delay in filing a petition for nullity, on the grounds of impotence or inability to enter into and sustain a normal marital relationship, does not necessarily imply acceptance of the marriage on the part of the petitioner. However, the longer the petitioner delays in filing a petition the greater the inference that there has been approbation. Each case depends on its own circumstances. The High Court held in *N.F. v. M.T.* (1982) that a delay of almost six years in seeking a decree of nullity did not amount to approbation in the case of impotence. The parties had lived together for three and a half years before finally separating, and the petitioner then waited a further two years before commencing proceedings. O'Hanlon J accepted the evidence of the petitioner that he had not presented a petition earlier as he had been dissuaded from doing so by the pleas of the respondent, and the intervention of her parents. He was also satisfied that the petitioner was legally advised at first that he would not succeed, and that it was only when the petitioner received a second legal opinion that he found out that he had good grounds for presenting the petition. In *C.M. v. E.L.* (1994) a husband who did not become aware that he could have the marriage annulled until shortly before he filed his petition, obtained a decree of nullity twenty three years after the date of the marriage ceremony, on the basis of the wife's inability to maintain a normal marital relationship.

Collusion

Because divorce was not available in this jurisdiction prior to the amendment of Article 41.3.2 of the Constitution and the Family Law (Divorce) Act 1996, the Courts had to be careful that unhappily married couples did not collude with one another to have their marriages annulled as a means of opting out of the marriage contract. Despite the fact that divorce is now available in this jurisdiction, the judges continue to satisfy themselves in proceedings for nullity that there has been no collusion between the parties. For example, in *J.W.H. (orse W.) v. G.W.* (1998) and *D.K. v. T.H.* (1998) O'Higgins J expressed himself satisfied that there was no collusion in either case and that the petitions were genuine.

Collusion is basically an agreement between the parties not to present the true case to the Court to facilitate the obtaining of a nullity decree. The Concise

Oxford Dictionary describes the word 'collusion' as 'fraudulent secret understanding, esp[ecially] between ostensible opponents as in a law suit'. The Supreme Court held in *M.v M.* (1978) that there must be very specific evidence to prove collusion. A mere suspicion by the trial judge that there had been collusion was not enough. In *E.P. v. M.C.* (1985) Barron J referred to the heavy onus that is placed on the petitioner to show that there has been no collusion, and held that the petitioner had not discharged that onus. In *N. (orse K.) v. K.* (1986) McCarthy J referred to the possibility of collusion as justification for the high degree of proof that is required to rebut the presumption that a marriage is valid.

Further Reading

Shatter, *Family Law*, 4th. Ed. Dublin: Butterworths 1997.

Binchy, *A Casebook on Irish Family Law*. Abingdon: Professional Books 1984.

Duncan & Scully, *Marriage Breakdown in Ireland: Law and Practice*. Dublin: Butterworths (Ireland) 1990.

O'Connor, *Key Issues in Irish Family Law*. Dublin: The Round Hall Press 1988.

Attorney General, *The Law of Nullity in Ireland*. Dublin: Stationery Office 1976.

Report of the Joint Oireachtas Committee on Marriage Breakdown. Dublin: Stationery Office, 1985.

Law Reform Commission, Report on Nullity of Marriage (LRC 9 - 1984).

CHAPTER FOUR

SEPARATION BY AGREEMENT

The Nature of a Separation Agreement

A separation agreement is essentially an agreement between husband and wife to live separately and apart. Such an agreement is governed by ordinary principles of the law of contract. Consideration is necessary unless the agreement is under seal in the form of a deed of separation. The fact that the spouses have already separated, or are estranged and about to separate, is evidence of their intention to be legally bound. In *Merritt v. Merritt* (1970) the Court held that since the parties had negotiated at arm's length and had decided to separate, any reasonable person would regard their agreement as intended to be binding in law.

A separation agreement need not take any particular form to be enforceable. It may be made orally or implied from conduct. In practice, however, because of the serious matters involved for the spouses, a separation agreement will normally be in writing and embodied in a deed. An agreement providing for future separation between spouses who are still cohabiting is void as against public policy unless it forms part of an overall reconciliation arrangement — *Re Meyrick's Settlement* (1921). A separation agreement may be void for mistake as in *Galloway v. Galloway* (1914), where the parties had entered into such an agreement on the basis that they were validly married. The marriage was in fact bigamous and therefore void.

A separation agreement, in addition to providing for the spouses to live apart, normally regulates such matters as maintenance, custody and access to dependent children, and the use and division of matrimonial property. The actual terms of the agreement depend entirely on the requirements of the parties. Full and frank negotiation of all the material terms should take place. An improvident agreement, or one induced by undue influence exerted by the party in the dominant bargaining position, may be subsequently set aside. For this reason it is important that both parties have the benefit of independent legal advice. As a separation agreement releases the spouses from their duty to cohabit, it will have the effect of terminating desertion where one spouse has previously deserted the other. This may have implications later on for one spouse petitioning for judicial separation on the ground of the other's desertion. In addition, social welfare allowances paid to a deserted spouse may be adversely affected.

Legislative Developments

Separation agreements as a means of regulating the affairs of estranged spouses have assumed greater significance in recent times owing to major legislative and judicial developments in the area of marriage breakdown. Sections 5 and 6 of the Judicial Separation and Family Law Reform Act 1989 require the solicitors acting for both spouses, prior to instituting or defending judicial separation proceedings, to advise their respective clients of the possibility of engaging in mediation to help effect a separation by agreement. Similar provisions are contained in sections 5 and 6 of the Family Law (Divorce) Act 1996 in relation to divorce proceedings. The importance placed on separation agreements by the legislation governing marriage breakdown is again evident in section 20(3) of the 1996 Act, which requires the Court, in determining what provision should be made for spouses and dependent children in divorce proceedings, to have regard to the terms of any separation agreement entered into between the spouses still in force. In the absence of any indication as to what weight should be given to the terms of a separation agreement, the Court might consider the circumstances in which the agreement was reached, the actual terms of the agreement and any change in the circumstances of the parties since the agreement was concluded. If the Court is satisfied that the separation agreement makes proper provision for the spouses and dependent children within the meaning of the 1996 Act, it might refuse to make ancillary orders or make such orders in the terms of the provision set out in the agreement. Otherwise, the Court could vary the terms of the separation agreement and grant such ancillary relief as it deemed fit.

Judicial Developments

The most significant judicial development is the decision of the Supreme Court in *P.O'D. v. A.O'D.* (1998) to the effect that a separation agreement that amounts in law to a binding contract is a bar to subsequent proceedings for judicial separation under the Judicial Separation and Family Law Reform Act 1989. This is so not only because the parties to a binding separation agreement are not permitted to go behind it, but also because the parties, by agreeing to live separately and apart, had rendered superfluous the granting of a decree of judicial separation. This is an important consideration to be brought to the notice of the parties in negotiating the terms of a separation agreement, since the extensive range of financial and property reliefs available under Part II of the Family Law Act 1995 (which replaced Part II of the 1989 Act) can only be made on granting a decree of judicial separation. For a more detailed consideration of the issues involved, see Chapter 5.

A separation agreement cannot act as a bar to divorce proceedings under the Family Law (Divorce) Act 1996, since a decree of divorce dissolves a marriage. By virtue of section 14(c) of the 1996 Act, the Court, in making a property adjustment order, can vary the terms of any ante-nuptial or post-nuptial settlement. In *P.O'D. v. A.O'D.* the Supreme Court indicated that a separation agreement could be considered a post-nuptial settlement in the context of divorces *a vinculo matrimonii* (divorce dissolving marriage).

Standard Clauses in Separation Agreements

The following are examples of clauses usually found in separation agreements:

(1) Agreement to Live Apart

This is a standard clause in separation agreements. As such a clause is deemed to terminate desertion, it should not be included unless the deserted spouse agrees to live apart. In the absence of agreement to live apart, the parties may enter a maintenance agreement which merely defines the extent and duration of a spouse's financial liability to the other and/or dependent children.

(2) Non-Molestation Clause

The spouses agree not to molest, annoy or disturb each other. In *Fearon v. Alyesford* (1884) it was held that a wife's adultery and the subsequent birth of a non-marital child was not a breach of this clause. There would have been a breach, however, had the wife represented the child as her husband's. For a further consideration of the meaning of the word 'molest', see Chapter 11.

(3) Maintenance Clause

This takes the form of one spouse (usually the husband) agreeing to make periodical payments to the other spouse and/or dependent children. Alternatively, maintenance may be paid in the form of a lump sum. Periodical payments can be secured by a charge on property. Provision may be made for the annual review of maintenance payments to take account of such matters as an increase in the consumer price index and the changed financial circumstances of the spouses or either of them. It was held in the English case of *Kirk v. Eustace* (1937) that, in the absence of a *dum casta* clause, a covenant by one spouse to pay maintenance for the other spouse's life is enforceable, even in the event of the other spouse committing adultery.

An agreement not to apply to the Court for maintenance for either a spouse or dependent children is void under section 27 of the Family Law (Maintenance of Spouses and Children) Act 1976. The Supreme Court held in *H.D. v. P.D.* (1978) that a clause in a separation agreement cannot oust the jurisdiction of the Court to consider what is proper maintenance. However, it is clear from the judgment of Murphy J in *O'S. v. O'S.* (1983) that a maintenance order made by the Court under section 5 of the 1976 Act cannot have the effect of varying a provision for maintenance in a valid separation agreement.

A separation agreement which makes provision for maintenance by periodical payments to a spouse and/or dependent children may be made a rule of court under section 8 of the Family Law (Maintenance of Spouses and Children) Act 1976. The Court will only make the agreement a rule of court where it is satisfied that it is fair and reasonable and adequately protects the interests of both spouses and any dependent children. The Supreme Court held in *D. v. D.* (1991) that where a separation agreement providing for such matters as maintenance is made a rule of court, it will have the same effect as a maintenance order made by the Court.

(4) Dum Casta Clause

It is usual for the spouse paying maintenance to require the inclusion of such a clause, to the effect that liability to pay will cease should the other spouse not remain chaste, i.e. commits adultery or cohabits with another man or woman. It was held in *Fearon v. Aylesford* (1884) that a *dum casta* clause must be an express term of the agreement, as it will not be implied.

(5) Custody and Access to Children

By virtue of section 6 of the Guardianship of Infants Act 1964, as amended, both spouses are joint guardians of their children and are entitled to joint custody. Guardianship consists of parental rights and obligations in relation to a child, while custody is the right to physical care and control of a child (see Chapter 14). By virtue of section 18 of the1964 Act there is nothing to prevent the spouses providing for custody and access to children in a separation agreement. Detailed provision is made whereby one spouse will have day-to-day custody of the children and the other spouse will have access on specified dates and times. Provision may also be made for joint custody. There will normally be agreement by both spouses not to remove a child outside the jurisdiction of the State without the prior consent of the other, such consent not to be unreasonably withheld. However, it should be borne in mind that as a result of the decision in *Cullen v. Cullen* (1970) an agreement as to custody and access will not be enforced by the Court unless it is in the best interests of the children.

(6) Agreement Relating to Property

It is important that agreement is reached in relation to the matrimonial home. Where the home is owned jointly by the spouses, and the wife and dependent children are remaining in the home, it is usual to provide that the husband is to continue with the mortgage repayments and other outgoings. Where the matrimonial home is owned solely by the husband, and he is not prepared to transfer it to the wife or partition it between them, it is important that the agreement provides a right of residence for the wife and dependent children, at least until the youngest child attains his majority. To avoid disputes at a later date about furniture and other household effects, an inventory should be prepared and included as a schedule to the agreement identifying what items belong to each spouse. Section 21 of the Family Law (Maintenance of Spouses and Children) Act 1976 provides that, in the absence of agreement to the contrary, any property bought out of a household allowance shall belong to the spouses jointly.

(7) Renunciation of Succession Act Rights

The legal right conferred on a spouse by section 111 of the Succession Act 1965 to share in the estate of the other spouse who dies testate will survive the execution of a separation agreement. Accordingly, it is usual to find a clause in the agreement to the effect that both spouses renounce any claim they might have to the estate of the other spouse. Section 111 of the Act quantifies the legal right share as one half of the net estate where there are no children, and one third where there are children. Section 113 provides that the legal right share may be renounced in a written ante-nuptial contract or in writing after the marriage. In *Moorehead v Tiilikainen* (1999) the parties to a separation agreement had mutually renounced their Succession Act rights to the estate of the other, but expressly provided that if they subsequently resumed cohabitation as man and wife by mutual consent for a continuous period of twelve months, their mutual renunciation of Succession Act rights should be null and void. The High Court held that the parties had in fact resumed cohabitation as provided for, thereby rendering the renunciation of Succession Act rights null and void.

(8) Life Assurance

It is usual for the spouse responsible for the payment of maintenance to expressly agree to continue with the payment of premiums on any life policies in which the other spouse is a named beneficiary. As regards pension schemes, it is not possible for the parties to come to a binding agreement in relation to the splitting of a retirement benefit or a contingent benefit under a pension scheme. Benefits under pension schemes can only be split or earmarked by means of a pension adjustment order on the granting of a decree of judicial separation or divorce. Neither the 1995 nor 1996 Acts make provision for the parties to a separation agreement to apply for court approval of an agreement as to pension splitting.

(9) Indemnity Clause

Both spouses agree to indemnify each other against all debts and liabilities howsoever arising.

Termination of Separation Agreement

Ordinary principles of the law of contract govern the termination or discharge of a separation agreement. In general, such an agreement may be terminated in the following ways:

(a) By mutual agreement.
(b) By resumption of cohabitation. Whether a resumption of cohabitation discharges maintenance and property provisions is a matter of construction of the agreement.
(c) By breach. The breach must be so fundamental as to show that the party in

breach no longer intends to be bound by the agreement, and the other party must treat the agreement as at an end — *Pardy v. Pardy* (1939).

Remedies for Breach of Separation Agreement

The usual remedies for breach of contract are available to the parties to the agreement. They are damages, specific performance and an injunction.

Damages

The purpose of an award of damages is to compensate the injured party for the loss flowing naturally from the breach of contract. Where possible, the Court should endeavour to place the injured party in the same financial position as if the contract had been performed. The rule in *Hadley v. Baxendale* (1854), which has been applied by Irish courts, provides that the damages must be such as were reasonably foreseeable, when the contract was made, as likely to result from the breach.

Specific Performance

This will only be granted where the agreement, including one under seal, is supported by consideration on the part of each spouse. Specific performance may be decreed instead of, or in addition to, damages. Specific performance requires the party in breach of contract to carry out his obligations. The Court can decree specific performance to enforce any of the covenants in a separation agreement. However, as the remedy of specific performance is an equitable remedy, it is discretionary and will only be decreed in exceptional cases where the remedy of damages is inadequate. On the authority of *Beswick v. Beswick* (1968), periodical maintenance payments under a separation agreement could be enforced by specific performance to avoid the necessity of a multiplicity of actions to enforce payment.

Injunction

An injunction is an order of the court which compels a person to carry out an act which he is legally obliged to perform or to refrain from conduct that is unlawful. Like specific performance, an injunction is an equitable remedy and will only be granted where damages are inadequate. Under general principles of equity, an injunction may be granted in certain circumstances to restrain the breach of a negative covenant in a contract — see *Lumley v. Wagner* (1852). Accordingly, an injunction may be granted to prevent the breach of a non-molestation clause in a separation agreement.

Further Reading

Shatter, *Family Law*, 4th. Ed. Dublin: Butterworths 1997.

CHAPTER FIVE

JUDICIAL SEPARATION

Where a marriage, valid at its inception, has broken down and the spouses wish to separate but do not wish to terminate the marriage, they may resort to the remedy of judicial separation. A decree of judicial separation merely releases the spouses from their duty to cohabit without dissolving the marriage. The decree of judicial separation replaces the decree of divorce *a mensa et thoro* which had its origins in the old ecclesiastical courts and was available on the grounds of adultery, cruelty and unnatural practices.

The law on judicial separation is now enshrined in the Judicial Separation and Family Law Reform Act 1989, as amended by the Family Law Act 1995. By virtue of section 31(4) of the 1989 Act, the Court may only entertain an application for judicial separation where it is satisfied that either of the spouses is domiciled in the State on the date of the application or is ordinarily resident in the State throughout the year ending on that date. Section 2 of the 1989 Act sets out six grounds on which a decree can be granted. The grounds for judicial separation are adultery, unreasonable behaviour, desertion, living apart for specified periods and the breakdown of the marriage. The 1989 Act makes judicial separation available in certain circumstances without the necessity for one spouse to prove conduct amounting to fault on the part of the other. There is also provision in the Act for the making of ancillary financial, property, custody and other orders.

It should be emphasised at this stage that a decree of judicial separation will not be automatically forthcoming where an applicant establishes one or more of the grounds set out in section 2 of the 1989 Act. Section 3(2)(a) provides that the Court cannot grant a decree where there are dependent children of the family unless it is satisfied that proper provision has been made for their welfare, or the Court intends making such provision. The High Court considered the implications of section 3(2)(a) in *S.(V.) v. S.(R.)* (1992). In that case, the wife appealed a Circuit Court decision refusing a decree of judicial separation. On appeal Lynch J, in granting a decree under section 2(1)(f), stated that the Court cannot grant a decree unless it is satisfied that it can make proper provision for dependent children.

Effect of Decree of Judicial Separation

Section 8 of the 1989 Act states that such a decree merely releases the spouses from their duty to cohabit. Non-cohabitation following a decree cannot amount to desertion. The parties remain husband and wife. Their succession rights remain intact, but either party may apply to the Court under section 14 of the 1995 Act for an order extinguishing the succession rights of the other. In addition, all the other ancillary reliefs available under the 1995 Act, as amended by the Family Law (Divorce) Act 1996, following the granting of a decree of judicial separation may be availed of. See Chapter 7.

Section 8 provides that at any time following the granting of a decree the spouses may apply by consent to have the decree rescinded. The Court may rescind the decree where it is satisfied that a reconciliation has taken place and that the spouses have either resumed cohabitation or intend to do so. Where a decree is rescinded, the Court can make any ancillary orders it deems proper with regard to any ancillary orders previously made.

The Supreme Court held in *F. v. F.* (1995) that a decree of judicial separation under the 1989 Act has the same effect as a decree of divorce *a mensa et thoro*, since both decrees release the parties from their legal obligation to live together. The 1989 Act merely extended the grounds for judicial separation. In that case the wife had instituted proceedings for a decree of divorce *a mensa et thoro* in 1986. The case was settled and the consent signed by both parties was made a rule of court. The wife instituted Circuit Court proceedings for judicial separation in 1992. Her main purpose was to claim certain ancillary orders available for the first time under the 1989 Act. On a case stated from the Circuit Court, the Supreme Court ruled that the bringing of proceedings for divorce *a mensa et thoro* under the old regime was a bar to subsequent proceedings under the 1989 Act. A decree of judicial separation does not affect the bond of marriage.

Separation by Agreement or Judicial Separation?

Spouses apply for judicial separation as opposed to separating by agreement for many reasons. Obviously, one reason is that they cannot reach agreement on all the pertinent matters associated with separation such as financial provision, property distribution and custody. Another reason is that the parties to a marriage that has broken down require some public recognition of the breakdown and a decree of judicial separation can fill this need. It is now widely accepted, however, that the main reason why proceedings for judicial separation are instituted is not because parties want a decree for its own sake, but because they wish to avail of the wide range of ancillary orders that the Court can make once a decree of judicial separation has issued.

Separation Agreement Bar to Obtaining Decree of Judicial Separation

In *P.O'D. v. A.O'D.* (1998) the Supreme Court held that where spouses had entered into a valid deed of separation prior to the 1989 Act, they were subsequently precluded from seeking a decree of judicial separation. This was so even in the absence of an express covenant in the separation agreement not to seek judicial separation. A separation agreement which took the form of a binding contract is a bar to an application for judicial separation, not merely because the parties to such a contract are not permitted to go behind it, but also because the parties by agreeing to live separately and apart had rendered superfluous the granting of a decree of judicial separation. The Court acknowledged that it might seem harsh to deprive a person who had entered into a separation agreement under the law formerly applicable to proceedings under the Married Women's Status Act 1957, of the right to seek the more extensive property transfer orders available under the 1989 Act. However, it was for the Oireachtas to balance possible injustices against the desirability of ensuring finality and certainty in settlements of family law disputes, and discouraging parties from re-litigating matters with the consequent trauma for all involved, particularly the children of the marriage. The Court cited with approval the case of *Courtney v. Courtney* (1923), which decided that a separation agreement, which constituted in law a binding contract, was a bar to subsequent proceedings for divorce *a mensa et thoro*, even though it contained no express covenant not to sue.

Judicial Separation and Divorce

Despite the availability of divorce in Ireland, it is likely that the remedy of judicial separation will continue to be availed of by spouses who satisfy the criteria for divorce. The finality of a decree of divorce may not prove attractive to couples. Also, many spouses may still have religious or conscientious objections to seeking the final dissolution of their marriages. A further reason why judicial separation may be the preferred option is that it is possible to get a judicial separation with agreement after living apart for one year or for other reasons, whereas with divorce the requirement of living apart for four of the previous five years is far more onerous, and many spouses will not want to wait that long to have the various issues that arise on the breakdown of a marriage sorted out.

This is borne out by statistics available from the Free Legal Aid law centres as of August 1999, which show that judicial separation continues to be a popular choice. Though the number of divorce applications has risen, there has been no corresponding decrease in the number of applications for judicial separation. According to the administrator of the Board, the steady demand for judicial separation is attributable to the fact that people must be separated for four years before they can apply for divorce. At the end of 1998, there were 1,019 judicial separation cases being dealt with by the law centres and 1,316 divorce cases (Irish Independent 4 August 1999).

Constitutional Considerations

Section 2(1)(f) of the 1989 Act provides for the granting of a decree of judicial separation where the Court is satisfied that a marriage has broken down to the extent that there has been no normal marital relationship for at least a year. In *T.F. v. Ireland* (1995) the plaintiff sought a declaration that the provision of extra grounds for obtaining judicial separation, in particular the ground set out in section 2(1)(f), was unconstitutional. He contended that this ground effectively allowed a spouse who had withdrawn consent to the continuation of a marriage, and was thus in breach of the marriage contract, to obtain a decree. This amounted to a failure by the State to protect the institution of marriage in breach of its obligation under Article 41. The Supreme Court, upholding the decision of the High Court, rejected the plaintiff's contention on the basis that even though the extension of grounds for judicial separation might interfere with the parties' personal and constitutional rights, such rights were not absolute and could be regulated in the interests of the common good. The Court emphasised the numerous safeguards provided by the Act to protect the institution of marriage. In this regard, the 1989 Act provides that no decree will be granted unless the Court is satisfied that provision is made for dependent children. It further provides that spouses are to be informed of the alternatives to judicial separation such as reconciliation, mediation and separation by agreement, and for the adjournment of the proceedings to assist reconciliation, and that applications can be made at any time, even after the granting of a decree, to rescind it.

The Grounds for Judicial Separation

Section 3(l) of the 1989 Act empowers the Court, subject to certain restrictions, to grant a decree of judicial separation where it is satisfied on the balance of probabilities that any of the grounds set out in section 2 have been proved. An application for judicial separation is not restricted to a single ground, and frequently a decree is granted on a number of grounds. For example, in *J.D. v. D.D.* (1997) the Court granted a decree pursuant to section 2(1)(a) (adultery) and section 2(1)(f) (absence of a normal marital relationship). The following are the grounds set out in section 2 of the Act:

(1) 'That the Respondent has Committed Adultery'— section 2(I)(a)
Adultery Defined
Adultery can be defined as voluntary sexual intercourse between a married person and a member of the opposite sex who is not the other spouse. As adultery must be a voluntary act, it was held in *Redpath v. Redpath* (1950) that a wife who is raped does not commit adultery. Sexual intercourse was described in *Dennis v. Dennis* (1955) as meaning penetration of the female by the male, however briefly.

Proof of Adultery

Since direct evidence of adultery is usually lacking, circumstantial evidence may be relied on, i.e. evidence of inclination and opportunity. In *Woolf v. Woolf* (1931) adultery was inferred from the fact that a couple spent the night together in the same bedroom. In *J.M.H. v. J.P.H.* (1983) Ellis J outlined the nature of the proof required. He stated that it is not necessary for the applicant to prove actual sexual intercourse by the respondent with another. Adultery is presumed if it is established, for example, that a married man spent the night with a woman in a brothel or spent the night with a woman other than his wife in a hotel bedroom. The onus then shifts to the respondent to prove that no adultery took place. In *B.L. v. M.L.* (1988) the husband's failure to deny adultery, or contradict evidence by the wife as to alleged incidents of adultery, led the Court to conclude that he had committed adultery. However, where the respondent denies adultery, the onus is on the applicant to prove it. The failure by the wife to produce evidence in support of her allegation of adultery against the husband in *S.(V.) v. S.(R.)* (1992) resulted in the Court refusing to grant a decree under section 2(1)(a) of the 1989 Act.

The value of independent corroborative evidence of circumstance and opportunity in cases alleging adultery is evident from the decision in *P.F. v. G.O'M. (orse. G.F.)* (1999). The husband instituted proceedings for judicial separation in the Circuit Court on the ground of the wife's alleged adultery with a married man, by whom she had been employed both before the marriage ceremony and afterwards. Subsequently, the husband petitioned for a decree of nullity in the High Court. See Chapter 5. The question of whether the wife and the other man were having an adulterous affair was irrelevant to the nullity proceedings, except in so far as the question of their credibility was concerned. Both the wife and the other man 'vigorously and persistently' denied the allegations. In addition to the evidence of the husband and wife, the High Court heard evidence from the wife of the other man and two neighbours. One neighbour said that he saw the wife shortly before the wedding 'embracing and kissing on the mouth' a man whom he subsequently identified at the wedding as the other man in question. Another neighbour, who lived five doors away from the parties, gave evidence of seeing the other man go into the parties' house when the husband was away. The other man would always park his car sixty to a hundred yards from the house. The car would be there at night and the following morning, which, according to O'Higgins J, was 'suggestive of Mr. K. staying there overnight' and 'suggestive of an affair'. The learned judge placed much reliance on the evidence given by the two neighbours and concluded that the wife 'had an affair with Mr. K. before and after the marriage'.

Admission by Errant Spouse

In some cases the errant spouse may be prepared to admit adultery. The weight to be attached to an admission of adultery is a matter for the discretion of the trial judge, i.e. the admission must be credible. In *M.M. v. C.M.* (1993) O'Hanlon J said that as the wife 'freely admitted a relationship with the priest in question', there was no need to rule on the admission of certain corroborative evidence given before an ecclesiastical tribunal. In *A.F. v. E.F.* (1995) the Court accepted the wife's admission of adultery when confronted by the husband as credible evidence, and granted a decree of judicial separation. It is significant that in *J.D. v. D.D.* (1997) McGuinness J refused to ignore the admitted adultery of the husband, which she felt was the event which finally killed off the marriage. Any chance of a possible reconciliation ended with the adultery. Accordingly, the learned judge granted a decree under both section 2(1)(a) and 2(1)(f) of the Act.

Bars to Obtaining Decrees based on Adultery
Section 4(l) of the 1989 Act provides that where the spouses have lived together for more than one year after it became known to the applicant that the respondent had committed adultery, the applicant shall not be entitled to rely on that adultery as a ground for judicial separation, although that adultery may be one of the factors that the applicant may rely on to prove 'behaviour' for the purposes of section 2(1)(b). By virtue of section 44 of the 1989 Act, connivance on the part of the applicant is a discretionary bar to obtaining a decree. An applicant who knows that adultery has taken place, but fails to protest or urge the respondent to discontinue that adultery, will be deemed to have connived in it. Condonation of the adultery is not a bar to relief. An applicant who forgives the respondent, having full knowledge that adultery has taken place, will be deemed to have condoned it.

(2) 'That the Respondent has Behaved in Such a Way That the Applicant Cannot Reasonably be Expected to Live with the Respondent — section 2(1)(b)

The Meaning of Behaviour
Behaviour can be described as some act, omission or course of conduct by one spouse which affects the other spouse in relation to the marriage. Although there is no limit to the kind of behaviour that might be considered under this ground, it was pointed out in the English case of *Dyson v. Dyson* (1953) that the conduct of a respondent in any particular case must be 'so grave and weighty as to make married life quite impossible'. However, it is important to distinguish grave and weighty conduct from what has been described as the reasonable wear and tear of married life. There must be some breach of the obligations arising from the marriage relationship that caused the applicant to consider life with the respondent unbearable. In another English case, *Pheasant v. Pheasant* (1972) the husband complained that the wife did not give him 'the spontaneous demonstrative affection which he craved.' Accordingly, he contended that he

could not reasonably be expected to live with her. The Court rejected his contention on the basis that the wife had given him all the affection she could. The parties had simply become incompatible.

Cruelty

Behaviour as a ground for judicial separation replaces cruelty which was a ground for divorce *a mensa et thoro* prior to the 1989 Act. Cruelty was described in *McA. v. McA.* (1981) as conduct 'which renders the cohabitation unsafe or which makes it likely that cohabitation will be attended by injury to the person or health of the party'. While it is no longer necessary to prove that the conduct of the respondent rendered cohabitation unsafe, clearly cruelty can amount to behaviour for the purposes of section 2(l)(b). There is no need to prove that the behaviour of the respondent was intentional, in the sense that the respondent intended to injure the applicant, nor is it necessary to prove that the respondent intended to behave in a particular way at all. All that has to be proved is that the conduct was deliberate in the sense that it was consciously adopted by the respondent. In holding that the husband's conduct amounted to mental cruelty in *McA. v. McA.*, Costello J said that it was immaterial that the husband had not set out deliberately to injure his wife's health. In *B.L. v. M.L.* (1988) the husband had subjected the wife to violent physical assault throughout the marriage. He also committed adultery on numerous occasions. His conduct forced the wife to leave the family home. The Court held that the cumulative effect of the husband's conduct destroyed the marriage relationship and created a situation whereby it would be unreasonable to expect the wife to resume cohabitation.

Mere incompatibility of the parties, without more, does not justify the granting of a decree of judicial separation on this ground. In *O'B. v. O'B.* (1984) the wife sought a barring order on the basis of the husband's conduct, but did not seek judicial separation. The alleged conduct of the husband included rudeness towards the wife in front of the children, lack of sensitivity in his manner to her and efforts at dominance in the running of the home. The Supreme Court held that the conduct of the husband did not justify the granting of a barring order nor could judicial separation have been granted on such grounds had it been sought.

The Test to be Applied

In considering applications based on the corresponding provisions of the Matrimonial Causes Act 1973, the English courts have formulated a test to decide whether the behaviour of the respondent in a given case makes it unreasonable to expect the applicant to live with the respondent. The test is mainly subjective, in that the Court must take into account the characters and personalities of the parties concerned. The respondent's alleged behaviour must be viewed in relation to the applicant and not in relation to a reasonable man or woman. For example, the Court might not expect an applicant who is a weak or timid character to endure a level of conduct that it might expect a stronger or more forceful applicant to withstand. In dealing with an application based on behaviour, the Court must take the conduct of the respondent into account and decide whether, in view of that conduct, the applicant can reasonably be expected to live with the respondent. In *Livingstone-Stollard v. Livingstone-Stollard* (1974) the Court held that a husband's constant and unjustified criticism, disapproval and belittling of his wife amounted to conduct that entitled the wife to succeed in her application for divorce. According to Dunn J, the question the Court must answer in the affirmative is:

> Would any right-thinking person come to the conclusion that this husband has behaved in such a way that this wife cannot reasonably be expected to live with him, taking into account the whole of the circumstances and the characters and personalities of the parties?

As behaviour connotes positive conduct and not just a state of mind or state of affairs, the question arises as to whether the behaviour of a spouse who is mentally ill can justify the granting of a decree. In cases involving a spouse who is mentally ill, the Courts have applied a subjective test. While making allowances for the illness and the temperaments of both spouses in any particular case, the Court must decide whether the behaviour of the sick spouse is more than the other should reasonably be expected to endure. In the English case of *Thurlow v. Thurlow* (1976) the wife suffered from epilepsy and a neurological disorder which caused her to be confined to bed for a few years. She was incontinent and abusive towards the husband. During her illness, she set fire to items of clothing and furniture. The husband was granted a divorce on the basis that he had made every effort possible to cope with caring for her. In both *M.K. v. A.K.* (1988) and *K. v. K.* (1993) the High Court held that the conduct of a wife suffering from a mental illness, in the form of a morbid jealousy, amounted to mental cruelty.

The Relevance of Adultery and Desertion in Proving Behaviour

To what extent can conduct of the respondent such as adultery and desertion be taken into account to prove behaviour as a ground for judicial separation? Since section 4(1) of the 1989 Act stipulates that cohabitation of more than one year after adultery is an absolute bar to reliance on that adultery as a separate ground, an applicant might want to plead the adultery of the respondent as evidence of behaviour. Section 4 itself expressly provides that in such circumstances, the adultery may be relied on as one of the factors required to prove behaviour for the purposes of section 2(1)(b). This seems to suggest that the adultery of the respondent, without more, would not be sufficient. It is probable that the applicant would be required to show that the adultery makes life with the respondent intolerable.

Similarly, desertion could be pleaded as one of the factors constituting unreasonable behaviour on the part of a respondent, where the desertion has not lasted for the required period of a year. However, it is significant that in *Stringfellow v. Stringfellow* (1976) an applicant, who could not establish the required two years' desertion as a separate ground for the purposes of the English Matrimonial Causes Act 1973, was not allowed to rely on the respondent's desertion to support an application for a decree of divorce based on behaviour. The Court held that section 1(2)(b) of the 1973 Act (the equivalent section 2(1)(b) of the 1989 Act) was not wide enough to cover conduct which the Act specified as a separate ground for divorce. Whether the Irish courts will adopt this approach remains to be seen.

(3) 'That There has Been Desertion by the Respondent of the Applicant for a Continuous Period of at Least One Year Immediately Preceding the Date of the Application.' — section 2(1)(c)

Proof of Desertion

Desertion occurs where one spouse, without the consent of the other spouse and without reasonable cause, leaves the family home with the intention of remaining permanently apart.

Physical Separation

There can be no desertion where the parties continue to live together as man and wife. In most instances of desertion, one spouse will move out of the house and live elsewhere. However, by virtue of section 2(3)(a) of the 1989 Act, the couple are to be treated as living apart 'unless they are living with each other in the same household.' Accordingly, it is possible for parties to be living separately and apart, even though they are living under the same roof, if they are living in such a way as to have established separate households under the same roof. In such a situation, there is no communal or joint life between the spouses. It was held in *Walker v. Walker* (1952) that a couple who were not sleeping together and used the same kitchen to cook their own meals were not sharing a communal life. On the other hand, in *Hopes v. Hopes* (1949) the couple slept in separate bedrooms and all sexual relations between them had ceased. The wife refused to wash or mend the husband's clothes. However, the husband joined the family for meals prepared by the wife and shared the rest of the house with the wife and children. The Court held that the spouses were not living separate lives. In *Le Brocq v. Le Brocq* (1964) the spouses occupied separate bedrooms and only spoke to one another when absolutely necessary. However, the Court held that the fact that the wife cooked her husband's meals meant that they were not living separate lives.

Lack of Consent by the Deserted Spouse

Where a husband and wife agree to live apart, neither is in desertion. A spouse will not be deemed to have consented to desertion by the other simply because he has not protested. Consent to separation may be express or implied. It is express where the couple enter into a separation agreement which provides for them living apart. Consent will be implied where the conduct of a spouse indicates that he does not desire to have the other spouse back. In *Joseph v. Joseph* (1953), a wife whose husband had deserted her obtained an order under Jewish law which had the effect of terminating the marriage. However, the order was not recognised under English law. The Court held that the wife, by her action, had shown that she intended to live apart from her husband and thereby impliedly consented to the husband's desertion.

The Intention to Remain Apart

The applicant must establish that the respondent intended to live apart from him permanently. The respondent must be capable of forming the intention to desert the applicant. Mental illness may prevent a spouse from forming the necessary intention. In the English case of *Perry v. Perry* (1963), a wife, under the insane delusion that her husband intended to kill her, left the family home. The Court held that she was incapable of forming the intention to desert the husband.

Lack of Just or Reasonable Cause

There may be reasonable cause for one spouse leaving owing to health or business requirements. Also, there may be reasonable cause for departure because of the conduct of the other spouse. Thus, it is not always the spouse who leaves the other that is in desertion. If one spouse is driven out of the house by the bad behaviour of the other spouse, then that other spouse may be in *constructive desertion*. However, the conduct must be grave, for a mere lack of care or consideration will not lead to constructive desertion. The term constructive desertion is defined in section 2(3)(b) of the 1989 Act as 'conduct on the part of one spouse that results in the other spouse, with just cause, leaving and living apart from that other spouse'. It was held in *Counihan v. Counihan* (1973) that constructive desertion requires an intention on the part of one spouse to disrupt the marriage or bring cohabitation to an end by forcing the other spouse to leave the home. The offending spouse will be presumed to have intended the natural and ordinary consequences of his conduct. That presumption is not rebutted by the offending spouse showing that he did not want the other spouse to leave. In *M.B. v. E.B.* (1980) the Court held that the husband's heavy drinking and irrational behaviour when he returned home drunk from the public house late at night, causing the wife to become concerned for the safety of the child, justified the wife leaving the family home. However, in *P. v. P.* (1980) the High Court held that a spouse who is unable to put up with the ordinary wear and tear of married life is not justified in leaving the family home.

The Period of Desertion

In addition to establishing that desertion has taken place, the applicant must show that it has lasted for at least one year immediately preceding the date of the application. Section 2(2) provides that no account will be taken of a period or periods during which the spouses lived together not exceeding six months, but such period or periods will be excluded when calculating the total period of separation.

The Termination of Desertion

Desertion will be deemed to have ceased where:

(A) COHABITATION HAS RESUMED

It was held in *Mummery v. Mummery* (1942) that there must be a bilateral intention on the part of both spouses to resume married life. The fact that the husband in that case spent the night with his wife and had sexual intercourse with her some years after he had deserted her was not sufficient, without more, to show that he intended to resume cohabitation with her.

(B) THE SPOUSE IN DESERTION OFFERS TO RETURN

The offer must be genuine and without unreasonable conditions. The deserted spouse must give the offer serious consideration. Should the deserted spouse reject the offer, he may thereafter be in desertion. It was held in *Hutchison v. Hutchison* (1963) that an offer by the husband to return to his wife on condition that there be no sexual relationship, a condition he knew she would not accept, was unreasonable.

(C) THE DESERTED SPOUSE HAS CONSENTED TO THE DESERTION

This occurs when the parties subsequent to the desertion enter into a separation agreement. Consent to desertion may be implied from the conduct of the deserted spouse, as in *Joseph v. Joseph* (1953), discussed above.

(D) JUST CAUSE ARISES SUBSEQUENT TO THE DESERTION

For example, where the deserted spouse is guilty of behaviour that is so grave and weighty as to justify the deserting spouse remaining apart, desertion may be terminated.

(4) 'That the Spouses Have Lived Apart from One Another for a Continuous Period of at Least One Year Immediately Preceding the Date of the Application and the Respondent Consents to a Decree Being Made' — section 2(1)(d)

This ground allows for judicial separation by consent. It requires both a period of living apart and the respondent's consent.

Living Apart

The concept of living apart entails more than the mere physical separation of the spouses. It is usually easy to establish that the parties are living apart in the physical sense. As has been pointed out when dealing with desertion, the parties live apart if they either live in different homes or live under the same roof in such circumstances that there is no communal life between them. However, the lack of a communal life is not always the determining factor. In *Fuller v. Fuller* (1973) the wife had left her husband to live with another man for four years, when the husband became seriously ill and unable to look after himself. The wife allowed the husband to move in with her lover and herself so that she could nurse him. Although the husband and wife occupied separate bedrooms, she cooked and washed for him. The Court held that the parties were not living with each other in the same household, as this phrase meant living with each other as husband and wife. The fact that spouses are living apart for business purposes, or because one spouse is in hospital or in prison, will not be sufficient to warrant a decree under this ground. Sachs LJ stated in *Santos v. Santos* (1972) that 'it is necessary to prove something more than that the husband and wife are physically separated — the relevant state of affairs does not exist whilst both parties recognise the marriage as still subsisting.'

With regard to the requirement in section 2(1)(d) that the parties are living apart continuously for at least one year, it is expressly provided in section 2(2) that a period during which they are living apart is not interrupted by a resumption of married life in the same household for one or more periods totalling less than six months. However, such period or periods do not count as part of the period of living apart.

Consent

The respondent must consent to a decree under this ground. He must therefore have the mental capacity to consent. This requires him to understand the implications of consenting to a decree. It was held in *Mason v. Mason* (1972) that an insane spouse can only consent where he is capable of understanding the nature and consequences of his actions.

(5) 'That the Spouses have Lived Apart from One Another for a Continuous Period of at Least Three Years Immediately Preceding the Date of the Application' — section 2(l)(e)

The main difference between this ground and the previous ground is that the length the parties must be living apart is three years instead of one, and the respondent's consent to a decree is not required. Section 2(l)(d) is availed of by spouses when they agree to obtaining judicial separation, whereas applications are made under section 2(1)(e) where one spouse is totally against the idea. Indeed, it is possible for the spouse who has caused the breakdown of the marriage to obtain a decree on establishing that he has been living apart from the other spouse for three years despite the fact that the latter may oppose the application.

(6) 'That the Marriage Has Broken Down to the Extent That the Court is Satisfied That a Normal Marital Relationship Has not Existed Between the Spouses for a Period of at Least One Year Immediately Preceding the Date of the Application — section 2(1)(f)

No Normal Marital Relationship

This is the most frequent ground relied upon by applicants for judicial separation. Although the vast bulk of the case law on judicial separation involves applications under this ground, consideration can only be given to a limited number of cases. A normal marital relationship requires that the parties live together as man and wife in a loving and caring relationship. There must be mutual trust and understanding and shared responsibility between the spouses. There cannot be a normal marital relationship where communication has ceased. Costello J stated in *D. v. C.* (1984) that there was more to marriage than its physical consummation, in that it 'requires for its maintenance the creation of an emotional and psychological relationship between the spouses'. In *T.F. v. Ireland* (1995) Murphy J, in the High Court, stated that a normal marital relationship does not exist between spouses if there is a breakdown 'which involves the loss of an essential ingredient of the marriage'. He went on to state that such an essential ingredient includes the consent of both parties, and that where one or other of the spouses is opposed to the continuation of the marriage, that fact 'must destroy the fundamental relationship.'

Evidence of Breakdown

Section 2(1)(f) of the 1989 Act requires the Court to be satisfied that the marriage has in fact broken down. Whether a marriage has broken down, to the extent that a normal marital relationship no longer exists, is a question of fact to be decided in the circumstances of the particular case. There is no need for the Court to identify the cause of the breakdown or attribute blame to either party. Indeed, it would appear that the Court is precluded from making an enquiry as to what caused the breakdown. In *M.M. v. C.M.* (1993) O'Hanlon J refused to apportion blame for the breakdown of the marriage between the parties, as he did not consider 'that it serves any useful purpose at this stage to do so, and it might well exacerbate the feelings of hostility which the husband and wife have at times felt for each other'. Referring to the conduct of both parties before and after the solemnisation of the marriage, which included adultery by the wife with a priest and excessive drinking and violence towards the wife by the husband, very often in the presence of the children, O'Hanlon J remarked that from before the marriage ceremony 'each of the two partners had embarked on a way of life which, if it continued — and as it has continued — was destined to lead inexorably to a break-down in the marriage'. In *T.F. v. Ireland* (1995) Hamilton CJ stated that under section 2(1)(f) 'all the court is entitled to look at is whether a normal marital relationship has not existed for the relevant period. It is not entitled to consider what caused this to occur'. The Court may grant a decree of judicial separation on a no-fault basis. Although the Court is not concerned with fault, it may choose not to ignore it and regard the conduct of a spouse as contributing to the breakdown. The Court refused to ignore the adultery of the husband in *J.D. v. D.D.* (1997) and *E.P. v. C.P.* (1998), discussed below.

In *S.(V.) v. S.(R.)* (1992) the wife sought a decree of judicial separation based on section 2(1)(a) (adultery), section 2(1)(b), (behaviour) and section 2(1)(f) of the 1989 Act. The husband denied the allegation of adultery and, as no evidence in support of the allegation was produced by the wife, her application on this ground failed. In relation to her claim based on the unreasonable behaviour of the husband, there was evidence of charge, denial and counterclaim, making it difficult for the Court to establish where the truth lay. An accusation by the wife that she had been physically abused by the husband was not corroborated. The Court refused a decree on this ground also. However, the Court was satisfied that over a considerable period the parties' relationship had deteriorated to the stage that sexual intercourse had ceased altogether. The wife had left the family home about half a dozen times. When she had been in the family home she and her husband had slept in different rooms and communicated with each other as little as possible. The wife rarely remained in the house when the husband was present unless one or both of the couple's two children were present. The couple had lived apart, each with one of the children, for about a year. Lynch J was satisfied that the marriage 'has broken down to the extent that a normal relationship has not existed between them for a period of at least one year immediately preceding the application, nor, indeed, for at least three and a half years.'

In *J.D. v. D.D.* (1997) the wife applied for judicial separation on the grounds set out in section 2(1)(a), (b) and (f) of the 1989 Act. The evidence showed that the marriage relationship had broken down over a long period. The husband spent very little time at home because of work commitments. When he was at home, there was very little communication between the parties. As the wife had given up work following the marriage to care for the children, she was dependent on her husband for money for her needs and those of the household. She was nervous spending more money than the husband approved, and was rather afraid of him. In her evidence, the wife painted a picture of general unhappiness When the wife was informed by a third party that the husband was having an affair, she confronted him. He did not deny the affair. He told the wife he very much loved the other woman and that the affair had been going on for some eight or nine months at that stage. He refused to go to a marriage counsellor and went to Dublin instead to meet his mistress. On his return, the wife asked him to leave the family home, which he did. When he returned to the family home after an absence of over eighteen months, the wife left with her 19 year old student daughter and went to reside at a house which she had acquired. In evidence, the husband expressed deep regret at the breakdown, which he accepted was irretrievable. The Court accepted that the combination of the husband's affair and the fact that the children, who were the main source of happiness for the wife in the marriage, were adults and largely had gone away from home, meant that the marriage had reached the stage of irretrievable breakdown. The Court granted a decree pursuant to section 2(1)(a) and (f) of the 1989 Act. Although urged by counsel for the husband to grant the decree pursuant to section 2(1)(f) only, the Court refused to ignore the husband's adultery which, in the words of McGuinness J 'put the final nail in the coffin of the marriage'.

The evidence before the Court in *E.P. v. C.P.* (1998) indicated a high level of conflict between the parties. The husband had left the family home five years previously and had not resided there since. He left originally because of a relationship with another woman whom he had since discarded in favour of his present partner. A doctor gave evidence of the effect of the marriage breakdown on the wife, which resulted in her attempted suicide and subsequent nervous breakdown, for which she was hospitalised. In his evidence the husband showed no sign of regret for the breakdown of the marriage and very little sign of a real sense of responsibility for the upbringing and financial backing of his children. McGuinness J granted a decree of judicial separation under section 2(1)(a) and 2(1)(f) of the 1989 Act, stating that it was clear 'that the parties have separated and that they are not going to live together again, and it is also clear that Mr P. is involved in other relationships'.

Reconciliation and Mediation

Sections 5 and 6 of the 1989 Act require a solicitor acting for an applicant or a respondent to:

(a) discuss with his client the possibility of reconciliation and supply the names and addresses of persons qualified to help effect a reconciliation;
(b) discuss the possibility of engaging in mediation to help effect a separation on an agreed basis and supply the names and addresses of persons qualified to provide a mediation service; and
(c) discuss the possibility of effecting a separation by way of a separation deed or written agreement.

The solicitor acting for the applicant must comply with these requirements before the institution of proceedings, and the solicitor for the respondent must do so as soon as possible after receiving instructions. Both solicitors must certify to the Court that they have complied with the requirements. In the absence of the required certification, the Court may adjourn the proceedings for a reasonable period to allow compliance with the statutory provisions.

Section 7 of the 1989 Act requires the Court to consider the possibility of reconciliation while the case is at hearing. The Court may adjourn the proceedings to afford the spouses the opportunity of considering reconciliation. Should the parties resume living together during such an adjournment, no account is to be taken of that fact in the proceedings. The Court may also adjourn proceedings at the request of the parties to facilitate agreement on the terms of the separation. Where the Court has granted an adjournment to facilitate reconciliation or an agreement on the terms of the separation, either party may request that the hearing resume, and the Court is bound to accede to that request.

It is worth noting that in *J.D. v. D.D.* (1997) McGuinness J stated that 'this is a marriage which might have been saved by counselling had it been undertaken in the early years, and even up to the time of the husband's affair the wife might well have struggled on in the relationship.' The learned judge did give consideration to the question of reconciliation, but felt that any slight hope of reconciliation that remained disappeared at the time the husband embarked on his affair.

Further Reading

Shatter, *Family Law*, 4th. Ed. Dublin: Butterworths 1997.

Duncan & Scully, *Marriage Breakdown in Ireland: Law and Practice*. Dublin: Butterworths (Ireland) 1990.

Walls & Bergin, *The Law of Divorce in Ireland*. Bristol: Jordans 1997.

Binchy, *A Casebook on Irish Family Law*. Abingdon: Professional Books 1984.

Law Reform Commission, Report on Divorce a Mensa et Thoro and Related Matters (LRC 8-1983).

CHAPTER SIX

DIVORCE

Divorce and the Constitution

Divorce is legal recognition that a marriage has ended. The parties to the marriage are no longer husband and wife and are free to remarry should they wish to do so. Judicial separation, on the other hand, merely relieves the spouses of their duty to cohabit but legally, they remain husband and wife. The constitutional bar on divorce in Ireland was finally removed in November 1995 when the people voted in a referendum to replace Article 41.3.2 of the Constitution, which prohibited the enactment of legislation providing for the grant of a dissolution of marriage, with the following provision:

> A Court designated by law may grant a dissolution of marriage where, but only where, it is satisfied that:
> i. at the date of the institution of the proceedings, the spouses have lived apart from one another for a period of, or periods amounting to, at least four years during the previous five years,
> ii. there is no reasonable prospect of a reconciliation between the spouses,
> iii. such provision as the Court considers proper having regard to the circumstances exists or will be made for the spouses, any children of either or both of them and any other person prescribed by law, and
> iv. any further conditions prescribed by law are complied with.

The Statutory Framework

The Family Law (Divorce) Act 1996, which came into operation on the 27 February 1997, makes provision for the Courts to grant decrees of divorce. The Act also enables the Courts to make certain preliminary and ancillary orders in relation to spouses and dependent children in or after proceedings for divorce. The power to grant a dissolution of marriage is set out in section 5 of the 1996 Act, which provides that the Court may grant a decree of divorce on the application of either spouse where it is satisfied that:

(a) at the date of the institution of the proceedings, the spouses have lived apart from one another for a period of, or periods amounting to, at least four years during the previous five years,

(b) there is no reasonable prospect of a reconciliation between the spouses, and

(c) such provision as the court considers proper having regard to the circumstances exists or will be made for the spouses and any dependent members of the family.

'No Fault' Divorce

The 1996 Act allows for divorce on a 'no fault' basis and reflects the position prevailing in most European countries. In other words, a divorce can be obtained without the need for one spouse to prove conduct on the part of the other spouse that led to the irretrievable breakdown of the marriage. It is interesting to note that by virtue of the Family Law Act 1996, England has moved to a purely 'no fault' divorce regime, thereby repealing the Matrimonial Causes Act 1973, which permitted divorce on proof of mixed grounds of conduct and 'no fault'. Divorce allows a spouse who has withdrawn consent to the continuation of the marriage, and is thus in breach of the marriage contract, to apply to have it dissolved against the will of a spouse who was not responsible for the break up. Critics of a 'no fault' divorce regime might view this as a breach by the State of its constitutional duty to protect the institution of marriage. This was the case put forward by the husband in his challenge to the constitutionality of section 2(1)(f) of the Judicial Separation and Family Law Reform Act 1989 in *T.F. v. Ireland* (1995), which provides for the granting of judicial separation where the Court is satisfied that the marriage has broken down to the extent that there has been no normal marital relationship for at least a year. The Supreme Court rejected his claim. See Chapter 5. Undoubtedly, the principles applied by the Supreme Court in that case will have equal application to divorce on a 'no fault' basis.

Both the constitutional provision and the 1996 Act ensure that divorce should only be granted where all reasonable attempts at reconciliation have failed. The four year period during which the spouses must be living apart is designed to ensure that they have time for reflection with a view to possible reconciliation. Where genuine attempts at reconciliation have failed, the marriage may be dissolved as the unavoidable consequence of the breakdown. The requirement that proper provision be made for spouses and dependent children prevents a 'clean break' situation arising on the question of financial and other supports for spouses and dependent children. This is in accord with the judicial view prevailing in Ireland that, while certainty and finality of litigation are important, a 'clean break' will not always be appropriate in cases of marriage breakdown.

The High Court granted the first divorce decree under Article 41.3.2 of the Constitution in *R.C. v. C.C.* (1997), even before the 1996 Act came into force. The application for divorce was brought by the husband, and the wife did not oppose it — her only concern was to ensure that proper provision should be made for her in accordance with Article 41.3.2.. The Court was satisfied that there had been no collusion between the spouses. As a preliminary issue, Barron J had to decide whether the provisions of Article 41.3.2 created a jurisdiction and, if so, whether it is exercisable by the High Court in the absence of regulatory legislation. The learned judge expressed himself satisfied that the High Court had the appropriate jurisdiction. The evidence showed that the parties were married and had lived together until the husband left the family home and went to live with another woman by whom he had a daughter. The parties lived apart continuously since the date of the separation, a period in excess of the four year requirement. Accordingly, this ground for divorce had been satisfied. Although the parties lived close to one another without bitterness, the Court was satisfied that there was no reasonable prospect of a reconciliation between them. There were three children of the marriage, none of whom were dependent. All three were in employment and their accommodation was adequate. The husband proposed to transfer substantial assets equally between them. He also proposed to transfer three properties to the wife. In the circumstances, the wife and children had been properly provided for.

Custody of Dependent Children

Section 5 (2) of the 1996 Act provides that on granting a decree of divorce the Court can give directions under section 11 of the Guardianship of Infants Act 1964 regarding the welfare, custody of, and access to dependent children. Additionally, the Court is empowered under section 41 of the 1996 Act to declare either of the spouses unfit to have custody of any dependent child of the family. Where the spouse to whom the declaration relates is a parent of any dependent child, that spouse shall not be entitled as of right to custody of such child on the death of the other spouse. By virtue of section 10(2) of the 1996 Act, both spouses remain joint guardians of dependent children on the granting of a decree of divorce.

Grounds for Divorce

The grounds on which a divorce can be granted are:

(a) that the spouses have lived apart for at least four years during the previous five years,
(b) that there is no reasonable prospect of reconciliation, and
(c) that proper provision exists or will be made for the spouses and any dependent members of the family.

Living Apart for the Requisite Period

The term 'living apart' is not defined in the 1996 Act. However, for the purposes of obtaining a decree of judicial separation, section 2(3) of the Judicial Separation and Family Law Reform Act 1989 provides that the parties are to be treated as living apart 'unless they are living with each other in the same household, and references to spouses living with each other shall be construed as references to their living with each other in the same household'. The Matrimonial Causes Act 1973, under which divorce decrees were granted in England prior to the enactment of the Family Law Act 1996, contained a similar definition of the term 'living apart'. There is a substantial body of case law in England dealing with the concept of living apart which will be of assistance to Irish courts in defining the term. A detailed account of the principles involved is contained in Chapter 5. In brief, spouses will be deemed to be living apart if they either live in different homes or live under the same roof in such a way as to have established different households. It should be emphasised that the concept of living apart entails more than the physical separation of the spouses. The fact that a couple are living apart for such reasons as business or because one spouse is in hospital or prison will not, without more, be sufficient to warrant the granting of a decree of divorce.

No Reasonable Prospect of Reconciliation

Since the marital breakdown must be irretrievable, a decree of divorce cannot be granted if there is a chance of reconciliation. The aim of both the constitutional provision and the legislation is to emphasise the desirability of a mediated resolution of the parties differences over an imposed solution. In *E.P. v. C.P.* (1998) the husband had left the family home to establish a relationship with another woman some five years earlier. This had such an effect on the wife that she attempted suicide and suffered a breakdown for which she was hospitalised. The husband had subsequently shown very little concern for the wife or dependent children and defaulted in maintenance payments. The children were being maintained mainly out of the separate earnings of the wife. In granting a decree of divorce, McGuinness J indicated that she was satisfied that the breakdown of the marriage was irretrievable when she stated: 'Both parties accept that there is no reasonable prospect of a reconciliation.' In granting a decree of divorce in *J.C.N. v. R.T.N.* (1999) McGuinness J stated: 'There is clearly no prospect of reconciliation; the husband has lived in a permanent second relationship since 1978'.

To ensure that only those marriages which have irretrievably come to an end should be dissolved, the 1996 Act provides that before embarking on proceedings, the spouses must be made aware of the possibility of reconciliation and the alternatives to divorce, namely, separation by agreement and judicial separation. Before instituting proceedings, the applicant's solicitor is required to discuss the possibility of reconciliation and to provide him with information on persons qualified to assist in the reconciliation process. The possibility of resolving differences by means of a separation agreement or judicial separation must also be discussed. Section 7 places a similar obligation on the respondent's solicitor before entering an appearance. Both solicitors must file a certificate in Court to the effect that they have fulfilled their respective obligations under sections 6 and 7.

When the application for divorce comes on for hearing, section 8 requires the Court to give consideration to the possibility of reconciliation between the spouses, and enables the Court to adjourn the proceedings for the purposes of the attempt at reconciliation. The parties must be willing to attempt reconciliation with or without third party assistance. The Court cannot insist on an attempt at reconciliation against the parties' wishes. The failure of an attempt at reconciliation indicates that the breakdown is irretrievable. Section 9 prevents communications between either of the spouses and a third party involved in reconciliation being used in evidence. Section 43 provides that the costs of reconciliation services shall be at the discretion of the Court.

Proper Provision for Spouses and Dependent Children

By virtue of section 5(1)(c) of the 1996 Act, the Court must be satisfied that 'such provision as the Court considers proper having regard to the circumstances exists or will be made for the spouses and any dependent members of the family'. The various orders available to the Court by way of the provision of ancillary relief are considered in Chapter 7. For the purpose of considering what provision should be made for the spouses and dependent members of the family, Section 26 of the 1996 Act enables the Court to discharge orders made under the Family Law (Maintenance of Spouses and Children) Act 1976, the Judicial Separation and Family Law Reform Act 1989 and the Family Law Act 1995 on granting a decree of divorce or other order under the 1996 Act. Unless discharged by the Court, any such order will remain in force. In *P.S. v. J.S.* (1999) White J, in the Circuit Court, made an order in divorce proceedings discharging a transfer of property order made some years previously on granting a decree of judicial separation. Under the previous order, made by consent of the parties, the family home was transferred into the names of both parties as tenants in common, with a right of residence in favour of the wife to the exclusion of the husband. The Court vacated that order and directed the transfer of the family home into the sole name of the wife subject to an outstanding mortgage. When the case had first come on for hearing before him, White J reserved judgment to enable him consider the question of whether the Circuit Court could vacate its previous orders. On the authority of the judgment of McGuinness J in *J.D. v. D.D.* (1997), to the effect that 'Irish statutory policy is totally opposed to the concept of the 'clean break' between spouses', White J was satisfied that he had power to vacate the previous orders.

A 'dependent person' is defined in section 2 as any child under 18 years of both spouses or adopted by both spouses or in relation to whom both stand *in loco parentis*, or a child of either spouse or adopted by either spouse or in relation to whom either spouse stands *in loco parentis*, provided the other spouse is aware he is not the parent of the child and has treated the child as a member of the family. A person over 18 years may be treated as a dependent person if he is in full time education and is under the age of 23 years, or is suffering from physical or mental debility and cannot maintain himself fully. It is significant that whereas section 5 of the 1996 Act refers to 'dependent members of the family', Article 41.3.2 of the Constitution refers to 'any children of either or both' the spouses. This gives rise to the possibility of a challenge to the constitutionality of section 5 of the 1996 Act. It should be noted that in granting a decree of divorce under Article 43.3.2 in *R.C. v. C.C.* (1997) Barron J examined the provision that had been made for the children, even though they were all of full age. Section 2 also provides that a reference to a spouse includes a reference to a person who is a party to a marriage that has been dissolved under the Act, and that a reference to a family includes a family where the marriage of the spouses has been dissolved under the Act.

Recognition of Foreign Divorces

A marriage which is recognised as at an end in one country and valid in another as a result of a divorce decree is referred to as a 'limping marriage'. The common law recognised the undesirability of such marriages and devised a mechanism whereby a divorce decree granted in one country would receive recognition in another country. The Courts were prepared to recognise a divorce granted by a country in which the parties were both domiciled at the time of the proceedings.

Because of the constitutional ban on divorce in Ireland prior to the passing of the 1995 referendum, the recognition of foreign divorces was of particular significance. Until the Supreme Court decision in *Mayo-Perrott v. Mayo-Perrott* (1958), there was some doubt as to whether Article 41.3.3. of the Constitution precluded the recognition of foreign divorces. A cursory reading of sub-section 3 would seem to suggest that a foreign divorce could not be recognised. The sub-section provides:

> No person whose marriage has been dissolved under the civil law of any other State but is a subsisting valid marriage under the law for the time being in force within the jurisdiction of the Government and Parliament established by this Constitution shall be capable of contracting a valid marriage within that jurisdiction during the lifetime of the other party to the marriage so dissolved.

The Court held that this provision did not expressly preclude the recognition of foreign divorces. It merely enabled the Oireachtas to enact legislation refusing to recognise foreign divorces. Since the Oireachtas had not enacted any such legislation, 'the law for the time being in force' was that carried into effect by Article 73 of the 1922 Constitution and Article 50 of the 1937 Constitution. As foreign divorces were then recognised by Irish courts where the spouses were domiciled in the country which granted the dissolution, Irish courts could recognise such a divorce under Article 41.3.3. The decision in *Mayo-Perrott* was followed in the later cases of *Bank of Ireland v. Caffin* (1971), *Gaffney v. Gaffney* (1975), and *T. v. T.* (1983).

Domicile

As the concept of domicile plays an important role in determining a person's status, marital or otherwise, a brief reference is made to the concept at this stage. Nobody is ever without a domicile. A person is domiciled in the country where he has a permanent home, whether he is a national of the country or not. In most cases, domicile and nationality coincide. However, the fact that a person changes his domicile does not mean that he changes his nationality or *vice versa*.

Domicile of Origin

This is the domicile that a person automatically acquires at birth. A marital child born during the lifetime of his father takes the domicile of his father. A non-marital child, or a marital child born after his father's death, takes the domicile of his mother.

Domicile of Choice

An adult can change his or her domicile and acquire a domicile of choice by establishing residence in another country with the intention of residing in the new country for an unlimited period of time. It was held in *M.(C.) v. M.(T.)* (1988) that a person's domicile of origin continues until it is proved to have been intentionally and voluntarily abandoned and replaced by a domicile of choice. The onus of proving a domicile of choice is on the person seeking to establish it. While statements of intention to abandon a domicile of origin are of evidential value, greater weight is usually given to conduct. The Court must take all the circumstances of the case into consideration. A person may change a domicile of choice as often as he wishes. In *Claire Proes v. the Revenue Commissioners* (1997) the High Court held that a domicile of choice is not abandoned unless there is evidence that a person no longer intended to return to reside in the country where he or she is domiciled. The appellant had acquired an English domicile of choice which she had not abandoned and, accordingly, her Irish domicile of origin had not revived. The loss of a domicile of choice automatically results in the revival of a domicile of origin, which lasts until a new domicile of choice is acquired.

Domicile of Dependency

A married woman's domicile of dependency was abolished by section 1 of the Domicile and Recognition of Foreign Divorces Act 1986. Indeed, before the passing of the Act, Irish judges had expressed serious doubts about the constitutional validity of the common law position which regarded a wife as domiciled in a country where her husband was domiciled, even though she had never set foot in that country. This view was shared by Barr J in *C.M. v. T.M.* (1990), Walsh J in *Gaffney v. Gaffney* (1975), and McCarthy J in *K.D. v. M.C.* (1985). In *W. v. W.* (1993) Egan J described the rule of dependent domicile of a married woman as possessing 'an element of absurdity' in that its application could mean 'that a married woman could be held to be domiciled in a country where she had never set foot and never intended to visit'.

As stated above, when dealing with domicile of origin, the domicile of a child depends on the domicile of a father or mother. The domicile of dependency of a child continues until he reaches the age of 18 years. Section 4(1) of the 1986 Act provides that where the father and mother of a marital child who is a minor are living apart, the child will have the domicile of the mother provided (a) he then has a home with the mother and does not have a home with the father, or (b) has at any time had the domicile of the mother by virtue of (a) and has not since had a home with the father. Section 4(2) provides that the domicile of a minor whose mother is dead shall be that of the mother, provided the minor was domiciled with the mother by virtue of subsection (1) at the date of her death and has not since had a home with the father.

Rules Governing Recognition

The whole question of recognition of foreign divorces is now regulated by the Domicile and Recognition of Foreign Divorces Act 1986. By virtue of section 5(1) of the Act, a foreign divorce will be recognised in this country if granted in a jurisdiction where either spouse was domiciled at the date of the institution of the proceedings. The wording of section 5(5), to the effect that the Act 'shall apply to a divorce granted after the commencement of this Act' (1st October 1986), was generally perceived to mean that the old rule on recognition, which required both spouses to be domiciled in the country where the divorce was granted, still applied to foreign divorces granted prior to the commencement of the Act. However, the decision of the Supreme Court in *W. v. W.* (1993) rejects this perception. The Court held that the rule of the dependent domicile of a married woman did not survive the enactment of the Constitution. Accordingly, the only basis for recognition of foreign divorces which would be consistent with both the Constitution and general principles of international law, would be to give recognition to a foreign divorce granted in a country in which either of the spouses was domiciled at the time of the proceedings for divorce.

The parameters within which a foreign divorce decree will be recognised in this country have been expanded still further by the decision of the High Court in *G.McG. v. D.W.* (1999). The Court ruled that a divorce decree granted in England to an Irish couple based on the ordinary residence of the wife for more than one year should be recognised. As the English decree was granted prior to the coming into force of the 1986 Act, the question of recognition had to be dealt with under the common law. The Court noted that the domicile-based recognition rule was expanded in English law over time to include such criteria as habitual or ordinary residence for a specified period. It was significant that the law in relation to divorce in Ireland had dramatically altered since the Supreme Court decision in *W. v. W.* (1993). Both the new Article 41.3.2 of the Constitution and the Family Law (Divorce) Act 1996 allowed for the granting of a decree of divorce where either spouse was resident in the State on the date proceedings were instituted, or where either spouse was ordinarily resident in the State for a period of one year on that date. McGuinness J regarded this as demonstrating 'a clear policy' by the legislature that jurisdiction in matrimonial matters was not limited to domicile, but also extended to a basis of ordinary residence for a period of one year before the issue of proceedings. The learned judge then went on to state:

> It would seem to me both logical and reasonable that the Irish common law recognition rule should similarly be extended to cover cases where under the statute law the Irish Courts claim entitlement not alone to dissolve marriages but also to annul them and to make far reaching declarations as to marital status. The well known policy of the comity of Courts alone would support such an extension of recognition.

An interesting consequence of the decision in *G.McG. v. D.W.* is that more flexible rules apply to recognition of a pre-1986 foreign divorce than to a post-1986 foreign divorce. This seems peculiar given the fact that the intent of the Domicile and Recognition of Foreign Divorces Act 1986 was to liberalise the recognition rules.

Section 5(3)(c) of the 1986 Act provides for the recognition in this State of a divorce obtained in Northern Ireland, where either of the spouses is domiciled in Northern Ireland at the time of the institution of the divorce proceedings. Section 5(4) provides for the recognition of foreign divorce decrees granted after the commencement of the Act where neither spouse is domiciled in the State. Such a divorce will be recognised if, though not granted in the country where either spouse is domiciled, it is recognised in that country, or both those countries.

Grounds for Non-Recognition

The fact that the requirement as to domicile under section 5 has been satisfied does not mean that Irish courts will automatically recognise a foreign divorce decree. Recognition may be refused where a divorce has been obtained by one spouse without the other being given reasonable notice of the proceedings or without being given a reasonable opportunity to contest the proceedings. In the English case of *Joyce v. Joyce and O'Hare* (1979) the Court would not recognise a decree granted in Quebec. The wife, who had been refused legal aid, had made every effort to tell the husband's solicitors in Quebec that she wished to defend the proceedings. The Court was not informed of this, or the fact that adultery and desertion had been found against the husband in proceedings in England.

A foreign divorce decree obtained in circumstances amounting to fraud as to the jurisdiction of the foreign court will not be recognised by Irish courts. In *Gaffney v. Gaffney* (1975) the Supreme Court refused to recognise an English divorce based on a false residential claim. To recognise a divorce in such circumstances would be contrary to public policy or contrary to natural justice. In *Kendall v. Kendall* (1977) an English court refused to recognise a Bolivian divorce where the English wife had been deceived into signing documents in relation to divorce proceedings. The documents, printed in Spanish, were represented to her by her husband as authorising her to take the children out of Bolivia. To recognise the Bolivian divorce in such circumstances would be contrary to public policy.

Collusion was the ground for non-recognition in *L.B. v. H.B.* (1980). The High Court refused to recognise a French divorce decree granted on the petition of the husband and cross-petition of the wife. The Court accepted that the parties were domiciled in France at the time of the divorce proceedings. The evidence established that both spouses wanted a divorce. For the husband's petition to succeed, he had to prove behaviour on the part of the wife which would justify the granting of a divorce. Evidence of behaviour was manufactured with the aid of the couple's lawyers and separate addresses were furnished to the Court, when in fact they were living together. The French Court could have refused the divorce on the basis of collusion which amounted to fraud, had it been aware of that fact. Barrington J stated that the divorce could not be recognised under Irish law as 'there was a substantial defeat of justice'. To recognise the French divorce would be a failure by the Courts, as an organ of the State, to uphold the institution of marriage under Article 41.1.2. of the Constitution.

There is no reported decision in Ireland as to the non-recognition of a foreign divorce obtained as a result of duress. Accordingly, one can only assume that an Irish court would decide the issue on the basis of the established principle of private international law giving domestic courts jurisdiction to refuse recognition of a foreign judgment where it does not comply with their public policy (Article 10 of the Hague Convention on the Recognition of Divorces and Legal Separations 1970). In *Gaffney v. Gaffney* (1975), the Supreme Court refused recognition of an English divorce on the ground that the spouses were not domiciled there. It emerged from the evidence that the husband had coerced the wife into petitioning for a decree. Walsh J observed that in a case involving duress it might be incumbent on the plaintiff to have the divorce decree set aside by the Court that made it, before she could successfully assert the status of wife. In the High Court, Kenny J expressed the view that a divorce obtained as a result of duress should be declared null and void. He accepted the approach of the Court in the English case of *Re Meyer* (1971) in refusing to recognise a divorce obtained by duress on the grounds of public policy.

Relief Orders Following Divorce or Legal Separation Outside State

Where a foreign divorce or legal separation is recognised in the State, section 23 of the Family Law Act 1995 enables the Court, on the application of either of the spouses or a person on behalf of a dependent member of the family, to make any of the ancillary orders (other than an order under section 6 or a maintenance pending suit order) that are available under Part 11 of the Act, subject to certain modifications, following a decree of judicial separation. A spouse who has remarried following a foreign divorce cannot apply for relief under section 23. A prospective applicant for a relief order under section 23 must obtain prior approval from the Court before bringing the application. This can be done by means of an *ex parte* application. The Court will only grant its approval where it is satisfied that it is appropriate to do so having regard to the matters set out in section 26, and that the requirements as to jurisdiction set out in section 27 have been met.

The matters which the Court must have regard to under section 26 are (a) the connection which the spouses have with the State, (b) the connection which the spouses have with the State that granted the divorce or legal separation, or any other State, (c) the financial provision already made on granting the foreign divorce or legal separation, (d) the extent to which relief orders already made in the State which granted the divorce or legal separation have been complied with, (e) the entitlement of the applicant spouse or dependent member of the family to seek relief in any other country, (f) the availability in the State of any property against which a relief order could be made, (g) the extent to which a relief order is likely to be enforceable and (h) the length of time that has elapsed since the date of the foreign divorce or legal separation.

By virtue of section 27, the Court can only make a relief order where it is satisfied that:

(a) either of the spouses was domiciled in the State on the date of the application for relief, or was so domiciled on the date the foreign divorce or legal separation took effect, or
(b) either of the spouses was ordinarily resident in the State throughout the period of one year ending on either of the dates aforesaid, or
(c) either of the spouses had a beneficial interest in land situate in the State on the date of the institution of the proceedings aforesaid.

Section 24 provides for the making of maintenance pending relief orders to cover the period between the granting of leave to apply for a relief order and the determination of an application for relief. The Court can order periodical payments or lump sum payments for either of the spouses or a dependent member of the family where it is satisfied that there is an immediate need of financial assistance and that the requirements as to domicile or ordinary residence set out in section 27 have been met. Section 25 enables the Court to make provision for a spouse out of the estate of the other spouse following a foreign divorce. Where one of the spouses dies following a foreign divorce, the other spouse may apply to the Court within 12 months (6 months in the case of an application after the commencement of the Family Law (Divorce) Act 1996) of the issue of a grant of representation to the estate of the deceased spouse for an order making provision for him out of the estate. The Court may make such provision for the applicant spouse as it considers appropriate. Provision cannot be made for a spouse who has remarried since the granting of the foreign divorce.

Where the Court is satisfied that a disposition of property by the deceased was made for the purpose of defeating or substantially diminishing the provision that the Court could make for the applicant spouse under section 25, it may order that the disposition shall be deemed never to have had effect as such and that the property the subject of the disposition is to form part of the deceased's estate. The donee of the property will be deemed a debtor of the estate for such amount as the Court may direct. By and large, the conditions for making an order under section 25 are similar to those that exist in relation to orders making provision for an applicant spouse out of the estate of the other spouse following a decree of judicial separation under section 15A of the Family Law Act 1995 and section 18 of the Family Law (Divorce) Act 1996. See Chapter 7.

Further Reading

Shatter, *Family Law*, 4th. Ed. Dublin: Butterworths 1997.

Walls & Bergin, *The Law of Divorce in Ireland*. Bristol: Jordans 1997.

'Divorce: A Clean Break With the Past', Seminar Report. Dublin: DIT 1999.

Conneely, 'The Family Law (Divorce) Act 1996: Some Observations'. (1997) 4 ILT 78.

Ward, 'Second Time Around — The 1995 Divorce Referendum'. (1995) 11 ILT 274.

O'Reilly, 'Recognition of Foreign Divorce Decrees'. (1971) 6 Ir Jur (n.s.) 293.

Duncan, 'Collusive Foreign Divorces — How to Have Your Cake and Eat It'. (1981) DULJ 17.

Law Reform Commission, Report on Domicile and Habitual Residence as Connecting Factors in the Conflict of Laws (LRC 7-1983).

Law Reform Commission, Report on Recognition of Foreign Divorces and Legal Separations (LRC 10-1985).

CHAPTER SEVEN

FINANCIAL AND PROPERTY PROVISION ON DIVORCE AND JUDICIAL SEPARATION

For the purpose of achieving a fair and equitable distribution of income and property between spouses, the Court, on granting a decree of judicial separation or divorce or at any time thereafter, has far-reaching powers to make financial and property provision for spouses and dependent members of the family. Part II of the Family Law Act 1995, in relation to judicial separation, and Part III of the Family Law (Divorce) Act 1996 in relation to divorce, enable the Court to make one or more of the following orders:

(a) preliminary orders under the Domestic Violence Act 1996, The Guardianship of Infants Act 1964 and the Family Home Protection Act 1976,
(b) maintenance pending suit orders,
(c) periodical payments and lump sum orders,
(d) property adjustment orders
(e) miscellaneous ancillary orders,
(f) financial compensation orders,
(g) pension adjustment orders,
(h) preservation of pension entitlement orders (in the case of judicial separation only),
(i) orders extinguishing succession rights (in the case of judicial separation only),
(j) orders for the sale of property, and
(k) orders for provision for spouse out of estate of other spouse.

Preliminary Orders

Where an application is made to the Court for a decree of judicial separation or divorce, section 6 of the 1995 Act and section 11 of the 1996 Act enable the Court, before granting the decree, where it appears proper to do so, to make one or more of the following orders:

(1) a safety order, barring order, an interim barring order or protection order under the Domestic Violence Act 1996,
(2) a custody or access order or other orders as to the welfare of a child under section 11 of the Guardianship of Infants Act 1964,
(3) an order under sections 5 or 9 of the Family Home Protection Act 1976 for the protection of the family home or household chattels and monies realised from their transfer or sale.

Maintenance Pending Suit Orders

Where an application is made to the Court for a decree of judicial separation or divorce, the Court can make an order under section 7 of the 1995 Act (section 12 of the 1996 Act) requiring either of the spouses to make either periodical payments or lump sum payments to the other spouse for his support, and for the benefit of any dependent member of the family. Payments on behalf of a dependent member of the family can be made to any person specified in the order. Periodical payments are to cover the period from the date of the application to the date of the granting or refusal of the decree.

Periodical Payments and Lump Sum Orders

On granting a decree of judicial separation or divorce or at any time thereafter, on the application of either of the spouses or any person on behalf of a dependent member of the family, the Court can make the following orders under section 8 of the 1995 Act (section 13 of the 1996 Act):

Periodical Payments Order

This is an order that either of the spouses should pay to the other spouse, or to some person on behalf of a dependent member of the family, a specific amount periodically, e.g. weekly or monthly.

Secured Periodical Payments Order

If the periodical payments order is secured, it is charged on specific assets owned by the paying spouse. Alternatively, property is transferred to trustees who pay the income to the payee spouse.

Lump Sum Order

This is an order that either of the spouses pay to the other, or to some person on behalf of a dependent member of the family, a fixed sum or sums of money. A lump sum order may be payable all at once or it may be payable by instalments. If the lump sum is ordered to be paid by instalments, the instalments can be secured on property owned by the paying spouse. A lump sum order cannot be varied by the Court under section 18 of the 1995 Act (section 22 of the 1996

Act). However, where it is to be paid by instalments, the instalments can be varied. Section 8(2) of the 1995 Act (section 13(2) of the 1996 Act) allows the Court to order payment of a lump sum to enable the applicant to meet liabilities and expenses incurred in maintaining himself or a dependent member of the family before the application for an order was made.

Whereas, a lump sum order can be made in any case, it is likely that such an order will usually be made in cases where the parties have been together for a great number of years and there are considerable financial assets. While there cannot be a 'clean break' situation following a decree of judicial separation or divorce in such cases, the Court should, where possible, consider the desirability of achieving certainty and finality in making provision for the spouses. There is support for this view in the decision of the High Court in *J.D. v. D.D.* (1997). In ordering the husband to pay a lump sum of £200,000 to the wife, in addition to making other ancillary orders, McGuinness J deduced the principle that:

> in the case where there are considerable assets the Court is not limited to providing for the dependent spouses actual immediate needs through a periodic maintenance order, but may endeavour, through the making of a lump sum order, to ensure that the Applicant will continue into the future to enjoy the lifestyle to which she was accustomed.

A periodical payments order or a secured periodical payments order shall begin not earlier than the date of the application for the order and cease not later than the death of either of the spouses concerned. Such orders also cease on the remarriage of the payee spouse, except as respects outstanding payments due on the date of the remarriage. A periodical payments order or a lump sum order cannot be made in favour of a spouse who has remarried after the date of the decree of judicial separation or divorce.

Under section 43 of the 1995 Act (section 13 of the 1996 Act) the Court may make an attachment of earnings order, within the meaning of the Family Law (Maintenance of Spouses and Children) Act 1976, at the same time as making a periodical payments order, if satisfied that the paying spouse has earnings. The Court must afford the paying spouse the opportunity to make representations as to whether he is in receipt of earnings, and is likely to honour the periodical payments order without the need to make an attachment of earnings order.

Property Adjustment Orders

On granting a decree of judicial separation or divorce or at any time thereafter, the Court, on the application of either spouse or a person on behalf of a dependent member of the family, can make the following property adjustment orders under section 9 of the 1995 Act (section 14 of the 1996 Act):

Transfer of Property Order

Where one spouse owns property, the Court can order him to transfer that property to the other spouse or a dependent member of the family or to any other person for the benefit of the dependent member. The term 'property' is not defined, but could include land, the family home, furniture, jewellery, cars and other tangible items. It could cover stocks and other investments. The item of property most likely to be transferred is the family home. In *A.S. v. G.S. and AIB* (1994) the Court made a transfer of property order in respect of the family home in favour of the wife, where the conduct of the husband was likely to lead to the loss of the home to creditors. As the conduct of the husband was not intentional, the Court could not make an order under section 5(1) of the Family Home Protection Act 1976 conveying the home to the wife. See Chapter 10.

B.S. v. J.S. (1999) involved an application by the wife for a decree of divorce and various ancillary orders, including an order transferring the family home into her sole name. A decree of judicial separation had been granted some years previously with various ancillary orders, made by consent of the parties, which included an order transferring the family home into the names of both parties as tenants in common, with an exclusive right of residence for the wife. White J was satisfied that he had the power to vacate the previous orders on the occasion of granting a decree of divorce, and directed the transfer of the family home into the sole name of the wife, subject to an outstanding mortgage on the property.

Settlement of Property Order

This is an order that one spouse settle specified property to which he is entitled for the benefit of the other and/or a dependent member of the family. There are no restrictions on the type of settlement that can be made. The power to make a settlement of property order could be used in relation to the family home as a means of providing a home for the wife and children, while at the same time preserving the husband's interest in the property. For example, the wife and children could be permitted to occupy the family home until the youngest child comes of age, and the home is then to be sold and the proceeds divided between the spouses.

Variation of Settlement Order

This is an order that any ante-nuptial or post-nuptial settlement (including such a settlement made by will or codicil) made on the spouses should be varied for the benefit of either spouse and/or any dependent member of the family. The settlement may have been made by the parties themselves or by a third party. The term settlement has been widely defined in the English case law interpreting the Matrimonial Causes Act 1973, where it has been held to cover a house bought by both spouses but transferred into the sole name of the husband, and an insurance policy taken out by the husband for the wife's benefit. The settlement must have a nuptial element. It was held in *Prinsep v. Prinsep* (1929) that the settlement 'must provide for the financial benefit of one or other or both of the spouses as spouses and with reference to their married state'. In *P.O'D. v. A.O'D.* (1998) the Supreme Court held that a separation agreement was not a post-nuptial settlement capable of being varied under section 9 of the 1995 Act. In *F.(R.) v. F.(J.)* (1995) the Court varied a settlement, which the husband had set up, whereby he had transferred funds to a trust, the beneficiaries of which were the two children of the marriage and his mother. The Court decided that the husband in effect controlled the trust and directed him to pay £25,000 to the wife and removed the mother as a beneficiary.

In *J.D. v. P.D.* (1997) the High Court held that the Court had no power to vary an ante-nuptial settlement which takes the form of a discretionary trust, under the terms of which the trustees had a discretion to appoint capital and income for the benefit of persons they may select, even if the spouses or either of them are within the class of persons they may select. However, such a trust could be taken into account under section 16(2) of the 1995 Act (section 20(2) of the 1996 Act) which requires the Court, in deciding whether to make a periodical or lump sum maintenance order, to have regard to 'other financial resources which each of the spouses concerned has or is likely to have for the foreseeable future'. McGuinness J cited with approval the English case of *Howard v. Howard* (1945), which decided that if the trust took the form of an ante-nuptial settlement of which the spouses alone were beneficiaries, the Court could vary such a settlement under section 9 of the 1995 Act (section 14 of the 1996 Act).

Order Extinguishing or Reducing an Interest in a Settlement

This order enables the Court to extinguish or reduce the interest of either spouse under an ante-nuptial or post-nuptial settlement.

Where a person is directed by the Court under section 9 of the 1995 Act (section 14 of the 1996 Act) to execute a deed or other instrument transferring property and refuses to do so, the Court may direct another person to execute the deed or instrument in the name of the transferor. Where a property adjustment order is made, a certified copy of the order must be lodged by the registrar or clerk of the Court concerned in the Land Registry or Registry of Deeds, as appropriate. A property adjustment order cannot be made in favour of a spouse who has remarried.

Section 9 of the 1995 Act (section 14 of the 1996 Act) shall not apply in relation to a family home in which either of the spouses resides with a new spouse on remarriage following a decree of judicial separation or divorce. When making a settlement of property order, a variation of settlement order or an order extinguishing or reducing an interest under a settlement, the Court can restrict or exclude the application of section 18 of the 1995 Act or section 22 of the 1996 Act (the power to vary orders) to the order.

Miscellaneous Ancillary Orders

On granting a decree of judicial separation or divorce or at any time thereafter, section 10 of the 1995 Act (section 15 of the 1996 Act) enables the Court, on the application of either spouse or a person on behalf of a dependent member of the family, to make one or more of the following orders:

(a) An order —
 (i) conferring on one spouse the right to occupy the family home to the exclusion of the other for life or for such other period (whether definite or contingent) as the Court may specify, or
 (ii) directing the sale of the family home and a division of the proceeds between the spouses and any other person having an interest.

In deciding whether to make either of these orders, the Court must have regard to the welfare of the spouses and any dependent member of the family. The Court must also take into consideration the fact that where a decree is granted it will not be possible for the spouses to live together and that proper and secure accommodation should, where practicable, be provided for a spouse who is wholly or mainly dependent on the other spouse and for any dependent member of the family. In *M.K. v. P.K.* (1991) the High Court made an order under section 16 (a) of the Judicial Separation and Family Law Reform Act 1989 (now replaced by section 10 of the 1995 Act) allowing the wife to reside in the family home for life to the exclusion of the husband. The Court did not consider an order for the sale of the family home appropriate to meet the circumstances of the case, as the youngest child went to school in the area and the wife had interests in the community.

(b) An order under section 36 of the 1995 Act determining any dispute between the parties as to the ownership or possession of any property.
(c) An order under the following sections of the Family Home Protection Act 1976:
 Section 4 (dispensing with the consent of a spouse to a conveyance of the family home),
 Section 5 (ordering the transfer of the family home from one spouse to another, or compensating a spouse who has been deprived of his residence in the family home),
 Section 7 (the adjournment of proceedings for possession of the family home by a mortgagee or landlord to enable the non-owning spouse to discharge arrears of mortgage instalments or rent), or
 Section 9 (restricting the disposal of household chattels, where that would make it more difficult for the other spouse or a dependent member of the family to reside in the family home without undue hardship).

(d) A safety order, a barring order, an interim barring order or a protection order under sections 2,3,4 and 5 of the Domestic Violence Act 1996.

(e) An order for the partition of property under the Partition Acts 1868 and 1876.

(f) A custody or access order or other orders under section 11 of the Guardianship of Infants Act 1964.

Financial Compensation Orders

A financial compensation order is a means of providing financial security for a spouse or dependent member of the family for loss of a potential benefit (for example, a benefit under a pension scheme) as a result of a decree of judicial separation or divorce. Section 11 of the 1995 Act (section 16 of the 1996 Act) provides that the Court, on granting a decree of judicial separation or divorce or at any time thereafter, can make a financial compensation order where (a) the financial security of the applicant spouse or the dependent member of the family can be provided for either wholly or partly by so doing, or (b) the applicant spouse or dependent member of the family, as a result of a decree of judicial separation or divorce, would forfeit the opportunity or possibility of acquiring a benefit and this loss can be compensated for wholly or in part by so doing.

A financial compensation order can direct a spouse to do one or more of the following:

(i)   to effect a life assurance policy for the benefit of the applicant spouse or a dependent member of the family,

(ii) to assign the whole or a specified part of an interest in an existing life policy to the applicant spouse or a person on behalf of a dependent member of the family,

(iii) to pay or continue to pay the premiums on the policy.

A financial compensation order can be made in addition to or in substitution for orders for periodical payments and lump sum orders under section 8 of the 1995 Act (section 13 of the 1996 Act), property adjustment orders under section 9 of the 1995 Act (section 14 of the 1996 Act), miscellaneous ancillary orders under section 10 of the 1995 Act (section 15 of the 1996 Act) and pension adjustment orders under section 12 of the 1995 Act (section 17 of the 1996 Act). In deciding whether to make a financial compensation order, the Court must consider whether proper provision, having regard to the circumstances, exists or can be made for the spouse concerned or a dependent member of the family by orders under sections 8,9,10 and 12 of the 1995 Act (sections 13, 14, 15 and 17 of the 1996 Act).

Where the Court subsequently makes an order under section 18 of the 1995 Act (section 22 of the 1996 Act) varying a financial compensation order, it can make provision for the disposal of the accumulated value of the insurance policy taken out in compliance with the financial compensation order. A variation order can also provide for the disposal of an interest under a policy which was assigned under a financial compensation order. A financial compensation order shall cease to have effect on the remarriage or death of the applicant spouse in so far as it relates to him, and the Court cannot make such an order if the applicant spouse has remarried.

Pension Adjustment Orders

Pensions Law

It is not possible to fully appreciate the nature and effect of a pension adjustment order without first considering the basics of pensions law. The Pensions Acts 1990 and 1996 regulate the operation of pension schemes, and are designed to protect the interests of those who are covered by individual schemes. The Pensions Board, established by the Pensions Act 1990, oversees the regulation and conduct of pension schemes. Pension schemes must register with the Board, which has power to monitor and supervise schemes, as well as laying down guidelines on the duties and responsibilities of trustees. Members of a pension scheme who are concerned about the operation of their scheme can seek the assistance of the Board, which has power to prosecute for breaches of the Act. As approved pension schemes qualify for generous tax concessions, the Finance Act 1972 provides for approval of schemes by the Revenue Commissioners.

Funded pension schemes are generally set up under a trust. The instrument setting up the trust will embody the rules under which the scheme operates and provide for the appointment of trustees. The powers and duties of the trustees are determined by the terms of the trust instrument, the Pensions Acts and trust law in general. Unfunded pension schemes, such as many in the public service, do not operate under a trust. Funded pension schemes approved by the Revenue Commissioners under the Finance Act 1972 enjoy considerable tax advantages. Contributions by employers and employees are fully allowed for tax relief, and the investments of pension funds are allowed to accumulate without paying tax on their income or capital gains. On the other hand, benefits payable in the form of income under a scheme are subject to tax under the PAYE system.

The purpose of a pension scheme is to produce income for a person after retirement and/or to provide benefits for his dependants on his death before or after retirement. State pensions are provided under the Social Welfare system. Persons who are self-employed or not in pensionable service make their own personal pension arrangements. Occupational pension schemes are provided through employer sponsored pension schemes. Occupational pension schemes usually make provision for benefits on retirement, death benefits (in the form of lump sums), pension increases, and benefits on leaving service (transfer of preserved benefits and refunds of contributions).

There are two types of occupational pension scheme, namely, defined benefits schemes and defined contributions schemes. Defined benefits schemes define clearly the benefits that will be paid to the members and/or their dependants, based on salary on retirement and on pensionable service in the employment or scheme. The rate of contributions by members is also defined. In defined contributions schemes, the amount of the member's benefit is determined by reference to the contributions paid into the scheme and the return on the invested contributions. The rate of the employer's and member's contributions is fixed. State benefits, in the form of contributory and non-contributory pensions, may be taken into account in an occupational pension scheme benefit structure. In some cases, benefits payable by the State may be deducted in calculating the pension payable under the occupational pension scheme. In other cases, such benefits may result in a reduction in the amount of salary which is taken into account for pension purposes.

A member of a pension scheme who is not entitled to full pension benefits on retirement, because he cannot meet the necessary qualifying criteria, may compensate by making payments under an additional voluntary contributions (AVCs) scheme. AVCs can also be availed of to improve benefits over and above those provided by a particular scheme. Approval of the Revenue Commissioners must be obtained for AVCs schemes to avail of taxation exemptions. Because AVCs are regarded as ordinary pension contributions, they are part of the normal pension regime and can only be taken out as benefits or, in very restricted circumstances, as a refund of contributions on leaving service. Where AVCs have been made by a member of a pension scheme, they must be taken into account by the Court in making a pension adjustment order.

Adjustment Orders

Benefits accruing under a pension scheme can be adjusted between spouses by means of a pension adjustment order under section 12 of the 1995 Act (section 17 of the 1996 Act). A pension adjustment order can be made by the Court on the application of either spouse or a person on behalf of a dependent member of the family. An order may be sought on the granting of a decree of judicial separation or divorce or at any time thereafter, and may be granted in addition to, or in substitution for, any of the orders available under sections 8 to 11 of the 1995 Act (sections 13 to 16 of the 1996 Act). It is important to emphasise that pension rights can only be adjusted by court order. A clause in a separation agreement, which purports to divide pension benefits between spouses, will not be enforceable against the trustees of a pension scheme. The trustees of a pension scheme must be given notice of an application for a pension adjustment order or a variation of such an order, and the Court in its deliberations must have regard to any representations made by them.

Before deciding whether to make a pension adjustment order, the Court must consider whether proper provision, having regard to the circumstances, exists or can be made for the applicant spouse or dependent member of the family concerned under sections 8 to 11 of the 1995 Act (sections 13 to 16 of the 1996 Act). In *J.C.N. v. R.T.N.* (1999), a case involving an application for a divorce, the Court considered the financial circumstances of both spouses, and held that it would be undesirable to order the payment of a lump sum under any heading to the wife. However, McGuinness J felt that the wife would be in a very precarious position should her husband predecease her, since the maintenance payments would cease and she had already waived her rights under the Succession Act 1965. While appreciating that the husband had built up the pension fund to benefit his present partner, the learned judge stated that she had to bear in mind the criteria set out in section 20 of the 1996 Act. She made a pension adjustment order in favour of the wife amounting to half the annual pension, the remaining half to be paid to the husband's partner.

As pension adjustment orders are, by their very nature, complex and costly, they should only be resorted to where necessary. For this reason, the Court is given a degree of discretion under section 12 of the 1995 Act (section 17 of the 1996 Act). Having taken pension benefits into account in its deliberations, the Court is not required to make an adjustment order where it is satisfied that a different type of order is sufficient to make proper provision for a dependent spouse and children.

Where it is inevitable that pension benefits will require adjustment by the Court in making proper provision for a dependent spouse and children, the parties should endeavour, where possible, to reach agreement on the manner in which benefits should be split and obtain the approval of the trustees of the pension scheme. This obviates the necessity of having the trustees attend court to make representations. Section 12 of the 1995 Act (section 17 of the 1996 Act) provides that the costs incurred by the trustees in making a court appearance must be borne by the parties, as the Court may determine.

Types of Order

A pension adjustment order may relate to retirement benefits (all benefits payable under a pension scheme to the member spouse or to others at or following retirement) and/or contingent benefits (benefits payable from a pension scheme in the event of the death of the member during the period of employment to which the scheme relates, and generally referred to as 'death-in-service' benefits).

Retirement Benefits Order

A *retirement benefits order* provides for the payment to the dependent spouse, or his personal representative, or a person on behalf of a dependent member of the family, of a benefit consisting of the whole, or a part, of that part of the retirement benefit that is payable under the scheme and has accrued at the time of granting the decree of judicial separation or divorce (the 'designated benefit'). In making a retirement benefits order, the Court must specify, (a) the relevant period over which retirement benefits were earned which is to be taken into account. The relevant period may be the duration of the marriage, but it need not necessarily be so provided it ends on a date not later than the date of the decree, and (b) the relevant proportion (percentage) of the retirement benefits earned during the relevant period which is to be allocated to the dependent spouse or dependent member of the family.

Where the Court makes a retirement benefits order in favour of a dependent spouse, and payment of the designated benefit has not commenced, that spouse has two options. He may elect to leave the designated benefit within the pension scheme, and payment of the designated benefit will commence at the same time as the retirement benefits fall due to the member spouse. Alternatively, the dependent spouse may request the trustees of the scheme to establish an independent benefit instead of retaining the designated benefit. For the purpose of establishing the independent benefit, a 'transfer amount' is calculated which represents the value of the designated benefit which might otherwise be payable. With the agreement of the trustees, the transfer amount is applied either as an independent benefit in the same scheme, or as an independent benefit in another occupational pension scheme (e.g. a scheme of which the dependent spouse is already a member), or as an independent benefit in an insurance policy approved by the Revenue Commissioners. Where the person for whom the independent benefit has been created does not elect to have it transferred to another scheme, the trustees may still transfer that benefit to another scheme, provided the designated benefit arises from the member spouse's participation in a defined contribution scheme.

Where a dependent spouse dies before the commencement of the designated benefit, an amount must be paid to his estate within three months of the date of death. The amount so payable is calculated as the transfer amount that would otherwise have been applied as an independent benefit immediately prior to the death of the dependent spouse. The death of a dependent spouse following the commencement of the designated benefit will result in payment to his estate within three months of death of an amount, calculated as the actuarial value of the designated benefit which would otherwise have been payable for so long as both the dependent spouse and member spouse were alive. In the event of a dependent member of the family dying either before or after the commencement of the designated benefit, no payment is made and the pension adjustment order ceases to have effect.

Where a member spouse dies prior to the commencement of a designated benefit, and no decision has been made to transfer the designated benefit to another scheme or policy, an amount is paid to the person in whose favour the order was made. The amount payable is the actuarial value of the designated benefit that would otherwise have been payable.

Contingent Benefits Order

A *contingent benefits order* provides for the payment to the dependent spouse or a dependent member of the family upon the death of the member spouse of the whole, or a part, of that part of a contingent benefit ('death-in-service' benefit) payable under a pension scheme. An application for a contingent benefits order must be made within twelve months of the making of a decree of judicial separation or divorce.

Cessation and Variation of Orders

A pension adjustment order will cease to have effect in the following circumstances:

(a) in the case of contingent benefits, where the member spouse no longer qualifies because the employment to which the pension scheme applies has been terminated,
(b) on the death of the dependent person named in the order,
(c) on the remarriage of the dependent spouse,
(d) where a dependent person ceases to be dependent.

A pension adjustment order may not be made in favour of a spouse who has remarried at the date of the application for the order. However, where an order has been made in relation to retirement benefits, it will not cease to have effect where a change occurs in marital status. An order in relation to contingent benefits ceases to have effect in relation to a dependent spouse where he or she remarries.

A pension adjustment order made in relation to retirement benefits may be varied under section 18 of the 1995 Act (section 23 of the 1996 Act), unless at the time of making the order the Court states that it cannot be subsequently varied. A contingent benefits order cannot be varied.

The Taxation of Benefits

Payments made under a pension adjustment order are treated as income and are chargeable to income tax under the PAYE system. Spouses who have separated will be treated as single persons for income tax purposes, unless they elect for joint assessment. Lump sum payments on retirement, which form part of a designated benefit or an independent benefit established following transfer, are paid free of tax. Payments made under a pension adjustment order in relation to retirement and contingent benefits following the death of a dependent member spouse are not liable to income tax, but may be liable to capital acquisitions tax.

In *B.S. v. J.S.* (1999) White J was reluctant to make a pension adjustment order under section 17 of the 1996 Act because of the respondent's circumstances due to the fact that at the date of the hearing he was unfit to return to work due to serious injury. The learned judge left open the question of apportioning his pension on retirement, but granted a pension adjustment order as to the contingent benefits, 'which would only come into play on the respondent's death'.

Preservation of Pension Entitlements

A decree of judicial separation may have the effect of disqualifying a dependent spouse from benefiting under a pension scheme, where it is a condition of the scheme that the spouses be living together at the time the benefit becomes payable. For this reason, section 13 of the 1995 Act enables the Court, on granting a decree of judicial separation or at any time thereafter during the lifetime of the member spouse, on the application of either of the spouses, to make an order directing the trustees of the scheme to disregard the separation of the spouses as a ground for disqualifying the dependent spouse from benefiting. The trustees must be given notice of the application by the dependent spouse, and the Court must have regard to any representations made by them before making an order under the section. Any costs incurred by the trustees must be borne by either or both of the spouses as the Court may determine.

An order under section 13 may be made in addition to or in substitution, in whole or in part, for orders under sections 8 to 11 of the 1995 Act. In deciding whether to make an order under section 13, the Court must consider whether adequate and reasonable financial provision exists or can be made for the dependent spouse by orders under sections 8 to 11.

Order Extinguishing Succession Rights

The mere fact that spouses are living apart as a result of a separation agreement or a decree of judicial separation does not automatically extinguish their succession rights to one another. However, as a decree of divorce has the effect of terminating a marriage, an order extinguishing succession rights is not available under the 1996 Act, a factor that may be taken into account by the Court when considering the making of ancillary orders. Where the parties separate by agreement, they may expressly renounce their mutual succession rights. In the case of a decree of judicial separation, section 14 of the 1995 Act enables the Court, on the application of either spouse, on granting a decree of judicial separation or at any time thereafter, to make an order extinguishing the share that either spouse would otherwise be entitled to in the estate of the other spouse as a legal right or on intestacy under the Succession Act 1965. The Court can make an order extinguishing succession rights where it is satisfied that adequate and reasonable financial provision exists or can be made for the spouse whose succession rights are in question under sections 8, 9, 10(1)(a), 11, 12 or 13 of the 1995 Act. The Court can also make such an order in the case of a spouse who has been refused ancillary financial relief under the above mentioned sections, or a spouse who would not be considered as meriting such relief had an application been made under those sections.

In *B.F. v. V.F.* (1994) the wife appealed against an order of the Circuit Court extinguishing her succession rights to her husband's estate. The High Court refused the appeal on the basis that the Court order had provided the wife with adequate maintenance, she had been provided with a mortgage-free apartment and her husband had also agreed to sign over to her the lump sum payable to him by his employers on his retirement or earlier death. The Court was satisfied that adequate and reasonable provision had been made for the wife. In extinguishing the succession rights of each spouse in the estate of the other, Lynch J said that 'the wife is a capable lady who will probably be free to obtain employment in eight or nine years time, if she so wishes'.

It is interesting to note that in *J.D. v. D.D.* (1997) the Court made an order under section 14 extinguishing the succession rights of both spouses, despite the fact that such an order had not been specifically sought in the pleadings. The Court considered that such an order was a necessary part of the balance of assets it had endeavoured to create between the spouses. The Court was satisfied that the provision already made by the husband for the wife, together with the lump sum maintenance order for £200,000 made by the Court in her favour, was 'adequate and reasonable' within the meaning of section 14.

Orders for Sale of Property

Section 15 of the 1995 Act (section 19 of the 1996 Act) provides that where the Court makes a secured periodical payments order, a lump sum order or a property adjustment order, thereupon, or at any time thereafter, it may make an order for the sale of property in which, or in the proceeds of which, either or both of the spouses has or have a beneficial interest. The Court may attach any conditions it considers appropriate to an order for the sale of property. In particular, the order may specify the manner of sale, name the potential purchaser, postpone the taking effect of the order, require the payment of the proceeds of sale to a specified person or persons, and specify the disposal of the proceeds of sale between the spouses and any other person having an interest in the property. The Court may not make an order for the sale of property so as to interfere with the right of a spouse to occupy the family home under another order made under the Act. Neither can such an order be made in respect of a family home in which, following the grant of a decree of judicial separation or divorce, either of the spouses concerned ordinarily resides with a new spouse, having remarried.

Where a spouse has a beneficial interest in any property and a third party also has a beneficial interest in that property, the Court shall give such third party an opportunity of making representations before making an order for the sale of that property, or orders under section 9 or 10(1)(a) of the 1995 Act (section 14 or 15(1)(a) of the 1996 Act) in relation to that property.

Orders for Provision for a Spouse out of the Estate of the Other Spouse

Section 15A of the 1995 Act (as inserted by section 52 of the Family Law (Divorce) Act 1996) provides an additional form of ancillary relief in cases where the succession rights of spouses have been extinguished by order of the Court under section 14, following a decree of judicial separation. Where one of the spouses subsequently dies, the other spouse may apply to the Court within six months of the issue of a grant of representation to the estate of the deceased spouse for an order making provision for him out of the estate. The Court may make such provision for the applicant spouse as it considers appropriate. In considering whether to make provision for an applicant spouse, the Court must have regard to all the circumstances of the case, including (a) any lump sum order or property adjustment order made in favour of the applicant spouse, and (b) any devise or bequest made by the deceased spouse to the applicant spouse. The provision made for an applicant spouse under section 15A cannot exceed in total the legal right share (if any) or the intestate share which the applicant spouse would have been entitled to in the estate of the deceased under the Succession Act 1965, had the Court not made an order under section 14 extinguishing the succession rights of the spouses.

Before making an order under section 15A, the Court must take into account the rights of any other person having an interest in the matter. In addition, the Court must be satisfied that proper provision was not made for the applicant spouse during the lifetime of the deceased spouse by way of maintenance, financial compensation, property adjustment or other miscellaneous ancillary orders. However, the reason for refusing such ancillary relief orders must not have been the conduct of the applicant spouse. The Court cannot make provision for an applicant spouse out of the estate of the deceased spouse where the applicant spouse has remarried since the granting of the decree of judicial separation.

Where an application is made under section 15A, the applicant spouse must give notice to the new spouse (if any) of the deceased spouse and to such other persons as the Court may direct. The Court, in deciding whether to make an order under the section, must have regard to any representations made by the persons entitled to receive notice of the application. The personal representative of a deceased spouse in respect of whom a decree of judicial separation has been granted shall make a reasonable attempt to bring the death to the notice of the other spouse concerned. Where an application is made, the personal representative of the deceased spouse must not, without leave of the Court, administer the estate until the Court makes, or refuses to make, an order.

Where the personal representative gives notice of the death to the other spouse, and (a) the other spouse intends to make an application for an order under section 15A, (b) the other spouse has applied for such an order, or (c) an order has been made under the section, the other spouse must, not later than one month after the receipt of the notice, notify the personal representative of such intention, application or order. Should the other spouse not notify the personal representative as aforesaid, the personal representative may distribute the assets of the deceased spouse, or any part thereof, amongst the parties entitled thereto. The personal representative shall not be liable to the other spouse for the assets so distributed unless, at the time of such distribution, he had notice of the intention, application or order aforesaid. Neither the failure of the other spouse to notify the personal representative as aforesaid, or the fact that a distribution of assets has taken place, shall prejudice the right of the other spouse to follow the assets into the hands of any person who may have received them.

An application can be made by either of the spouses at the time the decree of judicial separation is granted, or at any time thereafter during the lifetime of the spouses, for an order preventing either or both of the spouses from applying for an order under section 15A on the death of the other.

As a decree of divorce automatically extinguishes the Succession Act rights of the spouses to each other's estates, section 18 of the 1996 Act enables the Court, on granting a decree of divorce or at any time thereafter, to make an order making provision for one spouse out of the estate of the other. Similar criteria apply as in the case of an order made under section 15A of the 1995 Act in relation to judicial separation. Section 18(10) enables the Court, on granting a decree of divorce or at any time thereafter, on the application of either of the spouses during the lifetime of the other, to make an order that the other spouse shall not be entitled to apply for an order under section 18. In *J.C.N. v. R.T.N.* (1999) the Court made such an order under section 18, even though it was likely that the husband would re-marry subsequent to the decree and, thus, not qualify to apply for an order for provision out of his wife's estate.

Matters to be Taken into Account when Making Orders

Section 16 of the 1995 Act requires the Court, when granting a decree of judicial separation, to *endeavour to ensure* that proper provision exists or is made for each spouse and any dependent member of the family when making ancillary orders, and determining the provisions of such orders. Section 20 of the 1996 Act requires the Court, on granting a decree of divorce, to *ensure* that such provision will be made. The Court cannot make an ancillary order under either section unless it would be in the interests of justice to do so. In particular, when making provision for a spouse or dependent member of the family, the Court must have regard to the following matters:

(a) The Income, Earning Capacity, Property and Other Financial Resources Which Each of the Spouses Concerned has or is Likely to Have in the Foreseeable Future

All of the income and capital of both spouses, including income and property they are likely to have in the foreseeable future, must be taken into account. In *Calder v. Calder* (1976) the English Court of Appeal held that a husband's future entitlement under a family trust should have been taken into account by the lower court for the purpose of determining the size of a lump sum payment to the wife. In *J.D. v. D.D.* (1997) the High Court took into consideration the entitlement of the husband to benefit under a family trust.

Income includes both earned and unearned income, which may take the form of wages, bonuses, overtime, commissions, dividends and interest on investments. When considering a spouse's earning capacity, the Court should take into account any increased capacity which the spouse might reasonably be expected to have in the foreseeable future. Any promotion and better employment prospects resulting from retraining or continuing education would enhance a spouse's earning capacity. Property includes land and buildings, investments of all kinds and personal possessions. Financial resources include an award of damages for personal injuries. The fullest possible information must be disclosed to the Court in respect of the affairs of both spouses. This information is contained in the affidavits of means that each spouse must file in Court.

(b) The Financial Needs, Obligations and Responsibilities Which Each of the Spouses has or is Likely to Have in the Foreseeable Future (Whether in the Case of Remarriage or Otherwise)

Present and future living expenses of both spouses, such as food and clothing, mortgage repayments, rent, rates and other outgoings should be taken into account. Capital liabilities, such as the amount outstanding on a mortgage or a bank overdraft, should be taken into consideration when valuing the matrimonial home and other real property. Sections 16 and 20, respectively, expressly envisage a situation where a spouse might remarry or cohabit with a new partner. As a result, a spouse's obligation to support a new spouse or partner and the children of such a relationship must be taken into account. This will reduce the resources available for the support of the former spouse and dependent children. In the case of competing claims for support, the needs of the first family should be given priority. Where a new spouse or partner has an income, this will be taken into account to the extent that the new spouse or partner could contribute to, and thereby reduce, the needs of the party concerned. The High Court held in *Ennis v. Butterly* (1997) that a husband had no legal obligation to support a partner with whom he was cohabiting.

(c) The Standard of Living Enjoyed by the Family Before the Proceedings were Instituted or Before the Spouses Separated, as the Case may be

Ideally, the Court should endeavour to ensure that the breakdown of the marriage, and resultant separation, will have the least possible effect on the standard of living of the spouses. In *G.H. v. E.H.* (1998), which is discussed later in this chapter in connection with the power to vary orders, Barr J said that the wife was entitled to a lifestyle 'commensurate with' that available to the husband. In the majority of cases, however, separation usually results in a lowering of the living standards of the spouses owing to the necessity of maintaining two separate households. Finlay CJ recognised the detrimental effect of a separation on the living standards of spouses when delivering the judgment of the Supreme Court in *R.H. v. N.H.* (1986), a case involving an application for maintenance under the Family Law (Maintenance of Spouses and Children) Act 1976. See Chapter 8. It is only in cases where the family enjoys considerable wealth that living standards will remain unaffected. Where the means of the family are moderate, the Court should endeavour to ensure the same standard of living for both spouses.

(d) The Age of Each of the Spouses and the Length of Time During Which the Spouses Have Lived Together

The age of the spouses may be relevant to the Court's deliberations. Age can clearly affect the possibility of gaining employment. An elderly spouse in employment may have little or no promotion prospects. The age of a spouse could affect his prospects of obtaining a mortgage. The duration of a marriage must be taken into account. Generally, the younger the spouse and the shorter the marriage, the less likely it is that such spouse will be substantially provided for by the Court. Parties to a short marriage are less likely to have changed their position substantially, as might be expected in the case of a couple who have remained together for a long time. At the same time, even a short marriage between young spouses may result in the birth of a child or children. This would significantly alter the couple's position. Despite the duration of a marriage, it would appear from the English decision in *Krystman v. Krystman* (1973) that the Court will only take into account the time during which the spouses have cohabited. In that case, the marriage had lasted for twenty-six years, during which time the spouses cohabited for only two weeks.

Two fairly recent High Court decisions illustrate the practical application of the requirement to take both the age of the parties and the length of time they have lived together into account. In *J.D. v. D.D.* (1997), the parties had been married for some thirty years when the breakdown occurred. At the time the wife was aged fifty-five years. When the parties were first married the wife gave up her employment and engaged herself fully in caring for the home and family. Since the separation of the parties, the wife had retrained and obtained a 'permanent part-time' job in a college near her home, earning approximately £114 per fortnight net. While she was willing to work to help support herself, she had no great interest in a career outside the home. The Court accepted this as a realistic approach, given her relative lack of qualifications and age. On the basis that the marriage was a lengthy partnership of complementary roles (the husband as sole provider and the wife as homemaker), the Court decided that there should be a reasonably equal division of the accumulated assets, and ordered the payment of a lump sum of £200,000 by way of maintenance by the husband to the wife, in addition to him undertaking to finance the purchase of a residence for the wife. On granting a decree of divorce in *J.C.N. v. R.T.N.* (1999), the Court took into account the fact that the applicant was a lady of seventy-five years of age, that she had married the respondent forty years ago and lived with him for some twenty years, and that she was not able to earn a living for herself.

(e) Any Physical or Mental Disability of Either of the Spouses

This factor is closely linked with paragraph (b) above. Obviously, the needs of a handicapped spouse, particularly in financial terms, will require special consideration, bearing in mind their ability to gain or engage in meaningful employment. A handicapped person will have special needs in relation to treatment and care. Accommodation may have to be specially adapted for a person with a disability.

(f) The Contributions Which Each of the Spouses Has Made or is Likely in the Foreseeable Future to Make to the Welfare of the Family, Including Any Contribution Made by Each of Them to the Income, Earning Capacity, Property and Financial Resources of the Other Spouse and any Contributions Made by Either of Them by Looking After the Home or Caring for the Family.

In addition to taking into account any cash contributions made by the spouses, the Court must endeavour to place a value on the contribution the stay-at-home wife makes to the welfare of the family. Thus, the wife who gives up her job and devotes herself entirely to caring for the home and family, has the value of her services recognised. The significant contribution that the wife had made to the welfare of the family in caring for the home and bringing up the children, thereby enabling the husband to accumulate considerable assets, was recognised by the Court in *J.D. v. D.D.* (1997).

(g) The Effect on the Earning Capacity of Each of the Spouses of the Marital Responsibilities Assumed by Each During the Period When They Lived Together (with One Another) and, in Particular, the Degree to Which the Future Earning Capacity of a Spouse is Impaired by Reason of that Spouse Having Relinquished or Forgone the Opportunity of Remunerative Activity in Order to Look After the Home or Care for the Family

Under this heading, the Court will be able to assess the effect the marital responsibilities taken on by a spouse will have on that spouse's earning capacity, in particular, the adverse effect it has on the spouse who assumes the role of homemaker and gives up a salaried position. It is clear from the facts in *J.D. v.*

D.D. (1997) that the earning capacity of the wife was impaired by her having to give up her job to enable her take on the marital responsibilities of looking after the home and caring for the family. The Court took into account her contributions under paragraph (f) and her responsibilities under paragraph (g) in awarding her lump sum maintenance of £200,000.

(h) Any Income or Benefits to Which Either of the Spouses is Entitled By or Under Statute

All social welfare benefits that a spouse is entitled to are included under this heading.

(i) The Conduct of Each of the Spouses, if that Conduct is Such That in the Opinion of the Court it Would in all the Circumstances of the Case be Unjust to Disregard it.

The Court is obliged to take the conduct of each of the spouses into account if it is such that it would be unjust to disregard it. A number of English decisions dealing with the corresponding provisions of the Matrimonial Causes Act 1973 make it clear that it would be unjust to disregard conduct that was, in the words of Denning MR in *Wachtel v. Wachtel* (1973), 'obvious and gross'. See Chapter 8. As conduct is only one of several matters that must be considered, the Court would appear to have a considerable discretion. In exercising its discretion, the Court should emphasise the needs and responsibilities of the spouses rather than an individual spouse's misconduct. Where the Court decides to take conduct into account, it is not confined to matrimonial misconduct, as such. McGuinness J did consider the conduct of the husband in *J.D. v. D.D.* (1997), but stated that she did 'not think that any injustice would be done in this context by disregarding the adultery of the husband'. The learned judge also considered the husband's financial misconduct, but felt that she had dealt sufficiently with this aspect of the case by making an order pursuant to section 35 of the 1995 Act setting aside a disposition which constituted an effort by the husband to reduce the monies available for distribution to the wife.

(j) The Accommodation Needs of Either Spouse

The fact that the spouses have to live apart following a decree of judicial separation or divorce makes it necessary for them to have separate accommodation. The accommodation needs of the spouses must be taken into account by the Court when deciding to make financial and property provision orders. The need to establish separate households following a decree of judicial separation or divorce influences the size of periodical and lump sum payments. Usually, the spouse having custody of dependent children requires more ample accommodation than the non-custodial parent. Where possible, the spouse having custody should be allowed to remain in the family home, at least during the dependency of the children. The English courts have recognised this arrangement as the best solution where the assets of the family, excluding the family home, are ample to provide for the spouses — see *Clutton v. Clutton* (1991). The assets of the family in *J.D. v. D.D.* (1997) were substantial. As the wife had acquired a residence for herself in which she resided with the couple's 19 year old student daughter, the Court accepted the husband's undertaking to discharge the outstanding costs and expenses of the wife's residence, and allowed him to retain the family home.

However, where the family home represents the spouses' main or only asset, as is often the case, the Court may have to order its sale and a division of the proceeds so that the spouses can acquire separate accommodation. A typical case illustrating the difficulties faced by the Court in resolving the accommodation needs of the spouses where the family home is the main asset, is *L.C. v. A.C.* (1994). The wife obtained a decree of judicial separation and ancillary orders in the Circuit Court. One of the ancillary orders gave her the right to reside in the family home for life. The house would remain in joint ownership and the husband would continue with the mortgage payments. The husband appealed against this order seeking his share of the equity in the house. On appeal, the High Court noted that the parties agreed that it was desirable that the wife should continue to live in the family home with their son. However, the husband wanted to buy a house for himself, but could not do so without being able to raise capital. If the house was sold, it would raise £20,000 after the discharge of the mortgage, of which the husband's share would be £10,000. The wife said that she was unable to raise £10,000, but offered £2,000 which she could raise from her family. Murphy J felt that the most equitable solution was for the wife to purchase her husband's share. The existing situation whereby she had a right of residence and owned half the house was unsatisfactory, as it meant that the husband's equity was of no value to him. The learned judge recommended that the wife should purchase the husband's interest in the house for a fraction of his estimated value, the reduction reflecting her right of residence. Stating that he did not have the statutory power to order such an arrangement, he adjourned the case to enable the parties to reach a solution along the suggested lines.

(k) The Value to Each of the Spouses of Any Benefit (for example, a benefit under a pension scheme) Which by Reason of the Decree of Judicial Separation (divorce) Concerned That Spouse Will Forfeit the Opportunity or Possibility of Acquiring

Under this heading, the Court can compensate a spouse for the loss of any benefit, pension or otherwise. In the English case of *Trippas v. Trippas* (1973) the Court compensated the wife for the loss of a benefit she would have been entitled to had the parties not separated. The husband had promised the wife that, in the event of a sale of the family business, he would give her a share of the proceeds of sale. Shortly after the separation the business was sold. Where a spouse loses a pension benefit as a result of a decree of judicial separation, and the Court does not make a pension adjustment order, it can provide compensation for the spouse concerned by means of a periodical payments or lump sum order.

(l) The Rights of Any Person Other Than the Spouses but Including a Person to whom Either Spouse is Remarried

Where either or both of the spouses has remarried, the right of a new spouse to be supported by the spouse who has remarried must be taken into account. As mentioned under paragraph (d) above, a spouse's obligation to support a new spouse may reduce the resources available for the support of a former spouse and children. Priority should be given to the needs of the former spouse and children. In *J.C.N. v. R.T.N.* (1999) the Court took into account the husband's commitments to his partner and the two dependent children of their union. In particular, the Court acknowledged that the husband had built up the pension scheme after separating from his wife 'with a view to a pension being paid to his present partner'.

In relation to an application for a decree of divorce, section 20(3) of the 1996 Act requires the Court to take into account the terms of any separation agreement which has been entered into by the spouses and is still in force. Of course, the fact that a separation agreement contains a clause making property and financial provision for the spouses, does not prevent the Court making ancillary orders on granting a decree of divorce.

General Guiding Principles for the Court

In addition to taking into account the specific guidelines that are relevant to the making of financial and property provision orders, the Court has a wide area of discretion. In *Martin v. Martin* (1977) Ormond LJ, in discussing the corresponding provisions of the Matrimonial Causes Act 1973, emphasised the wide discretion conferred on the Courts in deciding on family provision when he stated that 'the Court should preserve, so far as it can, the utmost elasticity to deal with each case on its own facts'. In *J.D. v. D.D.* (1997) McGuinness J acknowledged that there was a dearth of case law in this jurisdiction that might be of assistance in regard to family provision. While emphasising that each case must be dealt with on its own facts, she was prepared to consider the large body of English case law in this area as instructive in establishing general principles.

In considering the English cases, it should be emphasised that the Courts in England favoured the 'clean break' principle, which advocated an equitable division of property and a lump sum order in place of continuing periodical payments. This was designed to make the spouses financially independent of one another. However, a clean break can only be achieved where there are considerable assets to compensate for a spouse's right to be paid maintenance on a continuing basis. In the average family, financial independence between the spouses cannot be achieved due to the modest assets available for a distribution between the spouses. Given that the tenor of the 1995 and 1996 Acts is against the concept of finality, Irish courts are prevented from operating the 'clean break' principle. Nevertheless, some of the English decisions decided on the 'clean break' principle will prove instructive and persuasive in guiding Irish courts. In *J.D. v. D.D.* the Court considered at some length the decisions in *Wachtel v. Wachtel* (1973), *Duxbury v. Duxbury* (1987) and *Gojkovic v. Gojkovic* (1990).

Wachtel v. Wachtel advocated the 'one third approach', a basic arithmetical approach of taking one third of the gross income and capital of the spouses. If the dependent spouse's assets are less than this third, the other spouse will be required to contribute assets to make up the difference. It should be emphasised that the one third approach is not a rule, but merely a starting point. It would serve in cases where the marriage had lasted for many years and the wife had been in the home bringing up the children. It could not apply where the marriage had lasted only a short time, or where there were no children and the dependent spouse could go out to work. Other circumstances that would justify a court ignoring the one third approach include obvious and gross misconduct, very low income and no capital. The one third approach is now out of favour.

The English courts now favour what has been described as a dual approach, depending on the income of the spouses. A 'subsistence level approach' is favoured in the case of low income families, to the effect that the Court will not make a periodical payments order where that would have the effect of reducing the paying spouse's income below subsistence level. In *Duxbury v. Duxbury* the Court approved the awarding of lump sums in the case of wealthy couples, to ensure that the wife of a wealthy man became financially independent following the breakdown of a marriage. In that case, the Court ordered an extremely wealthy husband to pay a lump sum of £600,000 to his wife to produce an income of £28,000 per annum, thereby guaranteeing her a luxurious lifestyle. In *Gojkovic v. Gojkovic* the husband owned property valued at £4 million. His wife had made an exceptional contribution to the creation of the family assets. She was awarded £1 million to help her start up her own business. In *J.D. v. D.D.* McGuinness J was not prepared to accept entirely the 'clean break' principle on which *Duxbury* and *Gojkovic* were decided, as advocated by counsel for the wife. She felt, however, that considerable reliance should be placed on lump sum provision, while periodic maintenance should also play an important part.

Provision for Dependent Members of Family

Section 16(4) of the 1995 Act (section 20(4) of the 1996 Act) empowers the Court to make the same types of order in favour of dependent members of the family, against either of the spouses, as it can in favour of the spouses themselves. For a definition of the term 'dependent member of the family', see section 2 of the 1995 and 1996 Acts. According to this definition, dependency normally ceases when a child reaches 18 years or, where a child is receiving full time education, 23 years. A child remains dependent for so long as he has a mental or physical disability and is unable to maintain himself.

In exercising its powers to make provision for a dependent member of the family under section 16 of the 1995 Act (section 20 of the 1996 Act), the Court shall have regard to (a) the financial needs of the member, (b) the income, earning capacity (if any), property and other financial resources of the member, (c) any physical or mental disability of the member, (d) any income or benefits to which the member is entitled by or under statute, (e) the manner in which the member was being and in which the spouses concerned anticipated that the member would be educated or trained, (f) the income and earning capacity of both spouses, their needs, obligations and responsibilities and the standard of living enjoyed by the family prior to the institution of the proceedings or the separation, as the case may be, (g) the accommodation needs of the member. Section 19 of the 1995 Act (section 23 of the 1996 Act) obliges the Court to disregard the conduct of the applicant spouse when deciding to make a periodical payments order or a lump sum order in favour of a dependent member of the family. Likewise, the Court must disregard the conduct of the applicant spouse when deciding to vary or discharge such orders under sections 18 and 22, respectively.

By virtue of section 18(3) of the 1995 Act (section 22(3) of the 1996 Act), that part of a Court order which makes provision for a dependent member of the family is discharged when the member ceases to be dependent on reaching the age of 18 or 23 years, as the case may be, and shall be discharged by the Court if it is satisfied that the member for any reason has ceased to be dependent.

Retrospective Periodical Payments Orders

By virtue of section 17 of the 1995 Act (section 21 of the 1996 Act), where the circumstances of the case suggest that it would be appropriate to do so, the Court, in making a periodical payments order, can direct retrospection to the date of the issuing of the proceedings. The Court can order that retrospective payments be paid in one sum and before a specified date, and that any payments made by the paying spouse to the applicant spouse in the period between the institution of proceedings and the grant of a decree of judicial separation or divorce be deducted from the lump sum.

Variation and Discharge of Certain Orders

In view of the fact that statutory policy in Ireland is totally opposed to the concept of the 'clean break', there can be no finality in respect of financial and property provision following the breakdown of a marriage. Accordingly, section 18 of the 1995 Act (section 22 of the 1996 Act) confers on the Court the power to vary or discharge certain orders. The Court may also suspend any provision of an order, revive the operation of an order or provision so suspended, further vary an order previously varied, or further suspend or revive the operation of an order or provision previously suspended or revived. An order under sections 18 or 22, respectively, may require the divesting of any property vested in a person under or by virtue of an order to which the section relates.

The orders to which section 18 of the 1995 Act (section 22 of the 1996 Act) relates are:

(a) a maintenance pending suit order,
(b) a periodical payments order (secured or unsecured),
(c) a lump sum order payable by instalments, whether secured or unsecured,
(d) orders for the settlement of property, the variation of a post-nuptial or ante-nuptial settlement and the extinguishment or reduction of an interest under a settlement, in so far as an application to vary is not restricted or excluded under section 9(2) of the 1995 Act (section 14(2) of the 1996 Act),
(e) an order relating to the occupation of the family home or the sale of the family home and the division of the proceeds of sale,
(f) a financial compensation order,
(g) a pension adjustment order, in so far as an application to vary is not restricted or excluded by section 12(26) of the 1995 Act (section 16(26) of the 1996 Act),
(h) a preservation of pension entitlements order,
(i) an order under section 18 of the 1995 Act itself (section 22 of the 1996 Act).

An application for an order under section 18 of the 1995 Act (section 22 of the 1996 Act), can be made by either of the spouses or by a person on behalf of a dependent member of the family. Where either of the spouses has died, an application may be made by any person who, in the opinion of the Court, has a sufficient interest in the matter. Under section 22 of the 1996 Act, in the case of the remarriage of either of the spouses, an application can be made by his or her spouse. In deciding whether or not to vary an order under section 18 or 22 the Court must have regard to any change in the circumstances of the case and any new evidence available since the making of the original order in regard to financial and property provision. The effect of inflation should be taken into account in considering an application to vary a maintenance order. In *K. v. K.* (1993) Finlay CJ said that the Court must 'try and ascertain as to whether, from the last effective order, the situation has changed so as to warrant either an increase or decrease in the amount of maintenance'. In *G.H. v. E.H.* (1998) the husband had attempted, by various means, to avoid liability for maintaining his wife. He made an application to the Court to vary downwards the maintenance payable by him to his wife because of his reduced financial circumstances. Barr J was not satisfied that there had been any change in the husband's circumstances to prevent him honouring his obligations to contribute towards the maintenance of his wife and son. Indeed, there was evidence to suggest that his fortunes had improved. In ordering the husband to pay continuing maintenance of £200 per week for the wife and dependent child and arrears of £7000, Barr J said that the wife had the 'right to the benefit of a reasonable lifestyle commensurate with' that available to her husband.

An order varying, discharging or suspending (a) an order for the settlement of property, (b) an order for the variation of a post-nuptial or ante-nuptial settlement, or (c) an order extinguishing or reducing an interest under a settlement is subject to any restriction or exclusion specified in that order. Such an order must not prejudice the interests of any person who has acquired an interest and is not a party to the marriage concerned or a dependent member of the family.

Avoidance of Dispositions

Section 35 of the 1995 Act (section 37 of the 1996 Act) is designed to ensure that no claim for financial or other material provision is defeated, limited or frustrated by the dishonest disposal of assets by the spouse liable to be ordered to provide it. Accordingly, where a claim for ancillary relief is pending and the applicant spouse satisfies the Court that the other spouse or any other person intends to defeat a claim for relief by disposing of or transferring out of the jurisdiction or otherwise dealing with any property, the Court may either restrain the other spouse or person from doing so or otherwise protect the claim of the applicant, or set aside any disposition already made, if satisfied that if the disposition were set aside the applicant would get relief or different relief.

The term 'disposition' is defined as any disposition of property howsoever made other than a disposition made by will or codicil. However, sections 35 or 37 do not apply to a disposition made to a *bona fide* purchaser for valuable consideration (other than marriage) without notice of the other spouse's intention to defeat the applicant's claim for relief. In the English case of *National Provincial Bank v. Hastings Car Mart* (1964) the Court set aside a sale by the husband of the family home to a company controlled by him, on being satisfied that his intention was to defeat his wife's claim for relief, the company having notice of his intention.

Any disposition made within three years of the date of the application for relief is presumed to have been made with the intention of defeating the claim of the applicant spouse. The onus is on the other spouse to rebut this presumption. In *J.D. v. D.D.* (1997) the wife had issued proceedings for judicial separation in October 1995. In May 1996 the husband transferred monies from a bank account in Cork to an account at the bank's branch in the Isle of Man, which he stated in evidence was for the benefit of his children. However, the Court was satisfied that his predominant motive was to reduce the monies available for distribution to the wife and thereby defeat her claim for relief. The Court refused to accept the husband's explanation of events as sufficient to rebut the presumption that the disposition was made with the intention of defeating the wife's claim for relief, and ordered that the disposition be set aside.

Section 26 of the 1996 Act provides that existing orders made under the Family Law (Maintenance of Spouses and Children) Act 1976, the Judicial Separation and Family Law Reform Act 1989 and the Family Law Act 1995 may be discharged on an application to the Court by either spouse for a decree of divorce. In so far as an existing order is not discharged, it will remain in force as if it were an order made under the 1996 Act, and may be varied or discharged under section 22 of that Act. *B.S. v. J.S.* (1999), discussed in Chapter 6 in the context of the requirement of the Court to make proper provision for the spouses and dependent members of the family on granting a decree of divorce, illustrates the power of the Court to discharge an order made in previous proceedings for judicial separation.

Further Reading

Shatter, *Family Law* 4th. Ed. Dublin: Butterworths 1997.

Duncan & Scully, *Marriage Breakdown in Ireland: Law and Practice*. Dublin: Butterworths (Ireland) 1990.

Gallagher, 'Pension Aspects of the Family Law Act, 1995', (1996) 7 GILS 201.

Martin, 'Judicial Discretion in Family Law'. (1998) 11 ILT 168.

CHAPTER EIGHT

FINANCIAL SUPPORT FOR SPOUSES AND CHILDREN

Husband's Common Law Duty to Maintain Wife

At common law, a husband was obliged to provide his wife with 'necessaries', that is, goods and services that were necessary for her maintenance, taking into account the standard of living which the husband had set for his wife and her actual requirements at the time. This rule stemmed from the doctrine of unity of husband and wife by marriage. As a result of this doctrine, nearly all a wife's property passed to her husband on marriage, which meant that she was incapable of contracting and providing for herself. A wife who deserted her husband lost her right to be supported by him while the desertion continued. The right to support was also lost if the wife committed adultery which the husband had not connived at or condoned.

While a wife's contractual and property difficulties existed at common law, the most significant method available to her for enforcing her husband's obligation to maintain her, was her common law power to pledge his credit for the purpose of purchasing necessaries. The power of the wife to pledge her husband's credit was based on implied agency. As a wife's property and contractual disabilities at common law were eroded by statute, and the Courts were given power to order a husband to pay his wife maintenance, it became largely unnecessary for a wife to pledge her husband's credit. However, a wife may still act as her husband's agent either by express appointment, estoppel or ratification.

The Legislative Framework

The Mutual Duty to Maintain

The law relating to maintenance is now set out in the Family Law (Maintenance of Spouses and Children) Act 1976, as amended. Section 5(1)(a) provides that the Court may make a maintenance order in favour of an applicant spouse and any dependent children of the family where it appears to the Court that the respondent spouse 'has failed to provide such maintenance... as is proper in the circumstances...'. As a result, the common law rule that a wife did not have to support her husband has been abolished. Either spouse can be ordered to pay maintenance to the other, regardless of whether the parties are living together or apart, if it appears to the Court that there has been a failure to provide proper maintenance. As an application for maintenance must be made by a spouse, it follows that where a marriage has been annulled by court decree or dissolved by a decree of divorce, a former spouse cannot avail of the section. Of course, where a marriage is dissolved, the Court, on the application of either party, can make the full range of financial and property orders that are available by way of ancillary relief under the Family Law (Divorce) Act 1996. Section 23 of the Family Law Act 1995 provides for the granting of ancillary relief where a foreign divorce is recognised in the State. The effect of a foreign divorce which is recognised in the State was considered in *C.M. v. T.M.* (1991). See Chapter 6.

Under section 5(1)(b) of the 1976 Act the Court may, on the application of any person, make an order for the maintenance of any dependent children of the family, where the spouse is dead, or has deserted or has been deserted by, or is living separately and apart from the other spouse. As a result of the foregoing provision, the application can be made by a person on behalf of dependent children even though such person does not have legal custody of them. Section 7 provides for the making of an interim order, on the making of an application for a maintenance order, for a definite period or until the application is adjudged, if it appears to the Court to be proper to do so having regard to the needs of the persons for whose support the maintenance order is sought and the other circumstances of the case.

Definition of Dependent Child

A dependent child for the purposes of the legislation is defined in section 3 of the 1976 Act, as amended by section 43 of the Family Law Act 1995, as any child under 18 years of age of both spouses or adopted by both spouses or in relation to whom both stand *in loco parentis*, or a child of either spouse or adopted by either spouse or in relation to whom either spouse stands *in loco parentis* provided the other spouse is aware he is not the parent of the child and has treated the child as a member of the family. A child over 18 years of age may be treated as dependent if he is in full time education and is under the age of 23 years, or is suffering from physical or mental debility and cannot maintain himself fully, in which case the dependency may be lifelong.

By virtue of the Status of Children Act 1987, a non-marital child is now regarded as a dependent child. Section 5A of the 1976 Act (as inserted by section 18 of the 1987 Act) provides that, in the case of a dependent child whose parents are not married to one another, either parent may apply to the Court for maintenance for the child. If it appears to the Court that the other parent has failed to provide such maintenance as is proper in the circumstances, the Court may make a periodical payments order or a lump sum order by way of maintenance in favour of the applicant parent.

Periodic and Lump Sum Payments

Originally, courts could only make maintenance orders by way of periodical payments. Such an order provided that one spouse should pay to the other a specific sum of money periodically, e.g. weekly or monthly. Section 41 of the Family Law Act 1995 enables the Court to make a secured maintenance order providing that periodic payments be charged against property owned by the paying spouse. Whereas, the death of the paying spouse automatically terminates an unsecured periodical payments order, it does not terminate a secured maintenance order, which can endure beyond the death of the paying spouse, as the property on which it is charged will still be in existence. Section 42 of the Family Law Act 1995 provides that the Court can make a lump sum maintenance order in addition to a secured maintenance order, or instead of such an order. A lump sum maintenance order requires the paying spouse to pay a fixed sum or sums of money in one payment or by specified instalments. If the lump sum is ordered to be paid by instalments, the instalments can be secured on property owned by the paying spouse. A lump sum payment order made by the District Court cannot exceed £5,000.

Assessment of Maintenance

Property, Financial Resources and Responsibilities of the Parties

Section 5(4) of the 1976 Act, as amended by section 38 of the Judicial Separation and Family Law Reform Act 1989, sets down the matters that the Court must assess when deciding whether to make a maintenance order, and in assessing the amount of maintenance that should be paid. The Court must take into account all the circumstances of the case and, in particular, (a) the income, earning capacity (if any), property and other financial resources of the spouses and of any dependent children, (b) the financial and other responsibilities of the spouses towards each other and towards any dependent children and the needs of any such children, including the need for care and attention and, (c) the conduct of each of the spouses, where in all the circumstances it would be repugnant to justice to ignore such conduct.

The Needs of the Family

In the absence of any clear guidelines as to what is proper maintenance in any given case, the Court must decide each case on its own particular circumstances, always bearing in mind that the needs of the family is the overriding consideration. Walsh J explained the purpose of the 1976 Act in *H.D. v. P.D.* (1978) when he stated:

> . . . the primary function of the Act is to ensure that proper and adequate maintenance will be available in accordance with the provisions of the Act

to spouses (and children) and that the basic question to be decided was whether at any given time there was a failure by one spouse to provide reasonable maintenance for the support of the other spouse . . . .

While the Court, in assessing the amount of maintenance that should be paid in any given case, must give priority to the needs of the applicant spouse and any dependent children, it must also ensure that the paying spouse will have sufficient resources left to live on. At the same time, any reduction in living standards should be borne primarily by the respondent, particularly where he has caused the breakdown of the marriage by his conduct. In *G.H. v. E.H.* (1998) Barr J was of the view that 'having regard to her financial liabilities and requirements', the wife was entitled 'to the benefit of a reasonable lifestyle commensurate with' that available to the husband. The evidence showed that the husband had considerable means. The Court refused his application to vary downwards his maintenance obligation to his wife and dependent child, and ordered him to continue payment of the weekly sum of £200 and arrears of £7000.

In the majority of cases however, it is a sad fact of life that when a couple separate they will experience a reduction in living standards. Finlay CJ painted a striking picture of the inevitable financial consequences of the breakdown of marriage in *RH. v. N.H.* (1986) when he stated:

> The court . . . must first have regard to the somewhat pathetic fact that upon the separation of a husband and wife and, particularly a husband and wife with children, it is inevitable that all the parties will suffer a significant diminution in the overall standard of living. The necessity for two separate residences to be maintained and two separate households to be provided for makes this an inescapable consequence of the separation.

The judgment of Finlay CJ in *L. v. L.* (1992) is clear authority for the proposition that mothers of dependent children, who have separated from their husbands and are required to maintain a second household, should not be obliged to work outside the home to supplement their income. The Chief Justice, in applying the principle set out in Article 41.2 of the Constitution, held that where a husband is capable of making proper provision for his wife, she should not be forced by economic circumstances to work outside the home to the neglect of her duties in it.

While it is usually the case that where spouses separate their living standards are thereby reduced, it is also true that in a limited number of cases a separation will not result in the lowering of living standards. This was the situation in *L.B. v. H.B.* (1980), where the High Court found that the husband, a man of substantial means, had failed to maintain his wife in the style she was entitled to expect and which she previously enjoyed. The husband was ordered to pay her £300 per week (which at that time was a substantial sum) so that she could maintain a sumptuous house which required the employment of a housekeeper and gardener.

The Relevance of Spousal Misconduct

As the conduct of the spouses must now be taken into account in certain circumstances, it is important to establish what type of conduct might be relevant. In *Wachtel v. Wachtel* (1973) Denning MR said that the Court should only take conduct into account where it was obvious and gross. In *Harnett v. Harnett* (1974) Bagnal J stated that a party was guilty of conduct that was obvious and gross where he 'wilfully persisted in conduct, or a course of conduct, calculated to destroy the marriage in circumstances in which the other party is substantially blameless'. A good example of the type of conduct that might be considered by the Court is the English case of *Kyte v. Kyte* (1987). The wife behaved callously when the husband, a manic depressive, made two suicide attempts. On the first occasion she was present and only called assistance at the last minute. When he again attempted suicide, she encouraged him by giving him alcohol and tablets and jeered him when he failed to carry out the attempt. The Court found that the wife wanted the husband dead so that she could inherit his money and share it with her lover.

Section 5(2) of the 1976 Act, as amended by section 38 of the Judicial Separation and Family Law Reform Act 1989, provides that desertion by the applicant spouse is a bar to relief unless, having regard to all the circumstances (including the conduct of the other spouse), the Court is of the opinion that it would be repugnant to justice not to make a maintenance order. Desertion is defined in section 3 of the 1976 Act as including constructive desertion. In *M.B. v. E.B.* (1980) the wife was forced by the drunken habits of the husband to leave the family home with their child. The husband resisted her application for maintenance for herself and the child, claiming that as she had deserted him he should not be obliged to maintain her. Barrington J was satisfied that the wife had just cause to leave the husband and ordered him to pay maintenance. In *K. v. K.* (1993) the wife was held to be guilty of constructive desertion. Her conduct, which amounted to mental cruelty, had forced the husband to leave the family home.

Effect of Second Relationship on Ability to Pay Maintenance

In very many cases, by the time the Court comes to decide what order to make, either or both spouses may have established a second relationship, and the new partner may have an income or property of his own. While a respondent will not have a legal obligation to support a partner with whom he is living in adultery, the question arises as to whether the Court can take into account the income or property of the partner in determining what maintenance should be awarded to the applicant. That there are conflicting views on this question is clear from two judgments delivered by Barron J in the High Court. In *O.'K. v. O.'K.* (1982) the learned judge ruled that neither the fact that the husband was living in an adulterous relationship, nor the fact that his partner was earning, is a consideration which should be taken into account. However, he came to a different conclusion in *McG. v. McG.* (1985), when he decided that where a husband has formed a permanent relationship with his new partner, the income of that partner should be taken into account, since it resulted in him having less expenses to pay. Accordingly, the relevant permanency of a second relationship is an important consideration for the Court in deciding whether to take into account the income or property of a partner. As any child born to a respondent spouse involved in a second relationship is a dependent child for the purposes of section 3 of the 1976 Act, the Court is obliged to take into account the respondent's obligation to support the child when assessing the amount of maintenance to be paid to the applicant spouse.

Effect of Separation Agreement

It is clear from the decision in *H.D. v. P.D.* (1978) that the spouses cannot, by the inclusion of a clause in a separation agreement, exclude or limit the power of the Court to exercise its statutory discretion to consider what is proper maintenance in any given case. In that case, an application for a decree of divorce *a mensa et thoro* commenced by the wife had been settled. The written agreement setting out the terms of the settlement was filed in court. A term of the agreement was that the wife was to be paid a lump sum of £10,000 in full and final satisfaction of her claim. Later, the wife applied to the Court under section 5 of the 1976 Act seeking a maintenance order. The Court overruled the husband's contention that the wife, by signing the earlier agreement, was estopped from seeking a maintenance order. By virtue of section 27 of the 1976 Act, any agreement that has the effect of excluding or limiting the power of the Court to consider what is proper maintenance in any given case shall be void.

Section 8 of the 1976 Act provides that an agreement entered into by the parties to a marriage, whereby one spouse undertakes to pay periodical maintenance to the other spouse and/or dependent children of the family may be made a rule of court, provided the Court is satisfied that the agreement is a fair and reasonable one which adequately protects the interests of both spouses and any dependent children. It further provides that any such agreement is to be considered a maintenance order for the purposes of section 9 of the Act, thus enabling the spouse who is entitled to maintenance under the agreement, to avail of the enforcement provisions of the Act, and to have payments made through the District Court for transmission to him.

Discharge and Variation

Section 6 of the 1976 Act, as amended by section 38 of the Judicial Separation and Family Law Reform Act 1989, provides for the discharge or variation of maintenance orders as follows:

(1) A maintenance debtor may apply to the Court to discharge a maintenance order at any time after the expiration of one year from the making of the order. The Court has power to discharge the order where it is satisfied that, having regard to the maintenance debtor's record of payments and to the other circumstances of the case, it would not prejudice the persons for whose support it was made to do so.

(2) The Court may discharge or vary a maintenance order at any time on the application of either spouse. Before discharging or varying an order, however, the Court must have regard to any circumstance which did not exist at the time the order was made, including the conduct of each of the spouses, where that conduct is such that it would be repugnant to justice to disregard it. The Court must also consider any evidence not available to the applicant at the time the order was made, or if it was varied, when it was last varied.

(3) Where the maintenance creditor deserts or continues to desert the maintenance debtor, the Court has power to discharge the maintenance order unless, in all the circumstances (including the conduct of the maintenance debtor) it would be repugnant to justice to do so.

(4) That part of a maintenance order which provides for the support of a dependent child is automatically discharged when the child reaches 18 years or 23 years (unless physically or mentally disabled), as the case may be. The Court may discharge a maintenance order in favour of a child if it is satisfied that the child has for any reason ceased to be a dependent child of the family.

(5) Desertion by, or conduct of a spouse shall not be a ground for discharging or varying any part of a maintenance order that provides for the support of dependent children.

Adultery by the maintenance creditor can no longer be specifically taken into account by the Court when considering an application for the discharge or variation of a maintenance order. It is suggested however, that where there is evidence of adultery, which has not been condoned or connived at by the maintenance debtor, that fact could be taken into account as 'conduct' where it would be repugnant to justice to disregard it.

Payment of Maintenance

Section 9 (1) of the 1976 Act provides that, unless the Court otherwise directs, payments under a maintenance order are to be made to the District Court clerk. The clerk is obliged to transmit the payments to the maintenance creditor. Where payments to the clerk are in arrears, he must, if requested in writing by the maintenance creditor, take reasonable steps to recover such arrears. This is without prejudice to the right of the maintenance creditor to proceed in his own name.

Enforcement of Maintenance Orders

Maintenance can be enforced by an attachment of earnings order, a distress order on the maintenance debtor's goods, or committal to prison.

Attachment of Earnings

An attachment of earnings order is probably the most effective method of enforcement where the maintenance debtor is in regular employment. Under section 10 of the 1976 Act, the Court can make such an order on the application of the maintenance creditor or the District Court clerk to whom payment is made. Section 43 of the Family Law Act 1995 provides that an attachment of earnings order can be made when the Court is making a maintenance order. The effect of an attachment of earnings order is a direction from the Court to the maintenance debtor's employer to pay to the District Court clerk or maintenance creditor the sum, known as 'the normal deduction rate', that the Court thinks is reasonable to deduct to meet the maintenance liability. The order must also specify the 'protected earnings rate', which is the sum below which the maintenance debtor's earnings must not be allowed to fall. The Court will not make an attachment of earnings order without the consent of the maintenance debtor except where he has defaulted in making maintenance payments.

The making of an attachment of earnings order, therefore, involves the determination by the Court of two amounts — first, the normal deduction rate, which is the amount the Court considers reasonable to satisfy payments as they fall due under the related maintenance order plus payment of arrears by instalments within a reasonable period; and, secondly the protected earnings rate, which is the amount below which, having regard to the resources and needs of the maintenance debtor, his earnings must in no circumstances be reduced.

Section 11 of the 1976 Act requires an employer upon whom an attachment of earnings order is served to comply with it after ten days have elapsed since the service. Where an order is served on an employer and the maintenance debtor is no longer in his employment or subsequently ceases to be in his employment, he must notify the Court. The employer must give a written statement to the maintenance debtor of any deduction from his earnings. An attachment of earnings order must be served on the employer to whom it is directed and on any subsequent employer of whom the Court becomes aware. Such service shall be effected by leaving the order or a copy at, or sending it by registered post to, the residence or place of business of the employer in the State.

The Court has power under section 13 of the 1976 Act to order the maintenance debtor or his employer to supply a statement of earnings. The maintenance debtor has an obligation under section 14 to inform the Court of any change of employment and a new employer is obliged to inform the Court if he knows that an attachment of earnings order exists in respect of any new employee.

Section 17 of the 1976 Act enables the Court to discharge or vary an attachment of earnings order on the application of the maintenance creditor, maintenance debtor or District Court clerk on whose application the maintenance order was made. An employer must comply with an order discharging or varying an attachment of earnings order on the expiration of ten days from service of the order on him. An attachment of earnings order lapses on notice from an employer to the Court that the maintenance debtor has left his employment but may be redirected to a new employer.

Where a maintenance debtor gives false or misleading information to the Court, he is guilty of an offence under section 20 and is liable, on conviction, to a fine not exceeding £200 or imprisonment for six months, or both. Under section 24, periodical payments under a maintenance order, variation order or interim order shall be made without deduction of income tax.

Distress Orders

This method of enforcement is rarely availed of in practice. It is available under the Enforcement of Court Orders Act 1940, as amended. Where the maintenance debtor is in arrears on payments, a District Judge may, if he thinks proper, direct that the sums payable be levied by distress, i.e. seizure and sale of his goods.

Imprisonment

Under the Enforcement of Court Orders Act 1940, as amended by section 29 of the 1976 Act, a maintenance debtor can be imprisoned for up to three months for default in making maintenance payments.

The International Dimension — Recognition and Enforcement of Maintenance Orders

Common Law

In the past, the recognition and enforcement of foreign maintenance orders in Ireland gave rise to certain problems. The decision of the Supreme Court in *Mayo-Perrott v. Mayo-Perrott* (1958) seemed to prevent the enforcement in the State of a maintenance order made consequent on a foreign divorce. In that case, the wife was granted a divorce, with costs, in England. She sued her former husband, who had come to live in Ireland, for arrears of costs. The Supreme Court, affirming the decision of the High Court, refused her claim on the basis that the award of costs could not be severed from the divorce decree. Were the Court to allow her claim for costs, it would amount to enforcing a divorce decree, which was contrary to the public policy of the State. However, in *Sachs v. Standard Chartered Bank (Ireland) Ltd* (1987) the Supreme Court, affirming the decision of the High Court, held that a maintenance order made in England ancillary to a divorce decree could be enforced. Finlay CJ was of the view that public policy did not prevent the enforcement of a foreign maintenance order. Indeed, the public policy of the State seemed to favour the enforcement of such an order, which would prevent a maintenance debtor from avoiding his liability towards his spouse and dependent children.

It is a general principle of private international law that a court should only enforce a foreign judgment which is final and conclusive. This seemed to pose a problem as far as the recognition of foreign maintenance orders at common law was concerned, since a maintenance order is by its nature subject to subsequent variation by order of the Court that made it. This issue was addressed by the High Court in *G. v. G.* (1984), where it was held that a maintenance order was to be regarded as final if the Court that granted the order had power within its jurisdiction to vary, rescind or alter the order retrospectively. In *McC. v. McC.* (1994) the High Court held that a maintenance order made in Hong Kong, which could be varied retrospectively under Hong Kong law, was enforceable on the basis of the principle of law enunciated in *G. v. G.*.

The Maintenance Orders Act 1974

The Maintenance Orders Act 1974, which applies to maintenance orders made before or after the commencement of the Act, provides for the enforcement in this jurisdiction of maintenance orders made in England and Wales, Scotland or Northern Ireland. A maintenance order is defined in section 3 the 1974 Act as including alimony and affiliation orders, and maintenance orders made in divorce proceedings. The Maintenance Orders (Reciprocal Enforcement) Act 1972 allows for the enforcement in the United Kingdom of maintenance orders made in Ireland.

Section 6 of the 1974 Act provides that when a request is received from the appropriate authority in a reciprocating jurisdiction for the enforcement of a maintenance order in the State, it is to be referred to the Master of the High Court for a determination on the matter. Having considered the matter privately, the Master must make an enforcement order, unless he considers that recognition and enforcement are prohibited by section 9. The decision of the Master, whether he orders enforcement or not, is notified to the maintenance creditor. Where the Master makes an enforcement order, notice of that fact must be given to the maintenance debtor under section 7. The notice must inform the maintenance debtor of his right to appeal to the High Court against the decision of the Master within one month of receipt of the notice. The maintenance creditor may appeal to the High Court under section 8 against a refusal of the Master to make an enforcement order. Notice of the appeal must be given to the maintenance debtor.

Section 9 of the 1974 Act provides that a maintenance order made in a reciprocating jurisdiction will not be recognised or enforced in the State (a) if it would be contrary to public policy to recognise or enforce it, or (b) where it was made in default of appearance, the person in default not being served with notice of the institution of the proceedings in sufficient time to enable him to arrange for his defence, or (c) if it is irreconcilable with a judgment given in a dispute between the same parties in the State. Section 14 empowers the District Court to enforce an enforceable maintenance order as if it were an order made under section 5 or section 5A or 21A of the Family Law (Maintenance of Spouses and Children) Act 1976.

The Maintenance Act 1994

The Maintenance Act 1994 has consolidated the law relating to the reciprocal recognition and enforcement of maintenance orders. The purpose of the 1994 Act is to give legal effect to the 1990 Rome Convention between the Member States of the European Communities on the simplification of procedures for the recovery of maintenance payments, and the 1956 New York Convention on the recovery of maintenance abroad. The preamble to the New York Convention recognises the urgency of the situation of persons in need dependent for their maintenance on persons abroad, and purports to provide a simplified means to solve the problem by overcoming serious legal and practical difficulties. Section 4 of the 1994 Act provides for the establishment of a Central Authority to discharge the functions required of it under the Act, or required of a Central Authority under the Rome Convention, or of a transmitting agency or receiving agency under the New York Convention. The Act is without prejudice to the provisions of the Maintenance Orders Act 1974.

Part II of the 1994 Act, which is to be construed together with the Jurisdiction of Courts and Enforcement of Judgments Acts 1988 - 1993, gives effect to the Brussels and Rome Conventions providing for the recovery of maintenance in a 'reciprocating jurisdiction' and Part III of the Act gives effect to the New York Convention providing for the recovery of maintenance in a 'designated jurisdiction'.

The Brussels and Rome Conventions
The Rome Convention requires Central Authorities to co-operate with each other, and promote co-operation between the competent authorities in their

respective States, to facilitate the recovery of maintenance payments due. Where a maintenance creditor in a contracting State seeks to have a judgment recognised or enforced in another contracting State, the maintenance creditor may request the Central Authority in the State of origin to transmit the application to the State addressed. On receipt of an application, the Central Authority in the State addressed shall take the necessary measures to (i) locate the maintenance debtor or his assets, (ii) have the judgment declared enforceable where appropriate, (iii) facilitate the transfer of maintenance payments to the maintenance creditor, and (iv) where the payments to the maintenance creditor are not made, use the necessary means of enforcement to permit recovery of those payments. The provisions of the Rome Convention are in addition to those of the Brussels Convention and are without prejudice to other existing international instruments.

Section 7 of the 1994 Act provides that where the Central Authority receives an application from a reciprocating jurisdiction for recognition or enforcement in the State of a maintenance order, it must send the application to the Master of the High Court for a determination on the matter. Having duly considered the matter, the Master shall make an enforcement order, unless it appears to him that recognition and enforcement are prohibited under the Brussels Convention. Where the Master makes an enforcement order, the Central Authority must serve notice of the order on the maintenance debtor, who has the right to appeal against the order to the High Court.

Article 27 of the Brussels Convention prohibits the recognition of a foreign judgment in circumstances broadly similar to those prohibiting recognition of a judgment under section 9 of the Maintenance Orders Act 1974. Additional grounds for non-recognition under Article 27 are (a) where recognition would conflict with the rules of private international law applicable in the State in which recognition is sought, and (b) if the judgment is irreconcilable with an earlier judgment given in a non-contracting State involving the same parties, provided that this latter judgment fulfils the conditions necessary for its recognition in the State addressed.

Section 8 of the 1994 Act provides for the admission in evidence of certain documents that are relevant to the recognition and enforcement of foreign maintenance orders. Section 11 confers on the District Court the power to enforce an enforceable maintenance order as if it were an order made by the District Court under section 5 or section 5A or 21A of the Family Law (Maintenance of Spouses and Children) Act 1976.

The New York Convention

The New York Convention lays down a procedure for the recovery of maintenance payments which is broadly similar in nature and effect to the recovery procedure outlined in the Rome Convention. For the purposes of the

New York Convention, a Central Authority means a transmitting agency or receiving agency in a State which is a contracting Party to the Convention. Whereas the Rome Convention uses the terms 'maintenance creditor' and 'maintenance debtor' for the purpose of reciprocal enforcement of maintenance orders, the New York Convention uses the terms 'claimant' and 'respondent'.

Section 14 of the 1994 Act deals with applications from a designated jurisdiction on behalf of a claimant for the recovery of maintenance from a person residing in the State. Where the Central Authority receives a request from a designated jurisdiction, and the request is accompanied by an order made in a contracting State, the Central Authority submits the request to the Master of the High Court for a determination on the matter. If the request is accompanied by an order made by any other court, and the Central Authority is of the opinion that the order may be enforceable in the State, the Central Authority may apply to the District Court for the enforcement of the order. If the request is not accompanied by such an order or if enforcement of the order is refused, the Central Authority may apply to the District Court or, where the amount claimed exceeds the amount which the District Court has jurisdiction to award, to the Circuit Court for the recovery of maintenance in accordance with the request. An enforcement order made by the District Court on foot of an order made in a contracting State, shall be deemed an enforceable maintenance order within the meaning of section 7 of the Jurisdiction of Courts and Enforcement of Judgments Act 1988. Where a request is not accompanied by an order made by a court in a contracting State or any other court, or where enforcement of the order is refused, an application made to the District Court or Circuit Court for the recovery of maintenance shall be deemed to be an application for maintenance under section 5 or section 5A or 21A of the Family Law (Maintenance of Spouses and Children) Act 1976.

Section 15 of the 1994 Act is designed to facilitate a claimant who wishes to recover maintenance from a respondent residing in a designated jurisdiction. The claimant may apply to the Central Authority to have the claim transmitted to the Central Authority in the designated jurisdiction, notwithstanding the existence of a maintenance order made against the respondent by a court in the State. The District Court may certify, on the basis of a sworn deposition made by the claimant, that the respondent owes a duty to maintain the claimant. A copy of the deposition and certificate is furnished to the claimant. Section 16 provides for the admission in evidence of certain documents that are relevant to the recognition and enforcement of maintenance orders. Section 17 deals with the obtaining of evidence from a designated jurisdiction, while section 19 relates to the taking of evidence for proceedings in a designated jurisdiction.

Part IV of the 1994 Act contains provisions that are common to reciprocating and designated jurisdictions. Section 20 confers extensive powers on the Central Authority to enable it obtain information that is necessary or expedient for the performance of its functions. The Authority may require any holder of a public office or body financed by the Oireachtas to provide information as to the whereabouts, place of work, or location and extent of the assets of the maintenance debtor/respondent. On an application by the Central Authority, the District Court may order any person or body, not being the holder of a public office or body financed by the Oireachtas, who is likely to have relevant information on the maintenance debtor/respondent to supply that information to the Central Authority.

Where proceedings are pending under Part II or Part III of the 1994 Act, section 21 provides for the admission in evidence of documents purporting to be signed by a judge or court officer in a reciprocating or designated jurisdiction, subject to authentication, as the Court may require. Other documents, such as tax certificates, certificates of earnings, medical certificates, letters, affidavits, documents establishing marital status, and documents in the nature of a power of attorney may also be admitted in evidence, subject to authentication, as the Court may require.

Section 22 of the 1994 Act provides that the recognition or enforcement of an order for recovery of maintenance made by a court in a jurisdiction other than the State may not be refused (a) by reason of the fact that the Court which made the order had power to vary or revoke it, or (b) on the ground that, under the rules of private international law of the State, the Court concerned had no jurisdiction, by reason of the fact that the respondent was not resident or present in that jurisdiction at the date of the commencement of the relevant proceedings, provided that at that date the claimant was resident there. Section 24 makes it clear that the 1994 Act shall not prevent the recognition or enforcement of an order for the recovery of maintenance which is made in a reciprocating jurisdiction or a designated jurisdiction and which, apart from the Act, would be recognised or enforced in the State.

Further Reading

Shatter, *Family Law*, 4th. Ed. Dublin: Butterworths 1997.
Duncan & Scully, *Marriage Breakdown in Ireland: Law and Practice*. Dublin: Butterworths (Ireland) 1990.
Binchy, *Irish Conflict of Laws*. Dublin: Butterworths 1988.

CHAPTER NINE

PROPERTY DISPUTES BETWEEN SPOUSES

Historical Developments

The early law which regulated the property of spouses was aptly described in the colloquialism that in law 'husband and wife are one and that one is the husband'. Thus, at common law, while the marriage subsisted, a married woman was deemed incapable of owning separate property. Any property brought into the marriage by her, or subsequently acquired by her, was regarded as owned exclusively by her husband. The husband was obliged to maintain her, unless her conduct disentitled her. This impediment was removed by the Married Women's Property Act 1882 which enabled married women to own and control their own separate property. By virtue of the Married Women's Status Act 1957 a married woman may sue to enforce both contractual and tortious remedies against both her husband and third parties.

The doctrine of community of property or of family assets is unknown in Irish law. Neither does it apply under English law, as is evident from the decision in *Pettit v. Pettit* (1970), where the House of Lords refused to consider whether property belonging to either spouse ought to be regarded as family property. An attempt was made by the Irish legislature in the Matrimonial Home Bill 1993 to confer equal rights in the ownership of the matrimonial home and household effects on each spouse. The Supreme Court, on a referral of the Bill to it by the President under Article 26 of the Constitution, found the Bill to be repugnant to the Constitution — *Re Article 26 and the Matrimonial Home Bill 1993* (1994). In the course of its judgment, the Court said that the right of a married couple to make a joint decision as to the ownership of the matrimonial home is a right possessed by the family and that the exercise of this right is an important part of the authority of the family under Article 41 of the Constitution. The Bill, as framed, was a disproportionate intervention by the State in the rights of the family and constituted a failure by the State to protect the authority of the family.

Nowadays, in many instances, the family home and household effects are owned jointly by the spouses, both as to the legal and beneficial interest, having been acquired out of joint savings or by one spouse with help from the other. As beneficial owners, both will have the right to occupy the home, and as legal owners, both will be able to enforce title against third parties. However, there are still cases where legal title to the home is in the name of one spouse alone, usually the husband. Accordingly, when a marriage breaks down the non-owning spouse will apply to the Courts for a declaration that he has a beneficial interest in the home based on contributions, direct or indirect, made towards its acquisition.

Procedure in Property Disputes

The jurisdiction of the Courts to determine any question arising between spouses as to the title to or possession of any property is based on section 36 of the Family Law Act 1995, as amended by the Family Law (Divorce) Act 1996, which repeals section 12 of the Married Women's Status Act 1957. Under section 36, the Court may make such order, and direct enquiries and give directions, in respect of the property in dispute as it considers proper, including an order that it be sold or partitioned. Either spouse, or a child of a deceased spouse, may apply to the Court under the section where it is claimed that the other spouse had in his possession or under his control, property (including money) belonging to that spouse or child and has not paid over the property or its value. Section 36 enables a spouse or a child to apply to the Court for an order tracing money which may represent the proceeds of sale of property in which that spouse had a beneficial interest, and property (other than money) to which that spouse was beneficially entitled.

For the purposes of section 36, the term 'spouse' includes a personal representative of a deceased spouse, either of the parties to a void marriage, whether or not it has been annulled, either of the parties to a voidable marriage that has been annulled, and either of the parties to a marriage that has been dissolved. Annulment or dissolution may be in accordance with the laws of the State, or a foreign annulment or divorce that is recognised in the State. In either case, an application under section 36 must be made within three years of the date of the annulment or divorce. Where a marriage is void but has not been annulled, an application must be made within three years of the parties ceasing to live together.

An application under section 36 may be brought even though there are no other matrimonial proceedings pending between the spouses. In contrast, however, the extensive powers vested in the Courts under the Judicial Separation and Family Law Reform Act 1989, as amended by the Family Law Act 1995, and the Family Law (Divorce) Act 1996, to make ancillary orders in relation to matrimonial property, are only available in the context of applications for judicial separation or divorce.

The Beneficial Interest

In the absence of a doctrine of community of property or family assets, the mere fact that both spouses use property which is registered in the name of one spouse only does not, of itself, give the non-owning spouse any interest therein. Where disputes have arisen between spouses as to the ownership of property, established principles of law have been applied by the Courts. Where the matrimonial property is vested in the sole name of one of the spouses, there is a rebuttable presumption that the beneficial interest also belongs exclusively to that spouse. To rebut this presumption the non-owning spouse must show that the other spouse held the property on trust for them both as beneficial owners.

Trusts may be categorised as express, implied, resulting or constructive. An express trust is created where one person sets up a trust for the benefit of another by means of a trust instrument. An implied trust arises where the conduct of the parties indicates that they intended to hold property jointly. A resulting trust arises where one person purchases property and has it transferred into the name of another. That other will be deemed to hold the property in trust for the person providing the purchase money (it 'results back') in the absence of an intention to make an out-right gift. However, where a husband purchases property and has it transferred into the name of his wife, the doctrine of advancement applies. The law implies an intention by the husband to provide for the wife by way of gift, in the absence of evidence to rebut this intention. In the case of a constructive trust, equity imposes a trust based on the conduct of the parties and the way the property is dealt with, irrespective of any intention, express or implied, of the parties. In *N.A.D. v. T.D.* (1985) Barron J distinguished between resulting and constructive trusts for the purposes of deciding whether a non-owning spouse has a beneficial interest in matrimonial property. He described the resulting trust as arising 'from the unexpressed but presumed intention of the parties where both contribute to its purchase either directly or indirectly and it is put in the name of one of them alone', and a constructive trust as 'imposed by operation of law independent of intention in order to satisfy the demands of justice and good conscience'.

Where the non-owning spouse has contributed, directly or indirectly, to the acquisition of the matrimonial home, in the absence of an express agreement between the spouses, the Court has to infer an intention concerning ownership using the device of the implied or resulting trust or, in some cases, a constructive trust. There is an abundance of Irish case law illustrating the principles to be applied in considering an application by a spouse for a declaration that he has a beneficial interest in property the legal title to which is vested in the other spouse. The starting point is the body of principles set out in two High Court cases, namely *Heavey v. Heavey* (1974) and, more significantly, *C. v. C.* (1976).

The judgment of Kenny J in *C. v. C.* is now generally regarded as the most authoritative statement of the law on the matter, and has been endorsed by the Supreme Court on a number of occasions since. In that case, the husband acquired the family home and had it vested in himself subject to a mortgage. The wife had paid the initial deposit and some of the mortgage payments, which amounted in total to about half the purchase price. When the marriage broke down as a result of the conduct of the husband, he left the home and refused to maintain the wife and the children of the marriage. The High Court held that the husband held the family home, as to half the beneficial interest therein, in trust for the wife. In delivering judgment, Kenny J outlined the principles involved as follows:

> I think that the correct and most useful approach to these difficult cases is to apply the concept of a trust to the legal relationship which arises when a wife makes payments towards the purchase of a house or the repayments of mortgage instalments when the house is in the sole name of the husband. When this is done, he becomes a trustee for her of a share in the house and the size of it depends upon the amount of contributions which she has made towards the purchase or the repayment of the mortgage. This approach also has the advantage that it gives that flexibility which is essential in dealing with domestic matters.

There is little difficulty in comprehending the approach of the Courts in dealing with the situation where the non-owning spouse has made direct contributions, as in *C. v. C.* However, where the contributions are indirect, the matter is not so straightforward. Accordingly, in an effort to set out as clearly as possible the principles applied by the Courts in resolving property disputes between spouses, it is proposed to deal separately with direct and indirect contributions.

Direct Contributions

While direct contributions may take any form, they usually take the form of the non-owning spouse paying part of the deposit and making contributions towards repayment of the mortgage out of her separate earnings or out of the proceeds of an inheritance. In *E.R. v. M.R.* (1981) the High Court decided that a wife, who had provided the entire purchase money out of an inheritance from her deceased mother to acquire lands which were transferred into the sole name of her husband, was beneficially entitled to the entire property, on the basis that the husband held it on trust for her. However, in *C.D. v. W.D. and Barclay's Bank plc* (1997) McGuinness J held that contributions by a wife to a family fund after marriage cannot give rise to a share in the matrimonial home, where it was purchased by the husband before marriage and had been unencumbered by any charges.

The Supreme Court had an opportunity to consider a non-owning spouse's direct contributions in *McC. v. McC.* (1986). It was agreed for the purposes of the proceedings that the wife had contributed one-third of the purchase price of the family home in Dublin. This house was sold and the wife allowed the husband to retain her one-third share. The husband subsequently purchased a house in Cork but did not provide any of the purchase money which was raised totally by means of a mortgage. The proceeds of sale of the Dublin property were used to

121

acquire furnishing and fittings for the new home. In the High Court, Costello J held that the wife was entitled merely to a one-third share in the furnishings and fittings. On appeal, the Supreme Court affirmed the decision of the High Court. In delivering the judgment of the Court, Henchy J stated the law as follows:

> [W]here a matrimonial home has been purchased in the name of the husband, and the wife has, either directly or indirectly, made contributions towards the purchase price or towards the discharge of mortgage instalments, the husband will be held to be a trustee for the wife of a share in the house roughly corresponding with the proportion of the purchase money represented by the wife's total contribution. Such a trust will be inferred when the wife's contribution is of such a size and kind as will justify a conclusion that the acquisition of the house was achieved by the joint efforts of the spouses.

Indirect Contributions

Indirect contributions usually take the form of the non-owning spouse managing or working in the family business or allowing her earnings to be paid into a family fund or making improvements to the property.

Unpaid Involvement in Family Business

Where a spouse does unpaid work for which he or she would normally be paid, as in the English case of *Nixon v. Nixon* (1969), where a husband bought a house largely from the profits of a business which the wife had helped to run without receiving any wages, the wife was held to have a half interest in the house. However, where a wife discharges the 'normal' functions of housewife and mother, she gains no interest in the home purchased by her husband, as the Courts do not regard this work as work which normally would be paid for. This is clear from the Supreme Court's decisions in *L. v. L.* (1992) and *N. v. N. and C.* (also known as *E.N. v. R.N.*) (1992).

The case of *K.v K.* (1978), while involving both direct and indirect contributions, is a good example of a wife doing unpaid work in a family business. She did not make any contributions towards the purchase of the family home. She had salaried employment for a period of two years and her wages were used to help with the mortgage repayments and to meet household expenses. Subsequently, the couple set up a business in which they each had a half share. The wife worked full time in the business, but the husband continued in his job and also worked in the business in his spare time. Neither party received a salary from the business but profits were used to cover family expenses and make mortgage repayments. When the marriage subsequently broke down, the wife instituted High Court proceedings claiming a beneficial interest in the family home. The Court held that she was entitled to a 28% share in the home, based on her initial direct contributions to the mortgage repayments while working in the supermarket and her subsequent indirect contributions through her participation in and part ownership of the family business.

N.D. v. A.D. (1982) involved a complex series of property transactions comprising acquisitions and disposals in New York, London and Kerry, culminating in the husband purchasing a licensed premises with living accommodation in Kerry. The property was conveyed into the sole name of the husband. The premises required substantial refurbishment before opening for business. The evidence showed that the business was run mostly by the wife and prospered to the extent that it provided the main source of income for the marriage during the period. The High Court awarded the wife a beneficial interest of 60% in the premises, and in doing so, took into account her contribution through her earnings to the purchase of the premises, 'and the later express or implied agreement between the parties' whereby the wife was left 'to create and develop the business in the premises by her own unaided efforts and business expertise'.

Contributions to Family Fund

That a wife, who did not contribute directly to the acquisition of the matrimonial home, can make indirect contributions towards its retention by allowing her earnings to become part of a general family fund, is clear from the decision of the High Court in *F.G. v. P.G.* (1982). The husband had acquired the home in his own name. He paid the deposit and the balance was borrowed and secured by a mortgage on the property. At this time, the wife did not work outside the home, occupying herself as mother and housewife. Subsequently, the parties emigrated to America, where the wife found employment and allowed her wages to be paid into a joint family fund until the parties separated following the breakdown of their marriage. The Court awarded the wife a beneficial interest of 30% in the home. Finlay P said that despite the fact that the wife never directly contributed to the purchase or maintenance of the house, it was part of family assets which were retained and acquired out of the joint family fund created by the earnings of both parties.

Indirect contributions, in the form of contributing to family assets, also came to be considered in *R. v. R.* (1979), where McMahon J held that there was no difference between money spent by the wife to provide necessaries for herself and money expended in meeting some household expenses, saying that 'in either case there is a saving to the husband and if that enables him *pro tanto* to meet the mortgage repayments the wife should be regarded as contributing to those repayments'. It is clear from this case that indirect contributions, which take the form of a wife using her earnings to defray personal and household expenses, is only relevant where the husband would not otherwise be able to afford the purchases.

In *McC. v. McC.* (1986) the Supreme Court gave its approval to the principle that indirect contributions taking the form of a spouse (in that case the wife) contributing earnings to a general family fund would enable the Court to infer a trust in favour of that spouse, 'on the ground that she has to that extent relieved the husband of the financial burden he incurred in purchasing the house'. In *L. v. L.* (1992) the Supreme Court approved of the doctrine of applying the constructive trust in cases where a spouse contributes to family assets. Finlay CJ acknowledged that a trust could arise from 'indirect contributions by the provision of earnings of monies into the family pool', but held that to extend the principle to a person 'who by carrying out the constitutionally endorsed activities of a wife and mother within the home' saved her husband from the expense of engaging outside home help, 'would be not to develop a doctrine, in my view, but to introduce a new one'. The case involved a successful appeal by the husband against the decision of Barr J to grant the wife a half share in the family home based on her indirect contributions by means of her work within the home.

Contributions to Improvements

Indirect contributions, taking the form of a spouse expending monies or carrying out work in the improvement of property which has been originally acquired by, and the legal ownership of which is vested solely in, the other spouse, have given rise to a considerable amount of litigation both here and in England. In *N.A.D. v. T.D.* (1985) Barron J, reviewing the law as it then stood, said that a claim based on a contribution to improvements should be dealt with by way of constructive trust, since a resulting trust could only arise where contributions were used towards acquisition of the property. The learned judge also said that the contribution to improvements must be substantial, and proceeded to set out the circumstances in which a constructive trust will arise:

> The constructive trust is imposed by operation of law independent of intention in order to satisfy the demands of justice and good conscience. Its imposition is dependent on the conduct of the person upon whom the trust is imposed and prevents him from acting in breach of good faith. There is no fixed set of circumstances in which such a trust is imposed.

Additionally, for a claim based on contributions to improvement to succeed, there must be an express agreement between the parties, or the person making the contribution must have been led to believe that he would be refunded. In *Heavey v. Heavey* (1974) the husband had made direct contributions towards the purchase of the property and carried out improvements. Kenny J stated that the husband had no claim to be repaid the sum he had spent 'even if he thought that the amount would be repaid . . . unless she led him to believe that it would be refunded'.

A wife's claim to a beneficial interest in a farm registered in the husband's name in *W v. W.* (1981) was based on work done by her in running a bloodstock business on the farm and carrying out improvements. In relation to the work done by the wife in the improvement of the property, Finlay P stated that she would have no claim in relation to the improvements unless she could prove 'that from the circumstances surrounding the making of it she was led to believe, or it was specifically agreed, that she would be recompensed for it', and that even where the right to be recompensed is established 'it is a right to recompense in monies only and cannot and does not constitute a right to claim an equitable share in the estate of the property concerned'. In *N. v. N. and C.* (also known as *E.N. v. R.N.*) (1992). Finlay CJ reviewed his own judgment in *W. v. W.* and stated that a direct contribution, even in money's worth, by a spouse towards improvements on a family home held in the sole name of the husband cannot, in the absence of an agreement, express or implied, constitute a claim to a beneficial interest.

No Beneficial Interest Based on Article 41.2 of the Constitution

In two very significant judgments delivered in 1992, namely *L. v. L.* and *N. v. N. and C.* (also known as *E.N v. R.N.*), the Supreme Court had to consider a wife's claim to a beneficial interest in the family home by virtue of her work as wife and mother based on Article 41.2 of the Constitution. In each case, the wife's claim failed, as the Court concluded that it did not have jurisdiction under Article 41 to make declarations concerning ownership of the family home except under the existing doctrines of resulting and constructive trusts. Were the Court to adopt such a course, it would amount to an interference with the separation of powers doctrine.

L. v. L. involved an appeal by a husband against the decision of Barr J in *B.L. v. M.L.* (as the case was called in the High Court) (1989) granting a beneficial interest in the family home to his wife based on Article 41.2. The husband had acquired a residential farm and had it transferred into his name. The wife had no outside earnings and engaged herself exclusively in running the home and rearing the two children of the marriage. She made no direct or indirect contributions in money or money's worth towards the acquisition of the property. Barr J acknowledged that the wife was not entitled to a beneficial interest on the basis of established authority, as she had not made direct or indirect contributions. However, he awarded her a 50% share in the family home, on the basis that under Article 41.2 she should have her work as homemaker and carer of her children taken into account. In allowing the husband's appeal, the Supreme Court accepted the desirable objective which the principle outlined by Barr J would achieve. However, Finlay CJ, who delivered the principal judgment of the Court, concluded that 'to identify the right in the circumstances set out in the case is not to develop any known principle of the common law, but is rather to identify a brand new right and to secure it to the plaintiff'. He went on to state that the creation of any such new right would 'constitute legislation and be a usurpation by the courts of the function of the legislature'.

It is interesting to note that Barrington J in *H. v. H.* (1989), while deciding the case on traditional grounds, approved the reasoning of Barr J in *B.L. v. M.L.*, on the basis that it would be inconsistent with the principles enshrined in Article 41 if a wife who could work outside the family home and contribute financially to the purchase of the family home was in a better position than the 'stay-at-home' wife.

N. v. N. and C (also known as *E.N. v. R.N.*) was an unsuccessful appeal by the wife against the decision of the High Court in *E.N. v. R.N.* (1990). Applying established principles, Barron J awarded the wife a one fifteenth share of the family home. While he recognised the soundness of the reasoning of Barr J, he refused to apply it. He stated that the provisions of Article 41 envisaged financial reward for the 'stay-at-home' wife as coming from outside the family rather than a distribution within the family.

Further Reading

Shatter, *Family Law*, 4th. Ed. Dublin: Butterworths 1997.

Duncan & Scully, *Marriage Breakdown in Ireland: Law and Practice*. Dublin: Butterworths (Ireland) 1990.

Binchy, *A Casebook on Irish Family Law*. Abingdon: Professional Books 1984.

O'Connor, *Key Issues in Irish Family Law*. Dublin: The Round Hall Press 1988.

Cooney, 'Wives, Mistresses and Beneficial Ownership'. (1979) 14 Ir Jur (n.s.) 1.

CHAPTER TEN

STATUTORY PROTECTION FOR THE FAMILY HOME

Where the family home is registered in the sole name of one of the spouses and the other spouse is unable to establish an equitable or beneficial interest in it, that spouse may invoke the protection of the Family Home Protection Act 1976, as amended, which prevents a spouse disposing of the family home without the prior written consent of the other spouse.

At common law, even though the whole of the legal and beneficial estate in the family home was vested in the husband, the wife, as wife, had a right to occupy it. However, this right could be defeated by a sale or mortgage to a third party, unless the wife could obtain a court order restraining her husband from disposing of the home without providing suitable alternative accommodation, as happened in *Heavey v. Heavey* (1974). In the English case of *National Provincial Bank v. Ainsworth* (1965) the House of Lords decided that a deserted wife without a beneficial interest was liable to be evicted from the family home by a *bona fide* purchaser from her husband, or the mortgagee of the premises, even though they knew of her presence and the fact that she was a deserted wife.

The 1976 Act does not give the non-disposing spouse 'any estate or interest' in the family home. It merely gives that spouse the right 'to veto the disposition' of it to a third party without his prior written consent. In *L. v. S.* (1981) McWilliam J stated in the High Court that the right of the non-owning spouse 'is a valuable right even though it does not constitute any estate or interest in the premises'. The precise nature of the right in question was explained by Henchy J in *Hamilton v. Hamilton* (1982) as follows:

> The Act of 1976 provides for the protection of the family home, presumably as an implementation of the constitutional duty that falls on the State to protect the family and to guard with special care the institution of marriage. To this end, the Act of 1976 (as I have pointed out) created a new right whereby (save in exceptional cases) the non-disposing spouse is given a right to veto the disposition to a third party of any legal or equitable interest in the family home.

In *Bank of Ireland v. Smyth* (1996), in delivering the judgment of the Supreme

Court, Blaney J endorsed this passage from the judgment of Henchy J in *Hamilton v. Hamilton* stating 'This passage emphasises an important aspect of the right given to the spouse — it is given for the protection of the family, and not simply for the protection of the spouse.'

Family Home

The term 'family home' is defined in section 2(1) of the 1976 Act as meaning 'primarily a dwelling in which a married couple ordinarily reside. The expression comprises in addition, a dwelling in which a spouse whose protection is in issue ordinarily resides or, if that spouse has left the other spouse, ordinarily resided before so leaving'. The Supreme Court decided in *National Irish Bank v. Graham* (1994) that the intention to occupy and reside in a home as a married couple did not constitute the home a family home for the purposes of section 2. Section 2(2), as inserted by section 54 of the Family Law Act 1995, defines a 'dwelling' as:

> any building or part of a building occupied as a separate dwelling and includes any garden or other land usually occupied with the dwelling, being land that is subsidiary or ancillary to it, is required for amenity or convenience and is not being used or developed primarily for commercial purposes, and includes a structure that is not permanently attached to the ground and a vehicle, or vessel, whether mobile or not, occupied as a separate dwelling.

The above definition of a family home is wide enough to include a flat or apartment occupied as a separate dwelling, and non-permanent structures such as mobile homes and house boats. The only requirement is that the structure is occupied as a family home. Expressly excluded from the definition is land that is being used for development for commercial purposes.

That a family home might form part of a larger estate in property can be gathered from the High Court decision in *Allied Irish Banks v. O'Neill* (1995), where it was held that a mortgage was valid against a residential holding of land, excluding the farmhouse which was occupied as a family home. In delivering judgment, Laffoy J, in interpreting section 2 of the 1976 Act, said that the charge could be severed on the basis that the Act recognised that the family home may constitute a portion only of a larger holding. In the earlier case of *Bank of Ireland v. Slevin* (1989) a husband mortgaged a farm which included the family home without the prior consent in writing of his wife. Johnson J held that the charge could be severed, with the result that it was void in respect of the family home only. On the question of severance, it is worth noting that in *Bank of Ireland v. Smyth* (1996) Blaney J, in the Supreme Court, refused to consider a submission by the bank that the charge could be severed and treated as void in relation to the family home and valid as regards the remainder of the land, on the basis that this issue had not been raised at the original trial. On the issue of severance, he considered the decision of Johnson J in *Bank of Ireland v. Slevin* (1989), but did not express any view on the correctness or otherwise of that decision.

The Need for Consent

The aim of the 1976 Act, as its long title suggests, is to provide for the protection of the family home. Section 3 of the Act, as amended by section 54 of the Family Law Act 1995, provides that where a spouse, without the prior consent in writing of the other spouse, purports to convey any interest in the family home to any person except the other spouse then, subject to stated exceptions, the purported conveyance shall be void. A conveyance shall not be deemed void until so declared by a court. Proceedings to declare a conveyance void shall not be instituted after the expiration of six years from the date of the conveyance. A 'conveyance' includes a mortgage, lease, assent, transfer, disclaimer, release or any other disposition of property. An enforceable agreement to convey property is to be treated as a conveyance. However, a will or a *donatio mortis causa* is not a conveyance. 'Interest' means any estate, right, title or other interest, legal or equitable.

Section 54 (3) of the Family Law Act 1995 provides that where a court, when granting a decree of judicial separation, orders that ownership of the family home shall be vested in one of the spouses, it shall, unless it sees reason to the contrary, order that section 3(1) of the 1976 Act shall not apply to any conveyance by that spouse of an interest in the home.

The Supreme Court had its first opportunity to consider section 3 of the 1976 Act in *Somers v. Weir* (1979). The husband and wife resided in a house registered in the sole name of the husband until the marriage broke down in 1973, when the wife left home with the children. The couple entered into a separation agreement in 1974, but the agreement made no provision for or any reference to ownership of the family home. The husband sold the house in 1976 and furnished the purchaser with a statutory declaration to the effect that his wife had no interest in the premises by virtue of the separation agreement. The purchaser subsequently agreed to resell the premises in 1977 to a third party who discovered, in the process of an investigation of title, that there had been no consent in writing by the wife to the conveyance of 1976 from her husband. The purchaser failed to obtain the wife's consent retrospectively and then successfully obtained a High Court order dispensing with her consent under section 4 of the 1976 Act. The Supreme Court reversed the decision of the High Court, and held that the purported conveyance of the husband in 1976 was void. The house was a family home within the meaning of section 2 of the Act and any conveyance of it required the wife's prior consent in writing.

In *Nestor v. Murphy* (1979) the Supreme Court held that where both spouses have joined in the conveyance there is no need for either of them to give a prior consent in writing. The defendant spouses were joint owners of the family home. They entered into a contract for the sale of the property but subsequently refused to complete the transaction on the basis that the wife had not given her consent in writing prior to the signing of the contract. The plaintiff obtained an order for specific performance of the contract.

Exempt Transactions

The exceptions referred to in section 3 of the 1976 Act include a conveyance of the family home by a spouse in pursuance of an enforceable agreement made before the marriage of the spouses. The most important exception, however, is a conveyance of the family home to a purchaser for full value, i.e. such value as amounts or approximates to the value of that for which it was given. The term 'purchaser' includes a grantee, lessee, assignee, mortgagee, chargeant or other person who in good faith acquires an estate or interest in property. The onus of proving that a conveyance of the family home is valid rests on the person alleging it. In *Somers v. Weir* the Supreme Court held that a person who fails to make the necessary enquiries to establish whether the premises is a family home, thereby necessitating the consent of the non-owning spouse, is not acting in good faith. In the earlier High Court case of *S.S. v. S.M.V.* (1978), Doyle J said that the question whether a person is a *bona fide* purchaser for value without notice resolves itself into an enquiry as to whether that person through his agent/solicitor 'did all that was reasonably necessary to acquaint himself with the circumstances of the vendor's title'.

Bearing in mind that a *bona fide* purchaser for value can defeat the right of a non-owning spouse to veto a conveyance of the family home, section 12 of the 1976 Act enables a spouse to register a notice in either the Registry of Deeds or the Land Registry to the effect that he or she is married to the owner of the property that comprises the family home. The registration of such a notice can effectively prevent such a purchaser defeating the right of veto of the non-owning spouse.

Limited Effectiveness of 1976 Act

The 1976 Act provides only limited protection to the non-owning spouse against creditors — a creditor who has obtained a judgment for an outstanding debt against the spouse who owns the family home, can register the judgment as a judgment mortgage against the home. In *Murray v. Diamond* (1982) the issue to be determined was whether a judgment mortgage obtained by the plaintiff constituted a purported conveyance by the defendant of his interest in the family home, such as would render it void under section 3(1) of the 1976 Act. The High Court decided that when a judgment mortgage is created, the spouse against whom the judgment is registered does not convey any interest in the family home. The judgment mortgage comes into existence by operation of statute and not by virtue of any positive act of the judgment debtor. Similar sentiments were expressed by Carroll J in the High Court in *Containercare (Ireland) Limited v. Wycherley and Anor.* (1982), when she stated that a judgment mortgage, which results from the unilateral act of the judgment creditor, 'is not a disposition by a spouse purporting to convey an interest in the family home'.

Fully-Informed Consent

The problems that can arise for banks and other lending institutions under the 1976 Act can be gleaned from an examination of some of the most recent decisions of both the High Court and Supreme Court, where the validity of the consent of the non-disposing spouse was in issue. The most significant of these decisions is *Bank of Ireland v. Smyth* (1996). The husband was registered as sole owner of a farm in Tipperary and resided with his wife in the family home on the land. With the prior written consent of his wife, he charged the house and land in favour of the bank for all present and future advances. The employee of the bank dealing with the transaction did not explain to the wife the possibility of her losing her home if her husband defaulted in payments, nor did he suggest to her that she should get independent advice before consenting to the creation of the charge. The wife believed that the charge did not affect the family home because the house had been built with the aid of a loan from another financial institution who had a mortgage over the farm. When the husband defaulted in repayments, the bank sought an order for possession of the house and lands in the High Court. Geogeghan J refused to make an order for possession on the grounds that the wife had not given an appropriate consent to the creation of the charge for the purposes of the 1976 Act. An appeal by the bank to the Supreme Court was dismissed. In delivering the judgment of the Court, Blaney J stated that the bank had the onus of establishing that the wife's consent was sufficient and it had failed to do this. A consent for the purposes of section 3 of the 1976 Act must be a fully-informed consent based on a knowledge of what that consent entails. As the wife believed that the charge affected only the land and not the family home, her consent was not a fully informed one and was thus invalid. The bank could not enforce the charge because it had constructive notice of the wife's lack of knowledge.

The validity of a wife's consent to the creation of a charge on the family home was again before the Supreme Court in *Allied Irish Banks v. Finnegan* (1996). The husband purchased the family home in his sole name with the assistance of a loan of £100,000 from the bank. Although the wife signed a document consenting to the creation of a charge on the home, she subsequently swore an affidavit to the effect that it had been agreed between the spouses that the purchase would be in their joint names, and that she would not have agreed to the purchase if she had known it was to be in the husband's sole name. She further averred that she signed the consent in the belief that the document related to the purchase in their joint names, and was not advised by her husband's solicitor as to the nature and effect of the document. The solicitor denied the wife's version of events in an affidavit, and stated that he told her that her consent was necessary for the creation of the charge as the house was being purchased in her husband's sole name. The High Court made an order for possession in favour of the bank on the basis that it was entitled to rely on the consent signed by the wife. As the bank was a *bona fide* purchaser for value, the mortgage was valid. On appeal, the Supreme Court held that because there was a dispute as to the circumstances in which the consent was signed, and as to whether the bank was a *bona fide* purchaser for value, the matter would have to be determined by a full oral hearing. The bank had to show that it did not have actual or constructive notice of the possible invalidity of the charge and this was not an issue that could be decided by the Court on affidavit.

Where a spouse whose consent is required for the purposes of section 3 of the 1976 Act receives independent advice before giving that consent, it will be difficult for the spouse to dispute the validity of the consent. Blaney J stated in *Bank of Ireland v. Smyth* (1996) that the bank did not owe a duty to Ms Smyth to suggest to her that she should get independent advice. In *ICC Bank PLC v. Michael A Gorman* (1997) the defendant made an issue of the fact that his wife did not have the benefit of independent legal advice in relation to giving consent. In the course of her judgment, wherein she held the consent of the wife to be a valid consent, Laffoy J stated:

> There is no requirement in law that a spouse who is giving a consent for the purposes of section 3 of the 1976 Act must have the benefit of independent legal advice in the sense of advice from a legal practitioner who is not acting for the mortgagor spouse or the mortgagee. What is required is that the consent should be a fully informed consent.

In *Bank of Nova Scotia v. Hogan* (1997) the Supreme Court upheld the decision of the High Court and rejected the wife's contention that her decision to lodge the title documents to the family home, owned solely by her, to secure her husband's indebtedness to the bank was the result of undue influence by the bank.

General Consents

Section 3(9) of the 1976 Act, as inserted by section 54 of the Family Law Act 1995, provides that a spouse may give a general consent in writing to any future conveyance of any interest in the family home. If the deed for any such conveyance is executed after the date of that consent, the consent shall be deemed for the purposes of section 3(1) to be a prior consent in writing of the spouse to that conveyance. General consents seem designed to cover the situation where a lending institution takes a charge on the family home to cover present and future advances. The High Court decided in *Bank of Ireland v. Purcell* (1988) that future further advances amount to a conveyance of an interest in lands for the purposes of section 3 of the 1976 Act, as each time there is a further advance the interest of the mortgagor in those lands is being altered and the value of the equity of redemption is also being altered. As a result of the Supreme Court decision in *Bank of Ireland v. Smyth* (1996) it will be essential to ensure that any general consent is a fully-informed one.

Dispensing with Consent

Section 4 of the 1976 Act gives the Court power to dispense with the consent of a spouse who omits or refuses to consent, subject to the provisions of the section. However, the Court shall not dispense with the consent of a spouse unless it considers that such spouse has been unreasonable in withholding consent, taking all the circumstances of the case into account, including the needs and resources of the respective spouses and any dependent children of the family and, where the spouse whose consent is required is offered alternative accommodation, the suitability of that accommodation. In exercising its discretion, it would appear that the Court will only dispense with the consent of a spouse where adequate provision is made for that spouse and any dependent children. In *R. v. R.* (1978) the husband wanted to create a further mortgage on the family home to raise money to set up another household for himself and another woman with whom he had formed a relationship. The Court refused to dispense with the consent of the wife on the grounds that the husband would be unable to meet the mortgage repayments, thus endangering the family home.

Section 4 also provides that where a spouse whose consent is required is unable to consent because of unsoundness of mind or mental disability, or cannot be found, the Court may give the consent on behalf of that spouse if it appears reasonable to the Court to do so. The Court must dispense with the consent of a spouse who has deserted and continues to desert the other spouse. Desertion, for the purposes of the section, includes constructive desertion. In *O'M v. O'M.* (1981) the conduct of the husband had forced the wife to leave the family home and set up home with her children in a council flat. The husband sought an order dispensing with the wife's consent to enable him sell the family home. In the circumstances, the Court refused to regard the wife as being in desertion, and would only consider dispensing with her consent provided that half the net proceeds of any sale of the premises were paid over to her to enable her acquire alternative accommodation for herself and the children. The judgment of Henchy J in *Somers v. Weir* (1979), makes it clear that there is no power to make an order dispensing with the consent of the non-disposing spouse after a disposition has been made, so that the dispensation acts retrospectively.

Section 5 Orders

Because the family home is available as a form of security to creditors who register a judgment mortgage against it, section 5 of the 1976 Act is designed to afford a limited form of protection to the non-owning spouse, by conferring a wide discretion on the Court, including a power to order the transfer of the family home from one spouse to the other. Even in a situation where a spouse has, by his conduct, deprived the other spouse, or a dependent child of the family, of his residence in the family home, the Court can order that the other spouse be compensated by that spouse. By virtue of section 5(1), where the Court is satisfied, on the application of a spouse, that the other spouse is engaging in conduct that might lead to the loss of the family home or render it unsuitable for habitation as a family home, with the intention of depriving the applicant spouse or any dependent child of the family of his residence in the family home, the Court may make such order as it thinks fit for the protection of the family home in the interest of the applicant spouse or dependent child. Before the Court can make an order under section 5(1), it must be satisfied that the conduct of the spouse who is putting the family home at risk is intentional, in the sense that it is wilful or deliberate.

Wilful or Deliberate Conduct

A spouse is not to be regarded as acting intentionally merely because he has been improvident or irresponsible in allowing himself to get into debt. In *E.D. v. F.D.* (1980) Costello J, while accepting that the husband who had got into serious financial difficulties by living 'on a scale wholly inappropriate to his family responsibilities' had acted improvidently, refused to regard that conduct as intentional within the meaning of section 5. However, Costello J adjourned the case to afford the husband the opportunity of making an arrangement with his creditors. When the case came before the Court again a year later (*E.D. v. F.D.* (1981)), the Court was satisfied that the husband's conduct was deliberate, in that he had done little or nothing to sort out his finances, and ordered that the family home be transferred to the wife. In *O'N. v. O'N.* (1989) the High Court ordered a wife who owned the family home jointly with her husband to transfer her share to the husband. The evidence showed that the wife had deserted the husband and had allowed a judgment mortgage to be registered against her interest in the premises in respect of a loan taken out after she had left her husband. Barron J held that the wife's conduct, which put the residence of the husband and children in the family home at risk, came within the ambit of section 5(1).

It is not enough for the Court to be satisfied that the offending spouse must have anticipated the natural and probable consequences of his actions. In *C.P. v. D.P.* (1983) Finlay P refused to construe the word 'intention' in the section as equivalent to 'the implied or imputed intention which can arise from the natural or probable consequences of an act or omission'. Similarly, in *S. v. S.* (1983), where the husband got into financial difficulties and put the family home in jeopardy, McWilliam J was of the view that although the husband acted improvidently and, possibly dishonestly, 'and the natural and probable consequences of his actions may have been that the family home would be the target of his various creditors', he had not intended to deprive the wife and children of their residence in the home.

A spouse, who is unable to satisfy the Court that the conduct of the offending spouse is intentional for the purposes of section 5(1) of the 1976 Act, may be able to overcome that problem by instituting judicial separation or divorce proceedings and seeking a transfer of property order under section 9 of the Family Law Act 1995 or section 14 of the Family Law (Divorce) Act 1996. In *A.S. v. G.S. and AIB* (1994) the High Court made a transfer of property order in favour of the wife under section 15 of the Judicial Separation and Family Law Reform Act 1989, (the 1995 Act was not then in force), where the circumstances of the case did not justify the making of an order under section 5(1) of the 1976 Act.

Where a spouse or a dependent child has in fact been deprived of his residence in the family home, that spouse may apply to the Court for relief under section 5 (2) of the 1976 Act. The Court has power to order the other spouse to pay compensation to the applicant spouse or dependent child, or to make such other order as is just and equitable to meet the circumstances of the case. It is generally accepted that, for the purposes of section 5(2), the loss of the family home must have been due to some blameworthy conduct on the part of the spouse in whose name the property is registered. In *A.D. v. D.D. and the Irish Nationwide Building Society* (1983) McWilliam J held that the husband's failure to pay mortgage instalments because of insufficient income would not be conduct sufficient to activate section 5(2). Only where the Court was satisfied that a spouse had sufficient means to pay the mortgage, but refused to pay resulting in the loss of an interest in the family home, would it grant relief to the other spouse.

Household Chattels

Section 9 of the 1976 Act is designed to prevent the disposal or removal of household chattels in circumstances that would make it difficult for the other spouse or a dependent child of the family to reside in the family home without undue hardship. 'Household chattels' are defined in the section as including the usual items of furniture and clothing and ordinary household effects. Consumable stores, garden effects and domestic animals are also included, but excluded are chattels used for business or professional purposes and money or security for money.

Section 9 provides that where matrimonial proceedings have been instituted by either spouse, neither spouse shall dispose of or remove household chattels without the consent of the other spouse or an order of the Court authorising the disposal or removal. In addition to incurring a sanction of a fine of £100 or imprisonment for up to six months on summary conviction, or both, a spouse who contravenes the section, or disposes of or removes household chattels, may be ordered to replace the chattels or pay a sum of money in lieu thereof. A disposal can include a sale, lease, pledge, charge or removal of chattels. The Court, on the application of a spouse, may by order, prohibit the disposal or removal by the other spouse on such terms as it thinks fit. Where a third person, to whom a spouse proposes to dispose of household chattels, has been informed in writing by the other spouse of his intention to institute proceedings under the section, the Court may make such order directed to the spouse or the third person as it deems proper in the circumstances.

Payment of Outgoings and Arrears by Non-Owning Spouse

Section 6 of the 1976 Act provides that any payment by a spouse in or towards satisfaction of any liability of the other spouse in respect of rent, rates, mortgage payments or other outgoings affecting the family home shall be regarded as being done by the other spouse, and shall be treated by the person to whom such payment is made as though it were made or done by the other spouse.

Recognising the perilous position that a spouse may find himself in where the other spouse is in arrears of mortgage instalments or rent, and faces the prospect of proceedings by the mortgagee or landlord for possession of the family home, section 7 of the Act provides an additional measure of protection. Where such proceedings are pending, the Court has power to adjourn the proceedings where it is satisfied that the applicant spouse desires, and is in a position financially, to discharge the accrued arrears and any future periodical payments that may arise. However, before exercising its discretion to adjourn the proceedings, the Court must have regard to the terms of the mortgage or lease and the interests of the mortgagee or landlord and the respective spouses.

Where the Court has adjourned the proceedings under section 7 of the Act on the application of a spouse, that spouse may subsequently apply to the Court under section 8. Where the Court is satisfied that all arrears due under the mortgage or lease, and all periodical payments due to date have been paid, and that payments falling due subsequently will be met, the Court may make a declaration to that effect. The advantage of such a declaration is that any term in a mortgage or lease to the effect that a default in payment will result in the capital sum advanced thereunder, or any other additional amount, becoming payable forthwith, shall have no effect for the purposes of the proceedings or any subsequent proceedings in respect of the sum becoming due.

Further Reading

Shatter, *Family Law*, 4th. Ed. Dublin: Butterworths 1997.

Duncan & Scully, *Marriage Breakdown in Ireland: Law and Practice*. Dublin: Butterworths (Ireland) 1990.

Binchy, *A Casebook on Irish Family Law*. Abingdon: Professional Books 1984.

O'Connor, *Key Issues in Irish Family Law*. Dublin: The Round Hall Press 1988.

Mee, 'The Family Home Protection Act: The Practical Implications of Bank of Ireland v. Smyth'. (1996) 8 & 9 ILT 188, 209.

CHAPTER ELEVEN

DOMESTIC VIOLENCE

The Domestic Violence Act 1996, which repeals the Family Law (Protection of Spouses and Children) Act 1981, now regulates the granting of interim and permanent relief for spousal misconduct and domestic violence generally. The long title describes the legislation as:

> An Act to make provision for the protection of a spouse and any children or dependent persons, and of persons in other domestic relationships, where safety or welfare requires it because of the conduct of another person in the domestic relationship concerned.

A 'dependent person' for the purposes of the Act means any child of either the applicant or respondent or both of them or adopted by either or both of them under the Adoption Acts 1952–1998 or in relation to whom either or both of them is or are *in loco parentis*, provided the child is under the age of 18 years, or over that age if suffering from mental or physical disability.

The 1996 Act breaks new ground in that for the first time cohabitees in a relationship outside marriage and their children are protected under the law and there is also provision for protecting parents from violent adult children. The Courts have power to make a long-term protection-type order, called a safety order, for a period of up to five years, renewable for a further five. The safety order protects an applicant and any dependent person against threats and intimidation without having the offending respondent barred. The period for which a barring order may be made has been increased to three years, with the power to renew for a further three years. One of the most radical innovations in the Act is the power conferred on a health board to apply under section 6 for a safety or barring order on behalf of an aggrieved person who may be too traumatised to apply on his own behalf, or too frightened to do so. A health board can make an application even without the authority of the person involved, but that person's wishes must be taken into account by the Court in any application before it. Both the District and Circuit Courts have jurisdiction to deal with applications under the Act. Proceedings under the Act are heard in private and are informal.

The protection now afforded to the victims of domestic violence is more comprehensive than under the repealed legislation. In this regard, it is worth pointing out that prior to the Family Law (Maintenance of Spouses and Children)

Act 1976, which legislated specifically for spousal misconduct for the first time, the only remedies available were an action for damages, a criminal prosecution and the injunction. These remedies were of limited value to victims. An award of damages was hardly likely to solve the problem of domestic violence, and in the case of criminal prosecution, the victim spouse did not have the final say, in that any such prosecution was at the discretion of the Garda Síochána. In any event, the victim spouse's main concern in seeking relief was to prevent further violence against her and any dependent children, and not the punishment of the offending spouse. An injunction could exclude the violent spouse from the family home and prevent further molestation of the victim but the District Court does not have jurisdiction to grant one. Whilst the injunction can still be availed of, it is not likely to be extensively used in practice, because of the simplified procedures involved in obtaining the range of orders available under the 1996 Act, which are available relatively inexpensively in the District Court. In addition, the extensive powers of arrest without warrant and entry into premises and the increased penalties provided by the 1996 Act make recourse to one of the orders more attractive.

The Orders Available

Safety Order — Section 2

An application can be made by:

(a) a spouse;

(b) a cohabitee who has lived with the respondent as husband or wife for at least six months in aggregate during the twelve months period immediately prior to the application;

(c) a parent of a respondent who is of full age and not dependent;

(d) a person of full age residing with the respondent in a relationship the basis of which is not primarily contractual. For the purpose of deciding whether the relationship is primarily contractual, the Court shall have regard to the time the parties have spent together, the duties performed by either party for the other, the absence of profit or payment for residing at the place concerned and any other relevant matters. The range of potential applicants under this last category includes brothers and sisters residing together, an adult relative of the applicant or the respondent, an adult child living with a parent and persons living in same sex relationships. Whether cohabitees who fail to satisfy the residence and ownership requirements of the Act are included under this category, is a matter discussed later in the chapter.

Where the Court is satisfied that there are reasonable grounds for believing that the safety or welfare of the applicant or dependent child so requires, it may by order direct that the respondent:

(1) shall not use or threaten to use violence against, molest or put in fear the applicant or dependent person, and,
(2) shall not watch or beset the place where the applicant or dependent person resides.

The term 'molest' is not defined in the section and the term has not been defined judicially in this jurisdiction. Accordingly, one must look to English decisions for the meaning of the term. In *Davis v. Johnson* (1978) it was held that molestation may occur without the threat or use of violence. In *Vaughan v. Vaughan* (1973) 'molest' was said to be synonymous with 'pester'. In that case, Stephenson J expressed his view in the following terms: 'Molest is a wide, plain word which I should be reluctant to define or paraphrase. If I had to find one synonym for it, I should select pester. Whether communication amounts to molestation is a question of fact and degree'. In *Fearon v. Aylesford* (1884) Brett MR defined molestation as follows: 'I am of the opinion that the act done . . . must be an act which is done with intent to annoy, and does in fact annoy'.

A safety order can be made for up to five years and it may be renewed for a further five year period. The Court has power to vary a safety order. The Court cannot make a safety order on an application for a barring order unless there is a separate application for a safety order before it.

Barring Order — Section 3

An application may be made by:
(a) a spouse,
(b) a cohabitee who has lived with the respondent as husband or wife for at least six months in the aggregate during the period of nine months immediately prior to the application,
(c) a parent of the respondent where the respondent is of full age and not dependent.

The same grounds, as in the case of a safety order, are provided for the making of a barring order in favour of an applicant or dependent child. If satisfied that sufficient grounds exist the Court may by order:

(1) direct the respondent, if residing at a place where the applicant or dependent person resides, to leave such place, and
(2) prohibit the respondent from entering such place (where the respondent is either residing in the place or living apart from the family).

A barring order may also prohibit the respondent from using, or threatening to use, violence, molesting or putting in fear the applicant or any dependent child or from attending at or in the vicinity of, or watching or besetting, a place where the applicant or any dependent child resides. For the meaning of the term 'molest' see above. A barring order can be made for up to three years and it may be renewed for a further three. The Court is given power to vary a barring order at any time. The Court cannot make a barring order on an application for a safety order unless there is a separate application for a barring order. An applicant or dependent person who has been prevented by the conduct of the respondent from residing in premises the subject matter of an application for a barring order, shall be deemed to be residing in the premises for the purposes of the section.

Interim Barring Order — Section 4

If on the making of an application for a barring order, or between the making of the application and its determination, the Court is satisfied that there are reasonable grounds for believing that there is an immediate risk of significant harm to the applicant or dependent child, or that a protection order would not be sufficient to protect them, the Court may make an interim barring order. Such an order has the same effect as a barring order and lasts until the Court determines the application for the barring order. Where the Court, in exceptional cases, considers it necessary or expedient in the interests of justice, an interim barring order may be made *ex parte* or notwithstanding the fact that notice of the application has not been served on the respondent. In effect, an *ex parte* order is made without the other side being told of the hearing or being given an opportunity to be present.

The Law Reform Committee of the Incorporated Law Society in its Report 'Domestic Violence: The Case for Reform' 1999 (referred to throughout this chapter as the Law Society Report) referred to the fact that an interim barring order, which may exclude a respondent from his place of residence, can be granted *ex parte* on what amounts to a *prima facie* review of the evidence, and stated that, for this reason, it is essential that an early return date is set for the hearing to determine the barring application. As a result of a survey carried out among practitioners, which revealed in some cases unacceptably long delays between the granting of an interim barring order and the return date for hearing the application for a barring order, the Report recommends that the District Court Rules be amended to provide an automatic early return date for interim barring orders. The Report also recommends that the District Court Rules be amended to require that *ex parte* applications for an interim barring order be made on affidavit, that the respondent automatically be provided with a note of all the evidence given at the hearing and that personal service of the barring summons be required in all cases or, at least, where the respondent is barred *ex parte*.

Protection Order — Section 5

In an emergency, particularly where violence is alleged, an applicant may require immediate protection and may fear the likely consequences of court proceedings being served on the respondent. To cover this situation, the Court may make a protection order to grant protection to the applicant and dependent children between making application for a barring order or safety order and the making of such order. If there are reasonable grounds for believing that the safety or welfare of the applicant or any dependent children so requires, an order may be made prohibiting the respondent from using or threatening to use violence against the applicant or child or from watching or besetting the place where the applicant or dependent child resides.

A protection order does not require a respondent to vacate the family home nor does it restrict his right to reside in it. A protection order shall cease to have effect on the determination by the Court of the application for a safety order or barring order. For the purposes of an application for a protection order, an applicant or dependent person who would, but for the conduct of the respondent, be residing at a place shall be treated as residing at such place.

As in the case of an interim barring order, a protection order may be made *ex parte* without the respondent being told of the application or being given an opportunity to attend the hearing. The Law Society Report recommends that applications for an *ex parte* protection order be made on affidavit and that the respondent be automatically provided with a note of all the evidence given at the hearing.

Applications by Cohabitees and Parents

Safety orders and barring orders are now available (in the circumstances outlined above) to couples who are merely cohabiting outside marriage and to parents against violent non-dependent children. Cohabitees and parents of non-dependent children may not apply for barring orders where they have no legal or beneficial interest, or where the respondent has a greater interest than the applicant, in the property in relation to which the order is sought. However the applicant's belief that he has an interest in the property is admissible in evidence. In the case of safety orders, there is no requirement that cohabitees or parents have a legal or beneficial interest in the property.

Cohabitees

In the case of cohabitees, section 3(13) of the 1996 Act (as inserted by section 4 of the Family Law (Miscellaneous Provisions) Act 1997) overcomes the anomaly that existed where a cohabitee wished to apply for a further barring order, by providing that, despite the fact that the parties were not living together at the time of the application as a result of the previous order, they would be treated as living together for the requisite period.

It appears that the restrictive ownership requirement imposed on cohabitees wishing to apply for a barring order was a precaution against constitutional challenge. It is significant that the English Domestic Violence and Matrimonial Proceedings Act 1976 did not impose any property restrictions on cohabitees, merely requiring that they are 'living with each other in the same household as husband and wife'. Initially, it was felt that a cohabitee could not claim relief under the English legislation unless he had a proprietorial or other interest in the home, but this view was rejected by the House of Lords in *Davis v. Johnson* (1978).

The 1996 Act requires that, in the case of cohabitees, the applicant must have 'lived with the respondent as husband or wife' for the requisite period, but does not define the term. Neither does the English Act of 1976 define the term 'living with each other in the same household as husband and wife'. It was held in *Adeoso v. Adeoso* (1980) that, just as husband and wife could be deemed to be living in separate households though living under the same roof, and thereby be deemed to be living apart, for the purposes of desertion or judicial separation, it was likewise possible for cohabitees to live in separate households under the same roof for the purposes of the 1976 Act. However, in that case, even though the parties were living separate lives, they were deemed to be living together because of the cramped nature of their accommodation. In the absence of any decision by the superior courts on the matter in this jurisdiction, there is nothing to indicate whether Irish courts will adopt a similar approach in determining whether cohabitees are living together.

The Law Society Report, while accepting that the residence and ownership requirements of the 1996 Act relating to a cohabitee applying for a barring order could be justified on constitutional grounds, could not find any justification for the residence requirement for a cohabitee applying for a safety order, since such an order does not exclude the respondent from living in his home or deprive a respondent of any property entitlement. The Report refers to a possible anomaly arising as a result of the residence requirement for a safety order, in that an applicant in a same sex relationship, who could seek protection under section 2(1)(a)(iv) of the 1996 Act as a person of full age 'who resides with the respondent in a relationship the basis of which is not primarily contractual', would enjoy a greater level of protection than a non-married applicant in a heterosexual relationship. The Report indicates that in practice, some District Judges allow couples who do not satisfy the cohabitation criteria to apply under section 2(1)(a)(iv) while on the other hand, some Judges do not. The Report recommends that the residence requirement be removed for cohabitees seeking a safety order. Recognising that there can be no constitutional justification for any residence requirement for cohabitees with sole ownership or tenancy rights in the home seeking a barring order, the Report also recommends the removal of such a requirement in such circumstances.

The Report of the Task Force on Violence Against Women, April 1997, has recommended that the requirement in the 1996 Act that a cohabitee must have lived with the respondent for at least six months before qualifying for a barring order should be reviewed subject to any constitutional requirements (see Paragraph 6.13). The First Report of the Steering Committee on Violence Against Women, March 1999, stated that, based on advice received from the Attorney General, there are no proposals to amend the requirement that a cohabitee must establish six months residence before obtaining a barring order. Neither are there proposals to amend the conditions in the 1996 Act that require cohabitants who apply for barring orders to have certain rights of ownership in the place of residence that is in question. The Report of the Task Force also recommended that the provisions of the 1996 Act should be extended to cover situations where couples have a child in common but do not live together (see Paragraph 6.12). The Report of the Steering Committee states that this proposal will be considered by the Department of Justice, Equality and Law Reform in the context of any legislation which may be brought forward in the area of family law.

Parents

As pointed out above, parents are now entitled to apply for the various protective orders against non-dependent children. As in the case of cohabitees, there is no requirement that a parent have a proprietorial interest in the home in the case of a safety order, but there is such a requirement in the case of a parent applying for a barring order. The Law Society Report highlighted the fact that there was no protection in the 1996 Act for parents or elderly relations against abusive relations other than an adult child, such as a son-in-law. Noting that such a relationship may be covered by section 2(1)(a)(iv) in respect of a safety order, the Report recommends that provisions be introduced permitting parents or elderly relations to apply for protective orders against abusive relations or persons other than an adult child.

Applications by Health Boards

Section 6 of the 1996 Act empowers a health board to apply on behalf of the aggrieved person for a safety order or barring order. The health board can make an application on behalf of an aggrieved person, who can either be a spouse or dependent person, where it becomes aware of an alleged incident or series of incidents that put into doubt the safety or welfare of that person. The health board must have reasonable cause to believe that the aggrieved person has been subjected to molestation, violence or threatened violence and is too traumatised or frightened to apply on his own behalf. The Court must take into account the wishes of the aggrieved person but can make the appropriate order without the authority of the aggrieved person.

On the occasion of an application by a health board on behalf of an aggrieved person, the Court is given power by section 7 to adjourn proceedings under the Act if it is satisfied that it would be more appropriate to make a care order or supervision order under the Child Care Act 1991 in relation to any dependent child. The Court may direct the health board to investigate the circumstances of the dependent child and make a report back with its recommendations as to whether or not it should make application for a care order or supervision order under the 1991 Act.

Ancillary Orders

Section 9 of the 1996 Act enables the Court, in addition to making orders under the Act, to make orders under other Acts where it appears proper to do so. Without the need to institute separate proceedings, the Court may make orders as to custody and access under the Guardianship of Infants Act 1964, orders as to maintenance under the Family Law (Maintenance of Spouses and Children) Act 1976, orders under the Family Home Protection Act 1976 and orders under the Child Care Act 1991.

The Principles Applied in Making Orders

The Court may make a safety order or barring order under sections 2 and 3 of the 1996 Act when 'it is of the opinion that there are reasonable grounds for believing that the safety or welfare of the applicant or any dependent person so requires'. Welfare is now defined in section 1 to include 'the physical and psychological welfare of the person in question'. It is not necessary for the applicant to prove actual violence or cruelty. The only condition that must be met is the safety or welfare of the applicant or dependent person. There is nothing in the 1996 Act to suggest that the Court is required, in making a particular order, to take the position of the respondent into account. When making a barring order, for example, the Court need not consider the hardship and inconvenience that exclusion from the family home will cause the respondent, even where a spouse who is barred does not have the means to acquire suitable alternative accommodation. The overriding consideration is the safety or welfare of the applicant or dependent person. For this reason, the Court will only make a barring order when absolutely necessary to secure the safety of an applicant or a dependent person.

Conduct

In a document to coincide with the introduction of the 1996 Act, entitled 'Protection from Domestic Violence — A Guide to the New Law', issued by the Minister for Equality and Law Reform, domestic violence is defined as 'any form of physical, sexual or psychological violence which puts the safety or welfare of a family member at risk'. Conduct of all types can be taken into account, but obviously, the more serious the conduct is, the more likely it is to have an effect on the success of the application. Violence and threats of violence are relevant, but lesser types of behaviour such as quarrelling, aggression and abuse which

An Introduction to Irish Family Law

undermine the welfare of an applicant or dependent person will suffice. Behaviour that has an effect on the applicant though not specifically directed at him, such as drunkenness, is also relevant. That it is not necessary to prove actual or threatened violence is clear from the High Court decision in *McA. v. McA.* (1981). The wife based her application on cruelty, but did not allege that the husband had been guilty of physical violence towards her. She claimed that her health had been adversely affected by the husband's conscious refusal over a considerable period of time to communicate with her except when absolutely necessary and then in the most formal way. Costello J made an order barring the husband from the family home, being satisfied that the husband's conduct, which the learned judge accepted was deliberate, had seriously affected the welfare of the wife. Costello J, in the course of his judgment, made it clear that even though he accepted that the husband's conduct was deliberate, he was satisfied that the husband had not set out deliberately to injure his wife's health. As a result of this decision, a spouse may be barred from the family home for conduct which was not intended to seriously injure the other spouse's health.

As the consequences of a safety order or barring order are far-reaching and have serious implications for the family unit, it is obvious that the conduct of the respondent must be so grave as to cause serious concern for the well-being of other family members. Mere insensitivity on the part of the respondent to the applicant, or the fact that the applicant finds it inconvenient to live with the respondent, is not sufficient. In *O'B. v. O'B.* (1984) the conduct of the respondent husband included rudeness in front of the children, a lack of sensitivity in his manner to his wife and efforts by him at dominance in running the home, as a result of which the wife suffered nervous strain. The Supreme Court refused to grant a barring order to the wife. O'Higgins C J stated that:

> The making of such an order requires serious misconduct on the part of the offending spouse — something wilful and avoidable which causes, or is likely to cause, hurt or harm, not as a single occurrence but as something which is continuing or repetitive in its nature. Violence or the threats of violence may clearly invoke the jurisdiction.

The Chief Justice also emphasised that irretrievable breakdown of marriage did not justify the exclusion of one of the spouses from the home.

Welfare — Absence of Statutory Guidelines

The definition of the term 'welfare' in the1996 Act does not require the Court to take any special criteria into account when making any of the protective orders. This is in marked contrast to the corresponding English legislation, which requires the Court to take into account such factors as the parties' behaviour, their respective needs and financial resources, the needs of any children and all the circumstances of the case. The 1996 Act merely requires the Court to consider 'the welfare of the applicant and any dependent person'. The Law Society Report made specific reference to the absence of statutory guidance as to the criteria to be taken into account in deciding whether to grant protective orders, and pointed to the confusion that exists as to whether the definition of welfare in the 1996 Act merely gives legislative effect to the decision in *O'B. v. O'B.* or changes the considerations to be taken into account. Referring to a divergence in interpretation between the majority in *O'B.* and the dissenting judgment of Griffin J (which some feel is more in accord with the concept of welfare as now expressed in the 1996 Act) who concluded that the husband had 'constantly indulged in ... conduct which no woman should be required to put up with' and which 'was bound to have an adverse effect on the physical and emotional health of the wife and children', the Law Society Report recommends the introduction of either detailed statutory guidance or a list of criteria to be considered by the Courts in determining whether to grant protective orders.

The 1996 Act does not specify any statutory conditions that must be met for obtaining any of the protective orders. Sections 2(2) and 3(2)(a) confer a wide discretion on the Court, which merely has to be 'of the opinion that there are reasonable grounds for believing that the safety or welfare of the applicant or any dependent person' requires the making of a protective order. The Law Society Report draws attention to the total absence of guidance as to the standard of proof necessary to establish abuse, and details the results of a survey carried out among practising solicitors involved in family law. Without going into detail on the matter, one set of figures from the Report reveals that in cases involving physical abuse, 72% of the solicitors surveyed replied that judges accepted the applicant's own unsupported evidence, 26% replied that evidence of the applicant supported by medical evidence was required, while only 2% replied that medical evidence was always required. These figures and other statistics in the Report show a marked lack of uniformity in court practice, which the Law Society feels inevitably renders the application of the law uncertain and creates obvious difficulty for lawyers in advising clients. Accordingly, one of the recommendations in the Report is that further statutory guidance be provided regarding the standard of proof necessary to establish abuse.

Effect and Enforcement

Section 10 of the 1996 Act provides that a safety order, barring order, interim barring order or protection order takes effect from the time it is notified to the respondent. Oral communication to the respondent by or on behalf of the applicant, together with the production of a copy of the appropriate order shall be sufficient notification. If the respondent is present in court when the order is made that will suffice as notice. A copy of the appropriate order must, under section 11, be given to the applicant, the respondent, the health board where it is the applicant, and the garda station in whose area the family home is situated.

Section 12 provides that an appeal from a safety order or barring order shall only stay its application where the Court or the appeal court so orders. An appeal from a protection order or interim barring order does not operate as a stay on the operation of the order. The Court is given power by section 13 to discharge a particular order on the application of the applicant, respondent or health board where it is of the opinion that the safety and welfare of the applicant or any dependent person does not require that a particular order continue in force.

As to the enforcement of orders made under the 1996 Act, it is one thing to obtain one of the protective orders designed to protect the applicant or dependent children and quite another to ensure that such order is obeyed. Whenever a protective order is broken, the problem of enforcing compliance arises. Enforcement is crucial to the effectiveness of a particular order. The Court cannot directly force respondents to comply with orders made under the Act, but it may punish respondents for disobedience, and hope that this will have the desired effect of compelling respondents to obey such orders in the future. Section 17 of the Act provides that a respondent who contravenes an order shall be liable on summary conviction to a fine of £1,500 or imprisonment for twelve months, or both. Where an order under the Act is made by any Court other than the District Court, an application can be made to the appropriate Court to treat the breach of the order as contempt of Court.

Where a member of the Garda Síochána suspects that there has been a contravention of the terms of an order made under the Act by the respondent, on a complaint being made to him in that regard by or on behalf of the applicant, the member may arrest the respondent without warrant under section 18. For that purpose, the member may enter, if need be by force, and search any place where he suspects the respondent to be.

Reform

In addition to the recommendations for reform made above, the Report of the Task Force on Violence Against Women, April 1997, recommends that courts dealing with domestic violence cases should have basic facilities, such as consultation rooms equipped with telephone and toilet facilities, and that separate and secure waiting room facilities should be provided for the use of victims and families. The design of courts should ensure that the victim does not have to come in contact with the accused, and enable the victim to give evidence from behind a screen at the discretion of the Court (see Paragraph 6.42). The First Report of the National Steering Committee on Violence Against Women, March 1999, states that the Minister has funded research on the effectiveness of the 1996 Act, which will include, *inter alia*, an examination of the structure of the Courts for processing domestic violence cases with a view to determining future legislative requirements. The Task Force Report also recommends that the option of allowing women in domestic violence cases to give evidence through a video link should be explored (see Paragraph 6.30).

Further Reading

Shatter, *Family Law* 4th. Ed. Dublin: Butterworths 1997.

Law Reform Commission, Report on Child Sexual Abuse. (LRC 32-1990).

Report of Task Force on Violence Against Women, Dublin: Stationery Office, April 1997.

First Report of National Steering Committee on Violence Against Women. Dublin: Stationery Office, March 1999.

Report of Law Society's Law Reform Committee, 'Domestic Violence: The Case For Reform'. Dublin: ILSI June 1999.

Davis, 'Mandated Victim Participation: A Criminal Law Response to the Problem of Domestic Violence'. (1999) 3 ILT 39.

CHAPTER TWELVE

THE STATUS OF CHILDREN

Position at Common Law

The legal effect of the relationship between parent and child is sometimes dependent upon whether the child was born to married or unmarried parents. Historically, the common law discriminated against the child born outside marriage (the 'illegitimate' child), particularly in the areas of succession and maintenance. A child born to unmarried parents had no rights against his father and, to begin with, no rights even against his mother. The 'illegitimate' child was regarded in law as *a filius nullius* (nobody's child). This treatment of the non-marital child was justified on the basis that to afford equal treatment to children born inside and outside marriage might be seen to promote promiscuity. The discrimination against the 'illegitimate' child was gradually eliminated by statutory intervention. For example, the Legitimacy Act 1931 conferred limited rights of succession on a non-marital child on the death intestate of his mother. By section 9 of that Act, where the mother of a non-marital child died intestate and was not survived by any marital children, the non-marital child would take any interest to which he would have been entitled had he been a marital child. However, in the areas of succession and maintenance, the unequal treatment of children depending on the marital status of their parents continued right up to the coming into force of the Status of Children Act 1987.

The main purpose of the 1987 Act was to equalise the rights of children and amend the law relating to their status. The Act abolished the concept of illegitimacy and established the principle of equal treatment of all children, whether born to married parents or not. We now refer to children who were formerly regarded as illegitimate as 'children whose parents have not married each other'. As this description is somewhat cumbersome, such children are referred to elsewhere in this text as non-marital. Whereas it should no longer be necessary to distinguish between marital and non-marital children, in practice it is sometimes necessary to so distinguish. It is mainly in the context of a father's rights to his child that some differences remain. In particular, the law on adoption distinguishes between children born within and outside marriage. The father of a non-marital child does not automatically become his joint guardian with the mother although, as will be seen later on, he has a defeasible right to apply to court to be appointed guardian and may become guardian by agreement of the mother.

New Rule Of Construction

Section 3 of the 1987 Act provides that for the purposes of the Act and all subsequent legislation, whenever a relationship between two persons is referred to, it will be traceable through both the father and mother regardless of whether or not they have married each other, unless a contrary intention appears. An adopted person's relationship shall be traced through his adopted parents from the date of the adoption order. This new rule of construction means that children born to unmarried parents will no longer have to be included expressly in a provision. If it is deemed necessary to distinguish between marital and non-marital children in any document or instrument having legal effect, then the person drafting the particular document or instrument will have to expressly designate which category of children is excluded.

The practical application of the new rule can best be seen in the area of succession. The old rule of construction meant that any reference to children in a will or other legal document meant only children born within marriage, unless it was expressly stated otherwise. One practical consequence of this rule was that section 117 of the Succession Act 1965, which enables the High Court to make provision for a child where a parent has failed in a 'moral duty to make proper provision for the child in accordance with his means', was not available to a child whose parents were not married to one another. Since the coming into force of the 1987 Act, the discrimination which previously existed against children born outside marriage has been completely abolished, and any reference to children or issue will include children born outside marriage, unless expressly stated to the contrary. In the area of succession, this means that on the death intestate of either parent, all children are treated equally for succession purposes, and the facility available to children under section 117 of the 1965 Act is now available to all children regardless of their status.

Legitimacy

At common law, there was a rebuttable presumption that a child conceived or born to parents who were validly married to each other, was legitimate. The burden of proving that such a child was illegitimate was a heavy one, i.e. proof beyond a reasonable doubt as in criminal cases. Section 44 of the 1987 Act provides that any presumption of law as to legitimacy or illegitimacy has been abrogated. However, certain presumptions of paternity and non-paternity are contained in section 46 of the 1987 Act, as follows: (a) where a woman gives birth to a child during a subsisting marriage to which she is a party, or within ten months of the termination of such a marriage by death or otherwise, the husband of the marriage shall be presumed to be the father of the child unless the contrary is proved on the balance of probabilities; (b) in the case of a married woman who is living apart from her husband under a decree of judicial separation or a separation deed, where any child is born to her more than ten months after the decree was granted or the deed was executed, her husband shall be presumed not to be the father of the child unless the contrary is proved on the balance of probabilities; (c) despite the presumption at (a) above, where the birth of a child is duly registered and the name of a person is entered as father of the child in the register, the person whose name is so entered shall be presumed to be the father of the child unless the contrary is proved on the balance of probabilities. It is to be welcomed that the standard of proof 'beyond reasonable doubt', which was the norm at common law, has now been replaced by the balance of probability rule, which is the normal standard required in civil proceedings generally.

The rule in *Russell v. Russell* (1924), which prevented a married couple from giving evidence that they did not have access to each other at the time of conception for the purpose of proving that a child born during their marriage was illegitimate, has been abolished by section 47 of the 1987 Act, which provides that 'the evidence of a husband or wife shall be admissible in any proceedings to prove that marital intercourse did or did not take place between them during any period'.

Determination and Declarations of Parentage

The determination of parenthood may be important for many reasons. Motherhood is rarely an issue. However, paternity frequently has to be determined and, unless it is admitted, it must be proved. The question of paternity generally arises in the context of matrimonial, guardianship or maintenance proceedings, or sometimes in disputes over wills.

Paternity can be established in a number of different ways. A man may formally acknowledge that he is the father of a particular child, or may be registered as the father in the Register of Births. There is a rebuttable presumption that a child born to a married woman is that of her husband. In *F. P. v Judge Thomas Ballagh* (1999) Smith J. said that where a child is born to a married woman, her husband is presumed to be the father of the child until a successful application is made to the Circuit Court persuant to section 35 of the 1987 Act. Evidence of paternity may consist of proof that a couple were cohabiting at the time of conception, as in *G.N. v. K.K.* (1998), where corroborative evidence by a third party that the mother and putative father of a child slept together in the same bed at the time the child was conceived, was regarded by the Court as significant in establishing paternity. However, none of these factors are conclusive and may or may not be accepted in any given case. Blood testing is now commonly used in determining paternity. The advent of 'DNA fingerprinting' has made a significant contribution to blood testing as a reliable method of establishing paternity.

The question of paternity can also be dealt with as an issue in its own right. Section 35 of the 1987 Act enables a person, other than an adopted person, to apply to the Circuit Court for a declaration that a person named in the application is his father or mother, as the case may be, or that both the persons named therein are his parents. An application may be made under section 35 even though the person named in the application as the father or mother is not alive. The Court will make the appropriate declaration where the application is proved on the balance of probabilities.

In *I.O'T. v. B.* (1998) the Supreme Court held that the right conferred on a person (other than an adopted person) under section 35 was clear, explicit and limited. It was the right to apply to the court for a declaration that 'a person named in the application' is his father or mother. In delivering his judgment Hamilton CJ stated, 'The right is a limited right to be exercised against a named person. The section cannot be interpreted to include a right to a declaration against an unnamed person, or to a right to be informed as to the identity of his/her natural parents'. The Chief Justice referred to the judgment of Keane J in the case where he stated, 'The Oireachtas has erected a barrier to the obtaining of a declaration under section 35, where the applicant cannot identify the putative parent or parents in respect of whom the declaration was sought'.

Part VII of the 1987 Act provides for the carrying out of blood tests in any civil proceedings where parentage is in question. Section 38 enables the Court to order blood tests of its own motion or on the application of any party to the proceedings. The Court may, at any time, revoke or vary a direction previously given by it under the section. Consent to the taking of blood samples is required under section 39. Generally, a blood sample may only be taken from a minor if the person having charge of or control over the minor consents. If more than one person has charge of or control over the minor and they cannot agree as to whether consent should be given, the minor shall be treated as not having consented. Where the Court considers that a person who is not of full age is capable of giving or refusing the necessary consent, it may accept that person's consent or refusal directly. Where a person is suffering from a mental disorder and cannot validly consent, the person who has care and control may consent to a blood test on his behalf. The patient's doctor must certify that the taking of the sample will not prejudice his care or treatment. Failure to comply with a direction on blood tests enables the court to draw such inferences, if any, from that fact as appear proper in the circumstances — section 42.

In *J.P.D. v. M.G.* (1991), a case involving a custody dispute between parents under the Guardianship of Infants Act 1964, the wife claimed that the husband was not the father of her two children, even though they were born at a time when the parties were lawfully married. In the course of the proceedings, the wife sought an order pursuant to section 38 that both the children and herself and the husband submit to genetic finger-printing (DNA testing). The High Court made the order and the husband appealed to the Supreme Court. McCarthy J, in delivering the judgment of the Court, stated that judicial discretion was required to be exercised in considering matters touching on the

153

welfare of children whose parentage is in question. He held that the trial judge had considered all the relevant matters and that his discretion was properly exercised.

In *G.N. v. K.K.* (1998) the plaintiff sought a declaration under section 35 of the 1987 Act that P.K., a party named in the proceedings, was his father. As P.K. was no longer alive, the Court directed that blood samples be taken from the defendant, who was a brother of P.K.. Despite the fact that the procedure was to be at the expense of the plaintiff, the defendant refused to consent to the taking of a blood sample. In the absence of the cold scientific evidence of DNA profiling and comparisons, the Court proceeded with the taking of evidence. The plaintiff's mother gave evidence of her relationship with P.K. and the circumstances which led to the conception and birth of the plaintiff. There was ample corroborative evidence from a number of people who knew P.K. and the plaintiff's mother. The Court was particularly impressed by the evidence of E.O., a sister-in-law of the plaintiff's mother, who stated in evidence that P.K. and the plaintiff's mother were often together in her house where they stayed overnight in the one bed in her guestroom. This was around the time the mother became pregnant in April 1974. E.O. further stated that she had known that P.K. was the father of the plaintiff, as he was the only person with whom the mother was going out. There was evidence from P.W., a brother-in-law of the plaintiff's mother, that he had helped her to cash a cheque for £600 she had received from P.K. after the plaintiff's birth. The Court was satisfied on the balance of probabilities that P.K. was the plaintiff's father and made a declaration accordingly.

Counsel for the defendant had submitted in *G.N. v. K.K.* that section 35 of the 1987 Act did not apply as it did not have retrospective effect, since the Act had not come into effect until 14 June 1988 and the putative father died on the 21 November 1987. Budd J rejected this contention, stating that taking past events into account did not amount to applying legislation retrospectively. It is worth noting that Budd J gave consideration to the making of an exhumation order for the purpose of obtaining a tissue sample from the putative father. However, he deemed such a course unnecessary, since the mother and brother of the putative father were alive. The learned judge noted that exhumation orders had been made for the purpose of obtaining samples in a Northern Ireland case.

Legitimation

Section 1 of the Legitimacy Act 1931 provides that a non-marital child is legitimated by his parent's subsequent marriage, provided the father is domiciled in Ireland at the time of the marriage. If at the time of the marriage the father was domiciled abroad, it must be shown that the law of the father's domicile recognised the legitimation — section 8 of the 1931 Act. Section 8 of the Status of Children Act 1987 has removed the requirement in section 1(2) of the 1931

Act, that had made it a condition of legitimation that the father and mother could have been lawfully married to each other at the time of the birth of the child or at some time during the previous ten months. It should be noted, however, that where the mother of a non-marital child marries a man other than the child's father, her husband has no rights or duties towards the child. The natural mother and her husband could apply to adopt the child, subject to the requirement that the natural father be consulted under the Adoption Act 1998, and his consent obtained where he had been appointed a guardian either by agreement with the mother under the Children Act 1997 or by order of the court under the 1987 Act.

Legitimation has the effect of placing the legitimated child in much the same position as a marital child. It was held by the Supreme Court in *K.C. and A.C. v. An Bord Uchtála* (1985), a case considered in more detail in Chapter 14, that a child legitimated by the subsequent marriage of its natural parents is to be regarded as the child of a family for the purposes of Articles 41 and 42 of the Constitution. In *Re J.* (1966) Henchy J, describing the status of a child legitimated by his parents subsequent marriage, stated:

> I find it impossible to distinguish between the constitutional position of a child whose legitimacy stems from the fact that he was born the day after his parents were married, and that of a child whose legitimacy stems from the fact that his parents were married the day after he was born'.

He expressed himself satisfied that section 1 of the 1931 Act operated to endow the child in the case with membership of a family founded on the institution of marriage.

Registering the Birth

The registration of births is governed by the Registration of Births Acts 1863 - 1996. As the majority of births occur in hospitals or maternity homes, the usual practice is for an employee of the particular hospital or home to supply the necessary particulars to the Registrar of Births to enable the birth to be registered. Of course, there is nothing to stop the parent or parents from registering the birth themselves. Where the parents of the child are not married to each other, the practice is for the hospital or home to register the mother's name only. Where it is desired to register both parents, section 7 of the Births and Deaths Registration Act (Ireland) 1880 (as inserted by section 49 of the Status of Children Act 1987) provides that both may attend the Registrar's Office and request that they be registered. Alternatively, either parent may attend alone and request registration of both names. In the case of the mother attending alone, she must acknowledge the identity of the father and produce a statutory declaration made by him acknowledging his paternity. Where the father attends alone, he must acknowledge his paternity and produce a statutory declaration made by the mother confirming his paternity. In the case of either parent attending alone, the production of a court order in which the father is named as father of the child, such as an order conferring guardianship on the father or a maintenance order, is sufficient to enable the Registrar place the father's name on the Register.

Re-Registering the Birth

Section 1 of the Legitimacy Act 1931 provides for the re-registration of a legitimated child whose birth is already registered. Where the birth of a non-marital child has been registered without the father's name appearing in the Register, the birth can be re-registered under section 7A of the Births and Deaths Registration Act (Ireland) 1880 (as inserted by section 49 of the Status of Children Act 1987). As with the registration of the birth of a non-marital child, the registrar shall re-register the birth so as to show the name of a person as father on the joint request of both parents, or on the request of either parent in circumstances similar to those set out above in relation to the registration of the name of the father of a non-marital child.

Further Reading

Shatter, *Family Law* 4th. Ed. Dublin: Butterworths 1997.

Horgan, 'The Financial Support of Illegitimate Children'. (1976) 11 Ir Jur (n.s.) 59.

Horgan, 'Affiliation Proceedings in the High Court: An Application by a Married Woman'. (1976) 11 Ir Jur (n.s.) 340.

Law Reform Commission, Report on Illegitimacy (LRC 4-1982).

CHAPTER THIRTEEN

ADOPTION

Adoption has the effect of severing the legal relationship between a child and his natural parents and replacing it with a similar legal relationship between the child and his adopters. Formal adoption was unknown to Irish law until 1952 when the Adoption Act of that year was passed. Prior to that time, informal adoption had existed. Since 1952, there have been Adoption Acts in 1964, 1974, 1976, 1988, 1991 and 1998. The law now makes provision for the adoption of marital, non-marital and foreign children, although it is only in exceptional circumstances that a marital child, other than an orphan, can be adopted under the Adoption Act 1988. The Adoption Act 1991 makes provision for foreign adoptions.

Only the Adoption Board (An Bord Uchtála), set up under the Adoption Act 1952, can make an adoption order. No Court has jurisdiction to make an adoption order. The role of the High Court in the adoption process is to consider applications by adoptive parents under section 3 of the Adoption Act 1974 to dispense with the consent of persons whose consent is required. The Court is given an additional jurisdiction under section 2 of the Adoption Act 1988 to order the Adoption Board to make an adoption order under section 3 of that Act involving marital children.

What is Adoption?

The legal effect of an adoption order is to extinguish the existing legal relationship between natural parents and their child, whether that child is marital or non-marital, and to create a new relationship of parent and child between adopter or adopters and the adopted child. An adoption order confers the same status on the adopted child in relation to his adoptive parents as a marital child. The adopted child acquires the same property, succession and citizenship rights as a child born in wedlock. As regards the succession rights of an adopted person, reference is made to the decision of Lardner J in *Stamp v. Redmond* (1993), where he held that adopted children are not regarded as children of a marriage and, accordingly, the word 'issue' used in the will in question did not include adopted children.

An adoption order, accordingly, permanently deprives the natural parents of any rights or obligations towards their child and confers such rights and obligations on the adoptive parents. However, it appears from the decision in

B. and B. v. An Bord Uchtála (1997), that the concept of permanence as an incident of adoption is not absolute in this jurisdiction, in that an adoption order may be set aside under section 22(7) of the Adoption Act 1952 and section 18 of that Act permits re-adoption in certain circumstances. Also, a second adoption order may be made in relation to a child in respect of whom an order is made by virtue of section 2 of the Adoption Act 1988. The Adoption Board must publish in Iris Oifigiúil a notice of every adoption order made. The notice includes the first name(s) of the adopted child and the address of the adoptive parents.

Placement for Adoption

Under section 34 of the Adoption Act 1952, only adoption societies registered with the Adoption Board and health boards are authorised to place children for adoption. Section 7B of the 1952 Act (as inserted by section 4 of the Adoption Act 1998) provides that an adoption agency can only place a child under the age of four weeks for adoption where the natural father indicates that he has no objection to the placement, or where the agency satisfies the Adoption Board that it has been unable to consult the father despite taking such steps as are reasonably practicable to do so. By virtue of section 7 of the 1998 Act a parent may place a child for adoption, if the person who intends to adopt the child is a relative of the child. The section prohibits a person who is not a relative of the child from receiving a child for the purpose of adoption otherwise than from an adoption agency. The term 'relative', in respect of a child, is defined in section 2 of the 1998 Act as meaning a grandparent, brother, sister, uncle or aunt of the child, whether of the whole blood, of the half blood or by affinity and includes the spouse of any such person, relationship to the child being traced through the mother or the father.

Eastern Health Board v. E., A. and A. (1999) involved *habeas corpus* proceedings by the Eastern Health Board against the owners of a pregnancy counselling agency in respect of a private placement for adoption. On the advice of the agency, a 21 year old unmarried woman gave her newly-born child for adoption to the couple who owned the agency. The High Court ruled that the placement was unlawful as being in contravention of section 7 of the 1998 Act. Laffoy J, in the course of her judgment, said that the circumstances of the case showed a 'glaring conflict of interest' in that a person 'who assumes the role of counsellor and adviser to a young girl in the later stages of a crisis pregnancy, proposes himself and his wife as prospective adoptive parents of the baby and proposes taking custody of the baby within days of the baby's birth'.

Who May Be Adopted?

Section 10(c) of the Adoption Act 1952 provides for the adoption of a child who is an orphan or a child whose parents have not married. Section 2 of the Adoption Act 1964 provides for the adoption of a child who has been legitimated under the Legitimacy Act 1931, but whose birth has not been re-registered. The Adoption Act 1988 permits the making of an adoption order in respect of a marital child, but only where the High Court authorises the Adoption Board to do so. Before authorising the Board to make the necessary order, the Court must be satisfied that the matters set out in section 3(1) of the Act have been complied with.

To be eligible for adoption, the child must be at least six weeks old and be under the age of 18 years. Where the child is over 7 years, he must be consulted and his wishes must be taken into account by the Board when making the adoption order. The Board does not have to concur with the child's wishes. Section 10(a) of the 1952 Act provides that the child has to be resident in the State, though not necessarily born here. Obviously, the requirement that the child be resident in the State does not apply in the case of foreign adoptions. Irish adoption legislation applies to children born outside the State to non-Irish parents — *T.M. and A.M. v. An Bord Uchtála* (1993). In reversing the decision of the High Court, the Supreme Court concluded in this case, that there were no grounds for holding that the provisions of the Adoption Acts 1952–1988 do not apply to children born outside the jurisdiction to non-Irish parents. In particular, the Supreme Court held that the 1988 Act which permits the adoption of illegitimate or orphaned children applies to all children whatsoever under the age of 18 years resident within the State.

Who May Adopt?

It should be emphasised that nobody has the automatic right, constitutional or otherwise, to adopt a child. Not even the natural mother has the right. Certain categories of persons have the right to apply to the Adoption Board to adopt a child. Section 10 of the Adoption Act 1991 now sets out the persons who are eligible to apply. The following conditions apply:

(1) The applicants must be a married couple living together, or
(2) The applicant must be the mother or father or relative of the child, or
(3) The applicant must be a widow or widower.
(4) The Board may make an adoption order in favour of an applicant who is not the mother or father or relative of the child or a widow or widower where the Board is satisfied that it is desirable to do so.
(5) Except in the case where the applicants are a married couple who are living together, an adoption order may not be made for the adoption of a child by more than one person.
(6) An adoption order may not be made in respect of an applicant who is married without the consent of the other spouse, unless the couple are living apart under a decree of divorce *a mensa et thoro* or judicial separation or a deed of separation or the spouse has deserted the applicant or the applicant

has been forced by the conduct of the spouse to leave the matrimonial home and live apart from him.

(7) The applicant and, if the applicants are a married couple, each of them must have attained the age of 21 years.

(8) The applicant or applicants must be ordinarily resident in the State and has or have been so resident during the year ending on the date of the order.

The religious requirements for adoption are now contained in section 4 of the 1974 Act. Where the applicants, the child and its parents or, if the child is non-marital, its mother, are not all of the same religion, an adoption order shall not be made unless every person whose consent is required knows the religion (if any) of the applicant or of each of the applicants when giving consent. Section 4 was enacted as the legislative response to the decision of the High Court in *J. McG. and W. McG. v. An Bord Uchtála* (1974), which ruled that section 12(2) of the 1952 Act, which required that the applicant or applicants be of the same religion as the child and his parents, or if the child was non-marital, its mother, was repugnant to the Constitution.

The Adoption Procedure

Section 13 of the 1952 Act provides that the Adoption Board cannot make an adoption order unless it is satisfied that each of the proposed adoptive parents is of good moral character. They must be financially capable of supporting the child and must be suitable to be parents. There is an intensive assessment process before a child is placed with prospective adoptive parents. When the prospective adoptive parents have been adequately screened and a report as to their suitability has been prepared by a social worker, and all other relevant documents (e.g. consents) are ready, the Board arranges an oral hearing. Section 5 of the 1998 Act provides that the following persons are entitled to be heard on an application for an adoption order: the applicant, the child, the mother of the child, the father of the child or the person who believes himself to be the father, the guardian of the child, a person who has charge or control over the child, a relative of the child, a representative of an adoption agency that has at any time been concerned with the child, an officer of the Adoption Board, any other person whom the Board decides to hear.

Consents Required to Adoption of Non-Marital Child

Before the Adoption Board can make an adoption order in respect of a non-marital child 'the consent of every person being the child's mother or guardian or having charge of or control over the child is required' — section 14(1) of the 1952 Act. Section 39 of the 1952 Act provides that before an adoption society accepts a child for adoption it must inform the person whose consent is required of the effects of an adoption order, and ensure that the person in question understands these effects.

Consent of Mother

In the case of the mother of a non-marital child, there are two stages in the consent process. Firstly, the mother must sign an agreement, in the prescribed form, to the placing of her child for adoption. The second stage is for her to consent to the making of the adoption order.

Agreement to place child for adoption

The consent to placement must be full, free and informed. The mother must be aware that she has a constitutional right to her child under Article 40 of the Constitution and that such right subsists up to the time when the adoption order is made. She must also be aware that she has the right to withdraw that consent, or refuse to consent further to the adoption, but that such right is subject to the possibility that the Court can, upon the application of the prospective adopters, decide that it is in the best interests of the child to dispense with her consent under section 3 of the 1974 Act. An application under section 3 can only be considered by the Court where there has been a valid agreement to place the child for adoption — *G. v. An Bord Uchtála* (1980).

The Supreme Court considered the consequences for the mother of agreeing to place her child for adoption in *M.O'C. v. Sacred Heart Adoption Society* (1996). The plaintiff became pregnant in 1992 and gave birth to a daughter in December of that year, when she was 21 years old. She signed the appropriate consent to placement for adoption in February 1993. She subsequently refused to consent to her child being adopted by the prospective adoptive parents and brought proceedings in the High Court seeking an order directing that they return her child to her. She claimed, *inter alia*, that her consent was not fully-informed because she was not expressly told that the right which she was surrendering was a constitutional right. The proposed adopters commenced proceedings seeking an order under section 3 of the 1974 Act authorising the Adoption Board to dispense with the plaintiff's consent to the making of an adoption order. They also sought an order granting them custody of the child in the interim. Morris J made an order authorising the Adoption Board to dispense with the plaintiff's consent and granted interim custody to the prospective adopters. The plaintiff appealed to the Supreme Court.

In delivering the judgment of the Supreme Court, which upheld the decision of the High Court, O'Flaherty J stated that placement for adoption could never amount, in itself, to an extinguishment of the mother's rights. Only on the making of an adoption order by the Adoption Board were the mother's rights finally extinguished. The right which a mother has to her child is constitutional in nature. However, the categorisation of this right as legal or constitutional is not an important distinction in the working of the adoption code. There was no doubt that placement for adoption was a giant step and might lead to the High Court dispensing with the consent of the mother to adoption. Therefore, the consequences of placement must be explained very clearly to the mother. The correct approach was to regard the mother's rights as subsisting up to the time of the making of the adoption order. Those rights would clearly have undergone a modification because she had placed the child for adoption. But placing the child was not by any means the end of the process. In concurring with the judgment of O'Flaherty J, Hamilton CJ said the decision of the natural mother to place the child for adoption was not an abandonment of her child, but was what she considered at the time to be in the best interests of her child. She showed her concern for the child by stipulating the type of home she required for the child and the nature of the family into which she wished the child to be integrated. She had met and approved the proposed adopters. These were the actions of a loving, caring and concerned mother, motivated to ensure the best interests of her child. The decision of the Court to dispense with the mother's consent was based on the best interests of the child and not in any way on the lack of fitness of the mother.

In *D.G. and M.G. v. An Bord Uchtála* (1996) the High Court held that the family circumstances prevailing at the time the mother placed her child for adoption, prevented her from making a free decision. For a consent to placement to be free and fully-informed, the mother must be aware of (i) her rights in relation to the child, (ii) the two-stage nature of the adoption process, (iii) the effect of the making of an adoption order on her rights, and (iv) the effect of section 3 of the 1974 Act and, in particular, the possibility that if she gives her initial consent to the placement, the Court may dispense with her final consent to the making of the adoption order. The facts of the case show that the mother's parents were very conservative and were shocked when she told them she was pregnant. Initially, her father suggested that she should have an abortion. Later, her parents suggested that the child should be placed for adoption. Laffoy J said that she made the decision to place the child for adoption 'because of fear which was a product of her upbringing, stress, anxiety, lack of maturity and deprivation of emotional support'. Because there had been no valid agreement to place the child for adoption, the issue did not arise as to whether it was in the best interests of the child to dispense with the mother's consent under section 3 of the 1974 Act.

The impact of surrounding circumstances on the validity of the consent of the natural mother was considered in *C. A. v. St Patrick's Guild Adoption Society* (1996). Acknowledging that fear, anxiety, stress and economic deprivations are frequently ingredients of the factual situations which give rise to an enquiry whether agreement by a mother to place her child for adoption was freely made in order to determine the applicability of section 3 of the 1974 Act, Flood J stated:

In my view, the presence of one or more of these features does not necessarily vitiate a mother's consent. The true test is whether, in the circumstances which prevail at the time she makes her decision, that decision reflects her will or the will of somebody else.

The Supreme Court held in *E.F. and F.F. v. An Bord Uchtála* (1997) that once the Court is satisfied that the mother appreciated the consequences that might flow from her consent to placement, it did not matter that the explanation given to her did not refer to the loss of her constitutional or other rights.

Consent to Adoption Order

The second stage in the consent process is for the mother to consent to the making of the adoption order. The 'final consent' (even though it may not actually be final) cannot be given until the child is at least six weeks old. This consent can be withdrawn at any time before the adoption order is made. Before signing the consent, the mother must have been informed, in writing, of the legal effect of an adoption order. She must sign a statement to the effect that she understands the effects of adoption. She must also be informed in writing of her right to withdraw the consent at any time before the adoption order is made.

Consent of Natural Father

The consent of the natural father must be obtained to the making of an adoption order where he marries the mother after the birth of the child, thereby legitimating the child — section 1 of the Legitimacy Act 1931. In the case of a non-marital child, the consent of the natural father is required where he has become guardian of the child either by agreement with the mother under section 4 of the Children Act 1997 or by order of the Court under section 6A of the Guardianship of Infants Act 1964 (as inserted by section 12 of the Status of Children Act 1987.) Otherwise, the consent of the natural father to the making of an adoption order is not required. This follows from the decision in the *State (Nicolaou) v. An Bord Uchtála* (1966). Nicolaou was the natural father of a non-marital child. The mother, without Nicolaou's consent, placed the child for adoption. The adoption order was made without his knowledge and the Adoption Board refused to hear him on the application for adoption. He challenged the constitutionality of section 16 of the 1952 Act on the grounds that the mother and himself were 'parents' within the meaning of Article 42 of the Constitution and that the mother, child and himself constituted a 'family' within the meaning of Article 41. The Supreme Court rejected Nicolaou's claim and held that the 'family' referred to in Articles 41 and 42 was that based on marriage. This discrimination against the natural father was justified by Walsh J in delivering the judgment of the Court, where he stated 'an illegitimate child may be begotten by an act of rape, by a callous seduction or by an act of casual commerce by a man with a woman, as well as the association of a man with a woman in making a common home without marriage in circumstances approximating to those of married life'.

The Impact of Keegan v. Ireland

On the question of the natural father's consent, one must now take into account the decision of the European Court of Human Rights in *Keegan v. Ireland* (1994), which found Ireland to be in breach of the European Convention on Human Rights and Fundamental Freedoms in permitting the adoption of a child born outside marriage without the father's knowledge and consent. When the case was before the Supreme Court in *J.K. v. V.W.* (1990), Finlay CJ, in interpreting section 6A of the Guardianship of Infants Act 1964, held that the Act only gave the natural father a right to apply to the Court to be appointed guardian, and not a right to be guardian, of his child. Neither did the father have a constitutional right or a natural right identified by the Constitution to guardianship of his child. In his application to the European Court of Human Rights, Keegan complained, *inter alia*, that there had been a violation of his right to a fair and public hearing under Article 6, and of his right to respect for family life under Article 8 of the Convention, in that his child had been placed for adoption without his knowledge or consent. The Court held that his rights under both articles had been infringed. In the course of its judgment, the Court restated its view that the notion of 'family' in Article 8 of the Convention is not confined to marriage-based relationships and may encompass other *de facto* ties where the parties are living together outside marriage. The Court stated that a child born out of such a relationship is *ipsa jure* part of that 'family' unit from the moment of its birth and by the very fact of it.

The facts of the *Keegan* case show that he met the mother of the child in May 1986 when they were aged 21 and 17 respectively. Having gone out together for a time, they lived together between February 1987 and February 1988. They decided to have a baby about Christmas 1987 and they later became engaged to be married. The mother found out she was pregnant in February 1988. The relationship broke down a short time later. During her pregnancy, the mother made arrangements to have the baby adopted. The baby was born in September 1988 and was placed with prospective adopters on the 17 November 1988. The mother informed Keegan of this by letter dated 22 November 1988. Keegan applied to the Circuit Court and was appointed guardian. On appeal by the mother, the High Court stated a case to the Supreme Court who ruled as outlined above. On reconsidering the appeal, the High Court refused to make the orders sought by the father, as the change in custody (the child had been with the prospective adopters for 15 months at that stage) might result in psychological trauma being suffered by the child, since it would involve her removal from a family recognised by the Constitution.

Guardian by Agreement with Mother

Section 4 of the Children Act 1997 allows a father, who has not married the mother of his child, to become guardian of the child by agreement with the mother, without the necessity of a court application. The father and mother must declare that they are the father and mother of the child, agree to the appointment of the father as a guardian of the child, have entered into arrangements regarding the custody of and, as the case may be, access to the child, and have made a statutory declaration to that effect as prescribed by the Guardianship of Children (Statutory Declarations) Regulations 1998 (Statutory Instrument S.I. 5/98).

The Adoption Act 1998

The Adoption Act 1998, *inter alia*, introduces a statutory procedure for consulting the father of a non-marital child before the child is placed for adoption, so as to afford the father an opportunity to apply to the Court to be appointed guardian of the child. The Act can be seen as a response by the State to the judgment of the European Court of Human Rights in *Keegan*, which required the State, 'where the existence of a family tie with a child has been created', to take the appropriate action to develop the family tie that exists between an unmarried father and his child and to create legal safeguards 'that render possible as from the moment of birth the child's integration in his family'. Section 4 of the 1998 Act inserts a new Part 1A (sections 7A to 7F) in the 1952 Act. The term 'father' for the purposes of the new Part 1A includes a person who believes himself to be the father of a child. The main provisions of the 1998 Act are:

(1) The father of a child has the right to notify the Adoption Board of his wish to be consulted in relation to the placement of the child for adoption by an adoption agency, or an application by the mother or any relative of the child to adopt him — Section 7D of the 1952 Act.

(2) Where an adoption agency proposes to place a child for adoption it must endeavour to ascertain the identity of the father, including requesting the Adoption Board to provide it with a copy of any notice received from the father under section 7D. The Adoption Board must inform the agency whether or not a notice has been lodged, and provide the agency with a copy of any notice. Where the adoption agency proposes to place a child for adoption and the identity of the father is known to the agency, it must take such steps as are reasonably practicable to consult the father, so as to inform him of the placement, explain to him the legal implications of, and the procedures related to, adoption and ascertain his attitude towards the proposed placement. Where the father indicates that he has no objection to the placement, the agency may proceed to place the child for adoption.

Where the father objects to the proposed placement, the agency must notify him and the mother that it is deferring the placement for a period of not less than 21 days for the purpose of affording him an opportunity to make an application to the Court for guardianship and/or custody of the child. If no such application is made by the father within the specified period, the agency may then place the child for adoption. If, on the other hand, the father is given guardianship of the child by the Court, his consent will be required for the adoption to go ahead — Section 7E of the 1952 Act.

(3) The Adoption Board may exempt an adoption agency from the requirement to consult the father in the following circumstances;

(a) where the agency is unable, after taking such steps as are reasonably practicable, to consult a father whose identity is known to it;
(b) where the nature of the relationship between the father and the mother or the circumstances of the conception of the child are such that it would be inappropriate to contact the father (e.g. in the case of rape);
(c) where the identity of the father is unknown to the agency and the mother refuses to reveal his identity.

The adoption agency need not consult the father where the mother makes a statutory declaration that she is unable to identify the father and the agency has no other practical way of ascertaining his identity — Section 7F of the 1952 Act.

It is significant that in *J.B. and D.B. v. An Bord Uchtála* (1998) the natural father of a child, conceived as a result of the father's rape of the mother, signed a consent to the adoption of his child by the prospective adopters. This would seem to indicate that, although the Adoption Board can exempt an adoption agency from the obligation to consult the natural father in such circumstances, he should be consulted where possible.

(4) New post-placement consultation procedures are set out where the applicant for an adoption order is not the father or the person who believes himself to be the father of the child and the placement was not arranged by an adoption agency. The Adoption Board must take such steps as are reasonably practicable to consult the father in relation to the application. The Board may arrange for a health board to assist it in carrying out its functions. Where the mother refuses to reveal the identity of the father to the Board, it must counsel her to attempt to obtain her co-operation, indicating to her (i) that the adoption may be delayed, (ii) the possibility of the father contesting the adoption at some later date, (iii) that the absence of information about the medical, genetic and social background of the father may be detrimental to the health, development or welfare of the child. The Board is exempted from the requirement to consult the father in the same circumstances as are

provided for in section 7F of the 1952 Act — Section 19A of the 1952 Act (inserted by section 6 of the 1998 Act).

Dispensing with Consent

There are two circumstances in which the consent of the natural mother can be dispensed with in the making of the adoption order. Under section 14(6) of the 1952 Act, the Adoption Board can dispense with consent where any person, whose consent is required, is incapable by reason of mental infirmity of consenting, or cannot be found. Under section 3 of the 1974 Act the High Court can order that consent can be dispensed with where any person whose consent is required and who has agreed to the placing of the child for adoption either (a) fails, neglects or refuses to give his consent, or (b) withdraws a consent already given. The High Court, in making any order under the section, must consider the best interests of the child. Hamilton CJ emphasised in his judgment in *M.O'C. v. Sacred Heart Adoption Society* (1996) that the decision of the Court to dispense with the mother's consent was based on the best interests of the child and not in any way the lack of fitness of the mother. *In J.B. and D.B. v. An Bord Uchtála* (1998) McGuinness J observed that in previous considerations of section 3 of the 1974 Act it had been pointed out that the use of the term 'best interests' as opposed to the term 'welfare' as used, for example, in section 3 of the Guardianship of Infants Act 1964 'implies a consideration of long-term factors affecting the child's future life in addition to matters which would affect the child's present welfare'.

The Best Interests of the Child

There is a substantial body of case law dealing with the circumstances in which the High Court can dispense with consent. The typical case involving a balancing of the competing claims of the natural mother and prospective adopters very often places the presiding judge in an unenviable situation. The judge is not required to find parental unfitness on the part of the mother before making an order under section 3. Such matters as the natural and biological ties between mother and child should be considered, whilst undue weight must not be placed on the fact that the prospective adopters are exemplary persons and are better suited to provide for the child's welfare. As the various authorities suggest, the extent to which the child has bonded with the prospective adoptive parents is very significant. At the end of the day, the judge must be satisfied that it is in the best interests of the child to make an order under section 3. In *M.O'C. v. Sacred Heart Adoption Society* (1996) O'Flaherty J described the judge's function in deciding whether to dispense with consent as not being anything as crude as to resolve a contest between opposing parties, but rather to engage in an enquiry to decide the child's best interests.

The Supreme Court considered the effect of section 3 of the 1974 Act in *G. v.*

An Bord Uchtála (1980), and held that when considering an application to dispense with the mother's consent, the Court must first decide whether the mother did agree to place her child for adoption. In considering whether the mother has validly agreed to place her child for adoption, the test is whether she has given a full, free and informed consent to the placement. It is only when the Court is satisfied that the mother has validly agreed to the placement that it can proceed to consider the best interests of the child. In *J.M. and G.M. v. An Bord Uchtála* (1986) Barron J concluded that the mother did not, when she consented to the placement of her child for adoption, fully realise that she might not be able to get her child back. There was, in the judge's view, 'no intention on the part of the mother to consent to any step which might result ultimately in her losing her child'. No one had given the mother 'any advice as to her rights in the circumstances which had occurred'. Accordingly, he held that there had been no agreement to place for adoption and he refused the prospective adoptive parents' application to dispense with the mother's consent under section 3.

The cases decided since *G. v. An Bord Uchtála* indicate that where there has been a valid agreement by the mother to place her child for adoption, and the child has been placed with prospective adoptive parents pending the making of an adoption order, the Court will consider the extent to which the child has bonded with the prospective adoptive parents and members of their extended families. Obviously, the Court will consider psychiatric evidence and decide the weight which should be attached to it. Examples of this approach being taken are *S. v. Eastern Health Board* (1979), where the Court accepted the psychiatric evidence which suggested that the child would suffer serious emotional damage if removed from the custody of the prospective adoptive parents, and *McC. v. An Bord Uchtála* (1982), where McWilliam J had the benefit of the evidence of two psychiatrists who agreed that 'a child becomes assimilated into its family or 'bonded' from the age of six months and that change after a year is usually difficult and may even be dangerous unless accomplished carefully'. In both of those cases, the Court decided that it would be in the best interests of the child in each case to remain with the prospective adoptive parents. McGuinness J in *J.B. and D.B. v. An Bord Uchtála* (1998) accepted the evidence of a very experienced child psychiatrist that the child 'has formed a strong and loving bond with both adoptive parents whom, naturally, he regards as his mother and father'.

J.B. and D.B. v. An Bord Uchtála (1998) involved an application to the Court by the prospective adopters for an order dispensing with the consent of the natural mother under section 3 of the 1974 Act, and an application by the natural mother for an order under section 11 of the Guardianship of Infants Act 1964 granting her custody of the child. The child was born as a result of the rape of his mother by the natural father. The natural father was subsequently convicted of the shocking and gruesome manslaughter of two women and given a lengthy custodial sentence. Prior to the birth of the child, the natural mother was fairly definite in her wish, which she frequently expressed to social workers, that the child be placed for adoption. She expressed no interest in advice regarding any alternative plan for the child's care. She stated that the child was the result of rape, and that she could not accept or care for the child of the natural father, given all the circumstances of its paternity and conception. The child was placed first in temporary foster care, and the mother signed the statutory form of consent to the placement of the child for adoption some three and a half months after his birth. She subsequently changed her mind on a number of occasions and eventually decided not to consent to the adoption order, as she had formed a relationship with another man whom she intended to marry.

In the course of her judgment, McGuinness J conducted a wide-ranging and in-depth review of the relevant authorities, and was satisfied from the evidence that the mother had placed the child for adoption within the meaning of section 3 of the 1974 Act. The learned judge then had to consider what was in the child's best interests. She was satisfied from the evidence of a social worker and a child psychiatrist that the child's placement with the prospective adopters was extremely successful. Indeed, the evidence of the psychiatrist suggested that, were the child to be removed from the prospective adopters 'it would cause him immediate and, in all probability, long-term psychological damage'. The history and future of the child's father, and the mother's reaction to it, had also to be taken into account. The mother's natural hatred and fear of the father could have a long term effect on her relationship with his child. Having carefully weighed up all the evidence available to her in regard to the child's best interests, McGuinness J dispensed with the mother's consent.

In a later judgment, in the case of *J.B. and D.B. v. An Bord Uchtála* delivered in January 1999 McGuinness J ruled that the adopters of a child who apply to the Court for an order under section 3 of the Adoption Act 1974 dispensing with the natural mother's consent can have the costs of the application awarded to them, despite the fact that there is no provision to this effect in the 1974 Act.

Adoption and the Marital Child

Whereas adoption in Irish law is essentially a consensual or voluntary arrangement, there are circumstances in which a child can be involuntarily adopted. The Adoption Act 1988 provides for the adoption of a child, marital or non-marital without parental consent, where it is in the best interests of the child to do so. However, it is only in the most extreme circumstances that the High Court will make an order authorising the Adoption Board to make an adoption order in respect of a marital child. Under section 3 of the 1988 Act the High Court can make such an order where it is satisfied:

(i) that

    (a) for a continuous period of not less than 12 months immediately preceding the time of the making of the application, the parents of the child to whom the declaration under section 2(1) relates, for physical or moral reasons, have failed in their duty towards the child,

    (b) it is likely that such failure will continue without interruption until the child attains the age of 18 years,

    (c) such failure constitutes an abandonment on the part of the parents of all parental rights, whether under the Constitution or otherwise, with respect to the child, and

    (d) by reason of such failure, the State, as guardian of the common good, should supply the place of parents,

(ii) that the child

    (a) at the time of the making of the application, is in the custody of and has a home with the applicants, and

    (b) for a continuous period of not less than 12 months immediately preceding that time, has been in the custody of and has had a home with the applicants, and

(iii) that the adoption of the child by the applicants is an appropriate means by which to supply the place of parents the Court may, if it so thinks fit and is satisfied, having had due regard for the rights, whether under the Constitution or otherwise, of the persons concerned (including the natural and imprescriptible rights of the child), that it would be in the best interests of the child to do so, make an order authorising the Board to make an adoption order in relation to the child in favour of the applicants.

The question of legislating for the adoption of marital children had been left in abeyance until the drafting of the Adoption (No.2) Bill 1987 because of fears that such a measure might fall foul of Articles 41 and 42 of the Constitution, and in particular the reference in Article 41 to the rights of the family being 'inalienable' and 'imprescriptible' and the reference in Article 42 to the 'natural and imprescriptible rights of the child' to education. The Bill, as passed by both houses of the Oireachtas, was referred to the Supreme Court by the President — *Re Article 26 and the Adoption (No. 2) Bill 1987* (1989). In upholding the constitutionality of the Bill, the Court was influenced mainly by the wording of Article 42.5 to the effect that 'in exceptional cases, where the parents for physical or moral reasons fail in their duty towards their children, the State as guardian of the common good, by appropriate means shall endeavour to supply the place of parents, but always with due regard for the imprescriptible rights of the child'.

Abandonment of Parental Rights

Because of the major change in Irish adoption law brought about by the 1988 Act, there have been a number of extremely important decisions as to what conduct on the part of parents amounts to 'an abandonment on the part of parents of all parental rights'. In *Re Article 26 and the Adoption (No. 2) Bill 1987* (1989) Finlay CJ, in delivering the judgment of the Court, made it clear that 'no mere inadequacy of standard in the discharge of the parental duty would, in the opinion of the Court, suffice to establish this proof'. Later on in the judgment he said 'a mere statement by a parent or parents that they wished to abandon a child would not necessarily constitute proof in any particular case of the fact of abandonment but may do so'. Just recently in *Southern Health Board v. An Bord Uchtála* (1999) the Supreme Court handed down a very significant judgment as to the type of conduct that will constitute 'an abandonment on the part of parents of all parental rights' for the purposes of section 3 of the 1988 Act. The Court found unequivocal evidence of non-accidental injuries occurring over a period of time to the child while in the custody of the parents. This evidence had not been challenged. There was psychiatric evidence to the effect that the post traumatic stress of the child would continue. It was also the view of the psychiatrist that the child should not be exposed to his parents until his late teens or early twenties, and then only if he wished to see them. In delivering the unanimous decision of the court, Denham J said that the word 'abandon' for the purposes of section 3 of the 1988 Act had a wider legal meaning than parents simply physically deserting a child, and that the word 'abandon' could be used where, by their actions, parents failed 'in their duty so as to enable a court to deem that their failure constituted an abandonment of parental rights'. The learned judge also said that there must be strong evidence to establish a failure of duty by parents towards a child for there to be 'an abandonment on the part of parents of all parental rights' for the purposes of section 3 of the 1988 Act.

In the intervening period between 1988 and 1999, the Supreme Court has had the opportunity of considering the effect of section 3 of the 1988 Act on a number of occasions. *T.M. and A.M. v. An Bord Uchtála* (1993) involved an application by the plaintiffs, both Irish citizens, to adopt an Indian child under the 1988 Act. The child had been abandoned by its unidentified parents at an orphanage in Delhi at birth. The plaintiffs had been appointed joint guardians of the child with their Indian attorney by a court in Delhi in 1980 to enable them bring the child back to Ireland for adoption under Irish law. In 1982, the plaintiff's application to adopt the child was refused by the defendant because of the absence of proof that the child was either born out of wedlock or an orphan. Following the enactment of the 1988 Act, the plaintiffs renewed their application to adopt the child. The defendant made a declaration pursuant to section 2 of the 1988 Act to the effect that, if an order was made by the Court under section 3(1) of the 1988 Act, it would make an adoption order in favour of the plaintiffs. The

High Court refused to make the appropriate order on the grounds that the 1988 Act did not apply to a child of 'alien parents'. On appeal, the Supreme Court held that the Adoption Acts 1952 - 1988 did apply to children of non-Irish or alien parents. It further held that the complete and total abandonment of a child within days of its birth is recognisable by an Irish court as a denial of the universally recognised rights of the child which are specifically protected under the Constitution. As the plaintiffs, in accordance with section 4(4) of the 1988 Act, had exhausted all reasonable and possible measures to ascertain the identity of the child's parents, to afford them the opportunity to satisfy the Court that they had not abandoned the child in accordance with the accepted standards of their duty as parents under Indian law, and as the proposed adoption was in the best interests of the child, the plaintiffs were entitled to an order under section 3(1) of the 1988 Act.

In *Southern Health Board v. An Bord Uchtála* (1995) the High Court granted an order pursuant to section 3 of the 1988 Act authorising the Adoption Board to make an adoption order in respect of the child of a travelling family. The facts of the case portray a grim picture of a child who suffered severe physical abuse at the hands of his parents to the extent of being abandoned by them. The evidence showed that when the child was a year old in December 1987, he had to be removed from the camp-site where he resided with his family by a welfare officer of the health board as he was suffering from pneumonia. In December 1989, the child was brought to Cork Regional Hospital where he was found to be suffering from fractures to his left arm which were not of recent origin. He had bruising all over his body. A doctor at the hospital was of the opinion that the injuries were non-accidental and recommended that the child be taken into care. The child was taken into care and placed with foster parents. When the child was examined by a consultant psychiatrist in January 1990, he was diagnosed as suffering from post traumatic stress disorder. The psychiatrist saw the child again in April 1994 and was satisfied that he had improved but that he should not be exposed to his parents until his late teens or early twenties, and then only if he expressed a wish to see them. In arriving at his decision, Costello P stated:

> I am satisfied that for twelve months prior to that date (the date of the application) F's parents had failed in their duty towards him. Their duty was to act as his guardians and as loving parents to further his welfare. They showed themselves unfit to discharge that duty and by their own actions made necessary the application of the law which disables them from fulfilling it because they have lawfully been deprived of his custody. Thus, since prior to December 1989 and up to the present time there has been failure to fulfil that duty to F. I am satisfied that the failure of F's parents to fulfil their duties towards him will continue until he attains the age of eighteen.

In *Western Health Board v. An Bord Uchtála* (1996) the Supreme Court upheld a High Court finding that a natural father's failure to fulfil his duty to his child did not constitute abandonment of all parental rights in the context of the 1988 Act. The case concerned a married couple who had three children. They had marital difficulties and separated. The wife was engaged in a relationship with another man. In February 1988, the husband came to the wife's house, spent the night there, forced himself on her and had sexual intercourse with her. She became pregnant and gave birth to a child the following November. The mother, believing her husband was not the father, placed the baby girl with foster parents and then with an adoption society for adoption. In May 1989, the child was placed with prospective adoptive parents. As the child was placed for adoption as a non-marital child, supporting sworn statements to verify this were required to enable the child to be adopted. One such statement was required from the husband that he was not the father. He refused to make the required statement on the basis that he could possibly be the father and blood and tissue tests clearly established that he was. The Supreme Court endorsed the finding of the High Court that the natural father's failure in his duty towards his child, which would continue, did not, *per se*, constitute his abandonment of all parental rights, referring to his expressed reluctance to give up the child and a claim to recover her.

Confidentiality and Anonymity

The adoption process is based on the necessity to maintain confidentiality and to preserve the anonymity of the parties involved in the adoption proceedings. The policy of the Adoption Board and the various adoption agencies is to maintain that confidentiality by refusing to reveal the identities of the parties involved. How much prospective adoptive parents should know about the background of the child they hope to adopt, and how much the child should be told about its natural parents, is a question for individual adoption agencies. Some detail about the child's background is usually given. For example, where the agency is aware that the child suffers from allergies, or that there are any hereditary diseases in the child's family, this information should be given to the adoptive parents. The natural mother may request the agency involved to give specific information to the adoptive parents.

Where an adoption agency considers it to be in the best interests of a child who has been placed with prospective adopters, it may arrange for the natural mother and the prospective adopters to meet. In *J.B. and D.B. v. An Bord Uchtála* (1998) McGuinness J acknowledged that such a meeting is in full accordance with present day adoption practice. She stated that such a meeting enables the natural mother to meet and approve the couple with whom her child is to be placed for adoption, and also enables the prospective adopters to have some knowledge of the natural mother which may, at a later stage, be passed on to the child. The meeting in this case, at which only Christian names were used and no details of identification were given, and which was in the presence of the social workers for both sides, appears to have gone well.

Although it may be in accordance with modern adoption practice to arrange such a meeting, it is important that a value judgment is made by the social workers in a particular case that a meeting will serve the best interests of the child. The successful outcome of the meeting in *J.B. and D.B. v. An Bord Uchtála* should be contrasted with the unfortunate consequences that stemmed from a meeting between the natural mother and the prospective adopters in *McC. v. An Bord Uchtála* (1982), where the meeting resulted in the natural mother and the adoptive mother becoming very emotional. Commenting on this meeting, McWilliam J stated: 'Unfortunately, one result of the July meeting was that the Plaintiff was able to discover the name and address of the adoptive parents and visit their house on several occasions'. The adoptive parents refused to return the child to the natural mother and she issued proceedings seeking custody of her child. The adoptive parents issued proceedings under section 3 of the 1974 Act seeking an order dispensing with the natural mother's consent. The Court made an order dispensing with the natural mother's consent.

The Adopted Children Register

When a non-marital child is born, the birth is registered in the normal way in the Register of Births. If that child is subsequently adopted, that fact is registered in the Adopted Children Register. Section 22 of the 1952 Act provides for the establishment of an Adopted Children Register by the Registrar General of Births, and the Adoption Board is obliged to send the Registrar particulars of each child in respect of whom an adoption order is made. In addition, the Registrar is obliged to keep an index so that the connection between each entry in the Adopted Children Register and the corresponding entry in the Register of Births can be traced, if required. The index is not open to public inspection, and no information from it can be given to any person except by order of a court or the Board. The Court can only order the furnishing of information from the index where it is satisfied that it is 'in the best interests of the child to do so': section 8 of the 1976 Act. In *C.R. v. An Bord Uchtála* (1994) the High Court held, *inter alia,* that the decision to furnish or withhold any information must be that of the Board. An adopted child had applied to the Board for particulars to enable him trace the connection between an entry in the Adopted Children Register and the corresponding entry in the Register of Births. The Board refused his application for reasons of confidentiality and stated that it would not depart from its practice of not providing access to birth records by adopted persons. The Board did not make any enquiry as to the merits of the application. On an application for judicial review, the High Court declared that the decision to furnish or withhold information must be that of the Board. However, in arriving at its decision the

Board had an obligation to consider the application on its merits and not simply refuse it as a matter of policy.

Discovery of Documents and Privilege

In interpreting section 8 of the 1976 Act, Finlay P held in *S.M. and M.M. v. G.M.* (1985) that the confidentiality of the Adoption Board's papers should be maintained, unless it is established to the satisfaction of the Court as a matter of probability that the best interests of a child concerned in a particular case require their discovery or production. In *P.B. v. A.L.* (1996) the mother of a non-marital child and her husband, who was not the father of the child, applied to the Adoption Board to adopt the child. The Board notified the natural father of the application, and correspondence took place between him and the Board. The natural father applied to the District Court for an order appointing him guardian of the child. The mother served a *subpoena duces tecum* on the Board requiring production of reports or notes prepared by it regarding the application for adoption and the submission made by the natural father. The Board claimed privilege on the ground of public policy in respect of the documents and records referred to in the *subpoena*. The District Judge stated a case to the High Court, which ruled that section 8 of the 1976 Act confers a privilege on the Board in respect of all its records and documents, and that the Board can only be ordered to discover its records and documents if such discovery is in the best interests of the child.

Intercountry Adoptions

Because of the decline in the number of children available for adoption in the developed countries of the world, more and more prospective adoptive parents are turning to developing countries in Eastern Europe, Asia and Latin America as a source of children available for adoption. In an Irish context, figures from the Central Statistics Office show that in 1970 non-marital births in Ireland represented 2.7% of all births, but by 1997 this had risen to 26.6%. Between 1986 and 1990, the percentage of mothers placing their children for adoption in one Dublin maternity hospital fell from 24.5% in 1986 to 7.1% in 1990. Only 100 Irish babies were available for adoption in 1998. The number of people hoping to adopt foreign children is now so great that by July 1999 more than 1,400 prospective adopters were left waiting three years or more to be assessed by health boards as suitable (Irish Independent, Monday, July 19, 1999). According to the annual report of the Adoption Board for 1999, 206 couples were given permission to adopt abroad in 1998, compared to 176 in 1997.

Recent media coverage of the subject of intercountry adoption suggests that couples in the highly-developed economies of Western Europe, including Ireland, and the United States of America are prepared to go to great lengths, and incur exorbitant expense, to find children to adopt. Media reports suggest that adoption agencies operating out of some countries are widely advertising their services and extracting large sums of money from couples who are desperate to adopt. In the United States of America, the Maine Adoption Placement Services quotes a range of prices on the Internet for couples hoping to adopt children from overseas, from about 10,000 dollars for a child from India to about 14,000 dollars for a child from Russia (*Irish Independent* 17 November 1998). For this reason, it is vital that current international instruments which seek to regulate intercountry adoptions are fully implemented and, where appropriate, incorporated into domestic law in those countries where the adoption of foreign children has become commonplace.

In the context of intercountry adoptions, Article 21 of the United Nations Convention on the Rights of the Child 1989 obliges those States that recognise and permit the system of adoption and have ratified the Convention (Ireland ratified on 21 September 1992) to ensure that the best interests of the child shall be the paramount consideration. In addition, they shall:

(a) take into consideration the interests of the natural parents and guardians of the child;
(b) recognise that intercountry adoptions may be considered as an alternative where foster care or adoption in the child's own country is not possible;
(c) ensure that the child concerned by intercountry adoption enjoys safeguards and standards equivalent to those existing in the case of national adoptions;
(d) take steps to ensure that those involved in intercountry adoption placements do not make improper financial gain;
(e) conclude bilateral or multilateral agreements to ensure that the placement of a child in another country is carried out by competent authorities or organs.

At present, Ireland has bilateral agreements with Romania, Thailand and China. The agreement with Romania states that it is guided by the principles set out in the United Nations Convention on the Rights of the Child. It contains a framework for the regulation of adoptions of Romanian children by Irish residents, providing for such matters as the eligibility of applicants to adopt, the assessment and approval in Ireland of applicants, and co-operation between the Adoption Board and the Romanian Committee for Adoptions.

Foreign Adoptions

Prior to the enactment of the Adoption Act 1991, the Adoption Board did not have any specific power to recognise foreign adoptions. The 1991 Act, as amended by the Adoption Act 1998, now makes provision for the recognition of foreign adoptions where, (1) they are effected or recognised in the place of domicile or habitual residence or ordinary residence of the adopters, and (2) the adopters are ordinarily resident in the State.

Adoption

The term 'foreign adoption' is defined in section 1 of the 1991 Act, as amended by section 10 of the 1998 Act. The key elements in the definition are:

(1) The child must be under the age of 18 (21 if the adoption was effected before the commencement of the Act).
(2) The adoption must have been effected in accordance with the law of the foreign country.
(3) The necessary consents or dispensations must have been obtained, either at the time the adoption was effected, or subsequent to that time so as to convert a 'simple' adoption (one which does not terminate all the rights of the natural parents) to a 'full' adoption which terminates the rights of the natural parents.
(4) The adoption must have, for so long as it is in force, substantially the same legal effect as respects the guardianship of the child as an adoption order made by the Board.
(5) The necessary enquiries into the prospective adopters, the child and the parents or guardian must have been carried out.
(6) The adoption must have been effected for the purpose of promoting the interests and welfare of the child.
(7) No payment, other than reasonable expenses, must have been made by the adopters.

Where a foreign adoption was effected or recognised as a valid adoption under the law of the particular State of the adopters' domicile (section 2) or habitual residence (section 3) or ordinary residence (section 4), it will be duly recognised as valid in this State, provided it satisfies the definition of an adoption in section 1 of the 1991 Act, as amended. There is a requirement in section 4 of the 1991 Act that in the case of habitual residence it must have existed for at least one year. Section 4A provides for the recognition in the State of a foreign adoption granted to persons who, while living in a country whose laws do not provide for the recognition of adoptions (e.g. certain Islamic countries), adopt a child in some other country.

Section 5 of the 1991 Act, as amended by section 13 of the 1998 Act, deals with the recognition of foreign adoptions where the adopters are ordinarily resident in the State. The following conditions must be complied with:

(1) The adopters must be eligible to adopt under section 10 of the Act.
(2) They must be ordinarily resident in the State on the date the adoption was effected.
(3) In case the adoption was effected before 1 April 1992, the Board must declare in writing that it is satisfied that the adopters are persons in whose favour an adoption order may be made under section 10.

(4) In case the adoption was effected on or after 1 April 1992, the Board must declare in writing before the date on which the adoption was made (i) that the adopters are qualified under section 10 and (ii) that following an assessment by the relevant health board or registered adoption society, the adopters are suitable persons under section 13 of the 1952 Act.

Section 6 of the 1991 Act provides that the Board shall establish and maintain a Register of Foreign Adoptions. The Board is required to recognise and register foreign adoptions on the application to it by an adopted person or the adopters to whom the adoption relates, where it is satisfied that the conditions set out in the section have been complied with. In *B.and B. v. An Bord Uchtála* (1997) the Supreme Court, on an appeal to it by the Adoption Board from a finding of the High Court, had to consider the Board's refusal to recognise and register applications to it by three couples who wanted to adopt Chinese children. The couples were found suitable to adopt children under section 5. However, the Board refused the applications on the grounds that it could not reconcile Irish and Chinese law relating to adoption. The Board's difficulties stemmed from the fact that it concluded that an adoption order under Irish law ends all legal bonds between natural parents or guardians and the child. The equivalent Chinese adoption order does not accord with Irish law in that it reserves to the child, parents or guardians and the adopters the right to review and/or rescind the adoption order. If the child is over 10 years old he must be consulted and his consent obtained. The applicants applied to the High Court by way of judicial review for an order of *certiorari* to quash the Board's decision. They also sought a declaration that the adoption of a child under Chinese law has the same legal effect as an Irish adoption order regarding the ending and creation of parental rights and duties. The High Court granted an order of *certiorari* and made the declaration sought by the applicants.

In dismissing the appeal the Supreme Court held that it was unlikely that the person in China who placed the child for adoption or the applicants would seek to terminate the adoption. It was also held that although the Adoption Acts 1952-91 do not contain provisions similar to Chinese law relating to termination, the Board is required by section 6 of the 1991 Act to recognise and register foreign adoptions, including those which were or might be liable to be set aside, annulled or rendered void under the law of the place where they were effected. Also, under section 22(7) of the 1952 Act an adoption order made in the State may be set aside and section 18 of the 1952 Act provides that adoptive parents may put up an adopted child for re-adoption, and there does not appear to be any statutory embargo on natural parents adopting their own child. Finally, there are no reasons why a child adopted under the provisions of the 1988 Act, on the basis that the adopters have failed in their parental duty in circumstances amounting to abandonment of the child, cannot be re-adopted. Accordingly, the concept of permanence of adoption is not absolute under Irish law.

Section 7 of the 1991 Act, as amended by section 15 of the 1998 Act, enables a person entitled to make an application to the Board under section 6 to recognise and register a foreign adoption, to apply to the High Court to rectify the Register. The Court may direct the Board to make a specified entry, to cancel an existing entry or to make a specified correction. Where a foreign adoption which has been recognised in the State is subsequently terminated under the law of the place where it was effected, the person seeking to have the recognition withdrawn must apply to the High Court to cancel the entry in the Register. The Court shall not give such a direction unless satisfied that it would be in the best interests of the adopted person to do so. Where the Court gives such a direction, it may make such orders as appears to it to be necessary, including orders relating to the guardianship, custody, maintenance and citizenship of that person.

Section 8 of the 1991 Act provides that where an application is made by a person or persons to have a foreign adoption recognised under section 5, the Board shall require a health board or registered adoption society to carry out an assessment of and make a report on such person or persons for the purpose of establishing their suitability as prospective adopters, within the meaning of section 13 of the 1952 Act. Section 8(1) requires a health board to carry out an assessment 'as soon as practicable'. The Supreme court held in *McC. and McD. v. Eastern Health Board* (1997) that the expression 'as soon as practicable' did not mean 'as soon as possible', and that, despite serious delays in carrying out an assessment, the health board was not in breach of its statutory obligation, taking into account the resources at its disposal and the large number of applications pending before it.

Proof of adoptions effected outside the State shall be established in the manner provided for in section 9 of the 1991 Act. Where an adoption is effected in a place outside the State, it shall be presumed, until the contrary is shown, that it was effected under and in accordance with the law of that place. An authenticated copy of an adoption order made outside the State will be accepted without further proof as a true copy and will be admissible as evidence of the adoption.

The Hague Convention

The Hague Convention on Protection and Co-Operation in respect of Intercountry Adoption 1993 provides a framework for the regulation of intercountry adoption and co-operation between countries of origin of adopted children and receiving countries. It is hoped that the adoption of the Convention by the various States involved will lead to the reduction, and eventual elimination, of the abuses of intercountry adoption and ensure that the best interests of the child prevail. Ireland has signed but not yet adopted the Convention. In September 1997, the Law Reform Commission issued a Consultation Paper on the implementation of the Convention, which contained a review of its main provisions, and made a number of recommendations as to its implementation. At the time of writing, the author has established that the consultation process has concluded and that the drafting of a Bill to give legal effect to the Convention has commenced.

The Preamble to the Convention recognises the necessity to take measures to ensure that intercountry adoptions are made in the best interests of the child, and takes into account the principles set forth in the United Nations Convention on the Rights of the Child and other international instruments.

The objects of the Convention, as set out in Article 1, are:

(a) to establish safeguards to ensure that intercountry adoptions take place in the best interests of the child and with respect for his fundamental rights as recognised in international law;

(b) to establish a system of co-operation amongst Contracting States to ensure that those safeguards are respected and thereby prevent the abduction, the sale of, or traffic in children;

(c) to secure the recognition in Contracting States of adoptions made in accordance with the Convention.

Article 2 provides that the Convention shall apply where a child habitually resident in one Contracting State ('the State of origin') has been, is being, or is to be moved to another Contracting State ('the receiving State') either after his adoption in the State of origin by spouses or a person habitually resident in the receiving State, or for the purposes of such an adoption in the receiving State or the State of origin. Article 2 also stipulates that the Convention covers only adoptions which create a permanent parent-child relationship.

Chapter II of the Convention sets out the requirements for intercountry adoption. Article 4 requires the State of origin to ensure that the child is adoptable; that a determination has been made, after considering the possibility of the child remaining in the country of origin, that intercountry adoption is in the best interests of the child; that all the necessary consents have been given; that, where relevant, the child has consented and his wishes have been taken into consideration. Article 5 requires the receiving State to determine that the prospective adoptive parents are eligible to adopt; that, where necessary, they have been counselled; and that the child will be authorised to enter and reside permanently in the receiving State.

Chapter III of the Convention provides for the setting up of a Central Authority in each Contracting State. Central Authorities are required to co-operate and exchange information. In particular, Central Authorities are required by Article 8 to take appropriate measures to prevent improper financial or other gain in connection with an adoption and to deter all practices contrary to the objects of the Convention.

Chapter IV of the Convention deals with the preparation of reports on the natural parents, the adoptive parents and the child. Provision is made for obtaining the necessary consents and the procuring of authorisation for the child to enter the receiving State. In particular, Article 17 regulates the placement of the child with the prospective parents. Before deciding to place the child, the State of origin must ensure that the prospective adoptive parents agree; that the receiving State has approved the placement; that both States agree that the adoption may proceed; that the prospective adoptive parents are eligible and suitable to adopt; and that the child will be allowed to enter and reside permanently in the receiving State. Article 19 provides that the child is not to be transferred to the receiving State until the conditions of Article 17 have been met.

Chapter V regulates the recognition and effects of a Convention adoption. Article 23 states that an adoption certified by the competent authority of the State of the adoption as having been made in accordance with the Convention, shall be automatically recognised by other Contracting States. Article 23 states that recognition may be refused in a Contracting State only if the adoption is manifestly contrary to the public policy of that State.

By virtue of Article 26.1, the recognition of an adoption includes recognition of (a) the legal parent-child relationship between the child and his adoptive parents; (b) parental responsibility of the adoptive parents for the child; (c) the termination of a pre-existing relationship between the child and his mother and father, if the adoption has this effect in the Contracting State where it was made. Article 26.2 states that in the case of an adoption having the effect of terminating a pre-existing legal parent-child relationship, the child shall enjoy in the receiving State, and in any other Contracting State where the adoption is recognised, rights equivalent to those resulting from adoptions having this effect in each such State.

Among the general provisions contained in Chapter VI of the Convention are Article 29, which places restrictions on contact between the prospective adoptive parents and the natural parents of the child before the adoption process has got under way and Article 30, which requires the competent authorities in a Contracting State to preserve information regarding the child's origin, in particular information relating to the identity of the natural parents and medical records. The competent authorities shall ensure that the child has access to such information, under appropriate guidance, in so far as is permitted by the law of that State.

Further Reading

O'Halloran, *Adoption Law and Practice*. Dublin: Butterworths Ireland 1992.
Shatter, *Family Law* 4th. Ed. Dublin: Butterworths 1997.

O'Connor, *Key Issues in Irish Family Law*. Dublin: Round Hall Press 1988.

Binchy, *A Casebook on Irish Family Law*. Abingdon: Professional Books 1984.

Law Reform Commission, Report on the Recognition of Foreign Adoption Decrees (LRC 29- 1989).

Law Reform Commission, Consultation Paper on Implementation of the Hague Convention on Protection of Children and Co-operation in Respect of Intercountry Adoption 1993 (LRC- September 1997).

CHAPTER FOURTEEN

GUARDIANSHIP AND CUSTODY OF CHILDREN

Parental Rights and Duties

The two central concepts governing parental rights and duties are guardianship and custody. A guardian is a person legally entitled to parental rights and duties in relation to a child. One of these rights is custody, which is the right to physical care and control of the child. Other parental rights include the right to decide where and with whom the child shall live; the right to impose discipline; the right to bring and defend proceedings on behalf of the child; the right to apply for a passport for the child and the right to consent to the child undergoing surgery. The duties include the duties to maintain, protect and educate the child.

The right to custody of a child is the most important parental right, from which all others flow. Where a parent is deprived of custody by court order he remains a guardian and retains a say in matters that are important to the child's welfare, i.e. the religious, moral, intellectual, physical and social welfare of the child. In *B. v. B.* (1975) Walsh J, in describing the effect of an order giving custody to one parent to the exclusion, total or partial, of the other parent, said that such an order 'does not deprive the parent who loses the custody of the other rights which accrue to him or her as guardian of the infant'. The right of the non-custodial parent to reasonable access to the child is normally expressly reserved under the court order. However, where the Court is satisfied that a parent is guilty of grave misconduct, to the extent that contact with the child would endanger his welfare, access may be denied. A parent deprived of custody can, of course, always apply again to the Court for a variation of the order.

At common law, the father of a marital child was his sole guardian, to the exclusion of the mother. The father would only be deprived of his right to custody where, in extreme circumstances, his conduct disentitled him. Equity, however, would more readily deprive a father of custody, even in the absence of misconduct, where the welfare of the child so dictated. The present position is that in matters relating to custody, the welfare of the child is the first and paramount consideration. In the case of a non-marital child, the mother alone was entitled to guardianship and custody. This continues to be the position in the absence of a court order conferring guardianship on the natural father or the mother agreeing to make him joint guardian. The natural father can apply to court seeking custody of his child and the right of access to it.

The Guardianship of Infants Act 1964

The law relating to guardianship and custody is now contained in the Guardianship of Infants Act 1964 as amended by the Status of Children Act 1987, the Judicial Separation and Family Law Reform Act 1989, The Family Law (Divorce) Act 1996 and the Children Act 1997. The term 'infant' was defined for the purposes of the legislation as a person under the age of 18 years. The word 'child' is now substituted for the word 'infant' by virtue of section 4 of the Children Act 1997.

Section 6(1) of the 1964 Act provides that the mother and father of a child born to them in wedlock are joint guardians of the child. The section gives statutory expression to the constitutional position, as identified by the Supreme Court in *B. v. B.* (1975), that parents have equal rights to and are joint guardians of their children. Section 10(2) provides that the parents as guardians are entitled to custody, again reflecting the constitutional position as outlined by Henchy J in *G. v. An Bord Uchtála* (1980):

> The Constitution does not pronounce specifically on rights of custody, but it is necessarily inherent in the provisions I have cited (Articles 41.1, 42.1, 42.5) that, in the case of children whose parents were or have become married, the primary right to custody is vested in the parents, for custody will normally be necessary for the effectuation of the parents' constitutional right and duty to provide for the religious and moral, intellectual, physical and social education of their children.

The mother of a non-marital child is the sole guardian of her child — section 6(4). The mother's right to custody of her child is to be found in section 10(2)(a). O'Higgins CJ recognised the unspecified constitutional right of the mother to guardianship and custody in *G. v. An Bord Uchtála* (1980), where he said:

> Suffice to say that this plaintiff as a mother, had a natural right to the custody of her child who was an infant, and that this natural right of hers is recognised and protected by Article 40.3.1 of the Constitution. Section 6(4) and section 10(2)(a) of the Guardianship of Infants Act 1964, constitute a compliance by the State with its obligation, in relation to the mother of an illegitimate child, to defend and vindicate in its laws this right to custody. These statutory provisions make the mother guardian of her illegitimate child and give the mother statutory rights to sue for custody.

The natural father of a non-marital child is given the right under section 6A (as inserted by section 12 of the Status of Children Act 1987) to apply to court to be appointed guardian. The *Keegan* case, referred to in Chapter 13, makes it clear that he has a defeasible right only, in that the Court has a discretion as to whether or not he should be appointed guardian. Section 2(4) (as inserted by section 4 of the Children Act 1997) provides that the mother and father of a non-marital child may agree to the appointment of the father as guardian of the child, provided they have entered into arrangements regarding the custody of, and as the case may be, access to the child, and have made a statutory declaration to that effect as prescribed by the Guardianship of Children (Statutory Declarations) Regulations 1998 (Statutory Instrument S.I. 5/98).

Custody Agreements

An agreement on custody made by a husband and wife on separation is valid under section 18(2). However, the Supreme Court ruled in *Cullen v. Cullen* (1970) that such an agreement will be enforced by the Court only if it is in the child's best interests. The mother of a non-marital child may sign an agreement granting custody to the natural father. In default of agreement, the father can apply to the Court under section 11(2) for custody or access to the child. The parents of a non-marital child cannot make a valid agreement that they shall have joint custody of their child. However, by virtue of section 11A (as inserted by section 9 of the Children Act 1997) the Court is empowered, if it thinks proper, to grant custody of a child to his father and mother jointly. Any agreement under which a parent, marital or non-marital, purports to give custody to a third party is void.

Access

There is now widespread acceptance of the principle established in the English case of *M. v. M.* (1973) that access is really a right of the child to see its own parent rather than a parental right, and that access to the child should only be denied in exceptional circumstances where the Court is satisfied beyond doubt that any degree of access under any conditions is likely to be seriously injurious to the welfare of the child. For example, in the English case of *Rashid v. Rashid* (1979) a father was refused access for seriously affecting his children's health by taking them to Pakistan in defiance of a court order. Where there is no dispute between the parents, the details as to access are left to be worked out between them. However, if they fail to agree, or their agreement does not take into account the welfare, needs and wishes of the child, the Court can make an order as to access and, if necessary, lay down in complete detail all matters relating to access. For example, the Court may stipulate the time, place and duration of the access, the frequency with which it is to take place and may, in appropriate cases, order it to be supervised by a suitable person. It emerged in evidence in *D.F.O'S. v. C.A.* (1999) that the South Eastern Health Board had been providing supervision for access by the mother to her young daughter who, by consent order, was in the custody of her father. It is interesting to note that the Board did not wish to continue the supervision as no child protection issue was involved.

The view that access is a right of the child, rather than a parental right, is reinforced by Article 9(3) of the United Nations Convention on the Rights of the Child, which requires State Parties to respect 'the right of the child who is separated from one or both parents to maintain personal relations and direct contact with both parents on a regular basis, except if it is contrary to the child's best interests'. In *Eriksson v Sweden* (1989) the European Court of Human Rights interpreted Article 8 of the European Convention on Human Rights as conferring an automatic right to access on the child which should only be denied where the welfare of the child so required.

There have been a number of cases over the years where such conduct on the part of a parent as adultery, desertion and suspected child abuse have resulted in the Courts imposing conditions under which access is to take place. In *MacD. v. MacD.* (1979), the High Court, in granting custody to the father, provided for liberal access by the mother on condition that it did not involve the children coming into contact with the other party to the adultery nor staying in his house whether or not he was there. On appeal, the Supreme Court reversed the decision and granted custody to the mother, with liberal access to the father. In *S. v. S.* (1992) the Court held that the mother of three young girls, who was involved in an adulterous relationship with another man, was not a suitable person to have custody of the children. In awarding custody to the father, the Court ruled that access for the mother was not to include overnight access. However, in *J.C. v. O'C.* (1980) a husband, who had been separated from his wife for four years and was living with another woman in an adulterous relationship, was permitted access to the children at the weekends and to take them on holiday within Ireland for a period of three weeks. In *N.A.D. v. T.D.* (1985) the High Court refused a wife who had deserted her husband access to her five children, as such access would not be of benefit to the children. The evidence revealed a natural reluctance on the part of the children to have anything to do with their mother. The Court accepted that the husband had not contributed to this reluctance. Barron J had met the two older boys in chambers, and was satisfied that the home circumstances of all the children was secure and well supported. In *O'D. v. O'D.* (1994) the High Court granted controlled access to the father where there was a reasonable suspicion that he might have sexually abused his child. The Court made it a condition of access by the father that one of his four sisters be present at all times.

Section 11B of the 1964 Act (as inserted by section 9 of the Children Act 1997) allows a person who is related to a child or the parent of a child by blood to apply to court for an order granting access to the child on such terms and conditions as the Court may order. The leave of the Court is a prerequisite to the making of a section 11B application. In deciding whether to grant leave the Court must have regard to (a) the applicant's connection with the child, (b) the risk, if any, of the application disrupting the child's life to the extent that the child would be harmed by it, and (c) the wishes of the child's guardian. By providing that the

Court may make an access order in favour of a blood relation, for example a grandparent or an uncle or an aunt of the child, the legislature is recognising that members of the child's family other than parents may have a valuable contribution to make to the child's future welfare.

Appointment of Guardian by Deed or Will

Section 6 of the 1964 Act provides that on the death of either parent, the survivor is guardian of any children of the marriage, either alone or jointly with any guardian appointed by the deceased parent or by the Court. Both parents have the right under section 7 to appoint a testamentary guardian, by deed or will, to act as joint guardian with the surviving parent. Where the surviving parent objects to the testamentary guardian, the dispute may be resolved by an application to the Court. This procedure also applies if the guardian considers the surviving parent unfit to act. The Court may (a) refuse to make an order (in which case the surviving parent shall remain sole guardian), or (b) make an order that the testamentary guardian shall act jointly with the surviving parent, or (c) make an order that he shall act as guardian of the child to the exclusion, so far as the Court thinks proper, of the surviving parent. Where the court orders that the guardian act to the exclusion of the surviving parent, it can order that parent to pay reasonable maintenance for the child to the guardian. If testamentary guardians are appointed by both parents they shall act jointly after the death of the surviving parent — section 9.

Appointment of Guardian by the Court

Where a child has no guardian the Court can, on the application of any person or persons, appoint the applicant or applicants to be guardian or guardians of the child — section 8. The section also empowers the Court to appoint a guardian in the absence of a deceased parent appointing one. Should the guardian predecease the parent who appointed him, or should he refuse to act, the Court can appoint one to act jointly with the surviving parent.

A guardian, however appointed, acquires most parental rights, powers and duties on the death of one or both parents. However, on the question of the child's education the parents wishes will prevail, unless they are contrary to the welfare of the child. A guardian is regarded as a trustee of the child's estate by virtue of section 10. Section 8(4) (as inserted by section 7 of the Children Act 1997) provides that a guardian appointed by will or deed or order of the Court, or holding office by virtue of an agreement between the mother and father of a non-marital child, may only be removed by order of the Court.

Custody after a Decree of Nullity

By virtue of section 46 of the Family Law Act 1995 the Court, on granting a decree of nullity, may declare either of the spouses unfit to have custody of any dependent member of the family who is a minor. Where such an order is made, that spouse shall not, on the death of the other spouse, be entitled as of right to the custody of that minor.

Custody on Judicial Separation and Divorce

Section 6 of the Family Law Act 1995 provides that the Court, on considering an application for judicial separation, may make a preliminary order as to custody or access or other order on any question affecting the welfare of the child pursuant to section 11 of the 1964 Act. On granting a decree of judicial separation, or at any time thereafter, on the application to it by either spouse, the Court may, *inter alia*, make an ancillary order pursuant to section 11 of the 1964 Act. By virtue of section 41 of the 1989 Act, where a Court grants a decree of judicial separation, it may declare either spouse unfit to have custody of dependent children. Where a spouse to whom such a declaration relates is a parent of any child of the family such spouse shall not, on the death of the other spouse, be entitled as of right to custody of that child.

Section 5 of the Family Law (Divorce) Act 1996 provides that on granting a decree of divorce, the Court may give directions under section 11 of the 1964 Act regarding welfare, custody of, or right of access to any dependent child who is an infant. Section 11 of the 1996 Act enables the Court to make preliminary orders pursuant to section 11 of the 1964 Act. By virtue of section 41 of the 1996 Act, where a Court grants a decree of divorce, it may declare either spouse unfit to have custody of any dependent member of the family who is a minor. Where such an order is made that spouse shall not, on the death of the other spouse, be entitled as of right to the custody of that minor.

Custody Disputes Between Parents

A dispute as to custody normally arises where parents are unable to resolve some outstanding difference over their child. Such a dispute can arise in the event of marital breakdown or where the parties are still living together. Section 11 of the 1964 Act, as amended, enables any person who is a guardian of the child to apply to the Court for its direction on any question affecting the welfare of the child. The Court may make any order it thinks fit in relation to such welfare.

Joint Custody

Most disputes between parents as to the custody of children are resolved by the Court granting sole custody to one parent and access to the other parent. However, it has long been acknowledged that joint custody can be granted where such an arrangement is best suited to the circumstances of a particular case. Section 11A of the 1964 Act (as inserted by section 9 of the Children Act 1997) now clarifies the position by confirming the Court's existing discretion to grant joint custody. In *B. v. B.* (1975) O'Dalaigh CJ appeared to suggest that joint custody might be a desirable option in certain cases, when he stated that, if the homes of the separated parents had been close enough to a single suitable school, he would have favoured maintaining the unity of the children 'by allowing them to reside for half the year with one parent, and the other half with the other'. In *E.P. v. C.P.* (1998) the Court granted decrees of divorce and judicial separation to the wife, but refused an application by the husband for joint custody. While acknowledging that joint custody is widely recommended at present, McGuinness J stated that it would not work in this case for the following reason:

> joint custody cannot work satisfactorily for the children if there is a high level of conflict between the parties and an opportunity for fights around every corner, as it were. If people cannot work together sensibly and happily in the interests of their children, an order for joint custody would not seem to be particularly suitable.

McGuinness J elaborated on her views on joint custody in *D.F.O'S. v. C.A.* (1999), when granting joint custody to the mother and father of a four and a half year old girl, and making arrangements as to where the child should live. McGuinness J found the case a difficult one to decide, as there was great hostility between the parties, and said that 'as a general rule where there is deep hostility between the parents I am very reluctant to make an Order granting joint custody, due to the probable inability of the parents to co-operate in caring for the child'. However, the learned judge went on to say that it appeared to her that if she granted custody in this case to one parent rather than the other, there was a danger that this might add to the bitterness and resentment.

The Welfare Principle

Section 3 of the 1964 Act sets out the principles upon which custody disputes will be decided:

> Where in any proceedings before any court the custody, guardianship or upbringing of an infant, or the administration of any property belonging to or held in trust for an infant, or the application of the income thereof, is in question, the Court, in deciding that question, shall regard the welfare of the infant as the first and paramount consideration.

The scope and meaning of the words 'shall regard the welfare of the infant as the first and paramount consideration' was considered by the House of Lords in *J. v. C.* (1970). In considering the corresponding English statutory provision, Mac Dermott LJ said that the words must mean more 'than that the child's welfare is to be treated as the top item in a list of items relevant to the matter in question'. The requirement that the child's welfare shall be the first and paramount consideration connotes:

a process whereby, when all the relevant facts, relationships, claims and wishes of parents, risks, choices and other circumstances are taken into account and weighed, the course to be followed will be that which is most in the interests of the child's welfare as that term has now to be understood. That is the first consideration because it is of first importance and the paramount consideration because it rules on or determines the course to be followed.

The approach of MacDermott LJ, as representing the proper approach, was approved by Henchy J in *MacD. v. MacD.* (1979).

Welfare is defined in section 2 of the 1964 Act as comprising the religious and moral, intellectual, physical and social welfare of the child. In *MacD. v. MacD.* (1979) Finlay P considered the various categories of welfare contained in the definition set out in section 2. He pointed out that a dominant position must not be given to any of these categories. The whole question of welfare must be looked at globally as the various categories of which it is comprised are interrelated. Social welfare means the type of welfare best suited to make a child a better member of the society in which he lives. Physical welfare is concerned with the health, bodily comfort, nourishment and hygiene of the child. Intellectual welfare is concerned with the child's education. Moral welfare means the moral and ethical code of the religion in which the child is being brought up as judged against moral standards and values of the society of which he is a member. Religious welfare is concerned with the education of the child in the practice of the religion in which he is being brought up.

Although the child's welfare is not the only consideration, the modern approach is to regard that welfare as the overriding consideration. In considering what course of action will most advance the welfare of the child, the Court will take into account other factors which might have a bearing on the welfare of the child, such as:

(a) The Conduct of the Parents

A distinction should be made between conduct of the parents which contributed to the breakdown of the marriage and such conduct in so far as it is relevant to the child's welfare. There may be no distinction in certain cases. In other cases, however, it is possible that a man who is a bad husband may be a good father. Equally, a woman who is a good mother may be a bad wife. The Court should not be concerned either to reward or punish parents in awarding custody. In this regard, it is worth noting the remarks of Kenny J in *M.O'B. v. P.O'B.* (1971) where he said that 'an award of custody is not a reward for good behaviour'. In that case, Kenny J awarded custody of four children, two boys aged 9 and 6 and two girls aged 10 and 7, to the wife, even though she was living with another man, on the basis that the learned judge refused to accept that a parent who has been guilty of matrimonial misconduct is necessarily unfit to have custody and that the 'innocent party is in every case the one who will best promote the interests of the child'.

Where a child is living in a stable and familiar environment with a parent whose conduct is far from exemplary, it is not desirable to uproot him unless the Court considers it necessary to guarantee the welfare of the child. In *M.B.O'S. v. P.O.O'S.* (1974) the Supreme Court reversed the decision of Kenny J in the High Court, and allowed three young children, a boy aged 5 and two girls aged 6 and 7, to remain with their father in the home which he had set up with another woman. The Court held that the bad example of the father in living in an adulterous relationship was a tragic fact of life which the children would have to come to terms with eventually. Noting that the children had been treated with care and had attained a degree of emotional security in the home of their father and his lover, Henchy J said:

> I do not think that they should be severed from that home in the hope that their youth will enable them to pass unscathed through the suggested change of custody, particularly when the evidence is that they dread the prospect of being removed to live with their mother.

In *MacD. v. MacD.* (1979) the mother of two young children, a girl aged six and a half and a boy aged four and a half, formed an adulterous relationship with a man named D. She had custody of the children on foot of an agreement with the father. On discovering that the mother allowed the children to come into contact with D, the father applied to the High Court for custody. Finlay J awarded custody to the father on the grounds, *inter alia*, that the wife by her actions had firmly and clearly repudiated the family as a fundamental and integral unit of Irish society as outlined by the Constitution and had failed to condemn and disapprove of adultery. On appeal, the Supreme Court reversed this decision. In delivering his judgment, Henchy J stated that 'custody is awarded not as a mark of approbation or disapprobation of parental conduct but solely as a judicial determination of where the welfare of the children lies'. Griffin J expressed the view that the conduct of parents was only relevant in so far as it affects the welfare of the children and went on to state:

> But the conduct of the parents is relevant in so far as inferences can be drawn from it to show where the priorities of the parents lie in relation to the children, as this is an important factor to consider in relation to their welfare.

As in *MacD. v. MacD.*, the conduct of the wife was the issue at the centre of a custody dispute between husband and wife in *S. v. S.* (1992). In the latter case, the Supreme Court upheld the decision of the High Court granting custody of three children, girls aged 13, 10 and 7 years, to the husband. In the High Court,

Morris J held that the wife had left the family home without justification, that she was involved in a relationship with another man and was often with him in the presence of the children, that she left the children on their own at night while she socialised in a public house and that, on the evidence, she had attempted to make a false and bogus allegation against the husband of improper sexual behaviour towards two of the children. The learned judge found the husband a thrifty, hardworking, responsible, retiring man, a non-drinker not interested in socialising and who believed strongly in traditional values and in his religion. On the negative side, the husband had difficulty relating to the children. In delivering the judgment of the Supreme Court, Finlay CJ, with whom McCarthy J and Egan J concurred, stated that the conduct of parents was relevant only in so far as it affected the welfare of children. However, in echoing the sentiments expressed by Griffin J in *MacD. v. MacD.*, the Chief Justice said that the conduct of the parents was relevant to show where the priorities of the parents lay in relation to the children. As much reliance was placed by counsel for the mother on *MacD. v. MacD.*, the Chief Justice distinguished both cases by pointing out that the findings made in *MacD.* concerning the qualities, character and approach of the wife to the upbringing of the children, and also the ages of the children in both cases, 'make it wholly different in detail from the case which is instantly before the Court on appeal'. The Chief Justice then made reference to the judgments of McCarthy J and Egan J in the case, and expressed himself in agreement with the statements contained in those judgments to the effect that:

> whereas general principles concerning questions of custody can be gleaned from the decisions of the courts made in individual cases those principles are very particularly to be applied to the special facts of each case which vary greatly.

(b) The Sex of a Parent

There is a certain amount of overlapping between this factor and parental conduct. In deciding the welfare of children, the Court very often has to consider the competing claims of parents in terms of the sex of either parent. The case law suggests a preference for the mother in the case of very young children, unless an award of custody to her would be detrimental to the welfare of the children. This reflects, in no small measure, the traditional role assigned to mothers by society. In *E.K. v. M.K.* (1974) Walsh J in the Supreme Court expressed the view that the removal of two children, a boy aged five and a half and a girl aged three and a half, from their mother would only be justified where it was found that 'the mother has been so greatly wanting in her duty to her children that the removal would be warranted'. The Supreme Court awarded custody to the husband on the basis that the wife was greatly wanting in her duty to her children, and that her adulterous relationship and unstable lifestyle were a manifest repudiation of the social and religious values with which the children should be inculcated. In

MacD. Henchy J articulated the preference for the mother as follows:

> In the case of very young children the person *prima facie* entitled to their
> custody, where the parents are estranged, is the mother, for by reason of her
> motherhood she will usually be the person primarily and uniquely capable
> of ministering to their welfare.

Later on in his judgment, he said that the 'risk that the religious and moral
welfare of the children will suffer' if the mother was given custody was
outweighed by 'the father's inability, during most of the week, to surround the
children with any direct parental presence or help'. Accordingly, he concluded
that 'the mother, for all the shortcomings of her situation, has the better capacity
to meet the amalgam of needs constituting the statutory definition of welfare'.

In *J.J.W. v. B.M.W.* (1971), a custody dispute involving children who were all
girls, Kenny J stated that 'fathers find it difficult to understand the minds and the
physical and psychological needs of young girls'. In *S. v. S.* (1992), where the
mother was deprived of custody of her three children because of her conduct,
Egan J acknowledged the fact that because they were girls meant that there could
be advantages for them in being looked after by their mother. It should be
stressed, however, that the view that very young children are better cared for by
their mother is not a rule of law, but a matter of common sense and human
experience. McGuinness J questioned this notion that young children,
particularly girls, are best cared for by their mothers in *D.F.O'S. v. C.A.* (1999),
where she granted joint custody of a four and a half year old girl to her parents.
Stating that she did not entirely accept what she termed as the old *'tender years'*
principle, she said that 'modern views and practices of parenting show the
virtues of shared parenting and the older principles too often meant the
automatic granting of custody to the mother virtually to the exclusion of the
father'.

(c) The Wishes of the Child

Section 25 of the 1964 Act (as inserted by section 11 of the Children Act 1997)
requires the Court, as it thinks appropriate and practicable having regard to the
age and level of understanding of the child, to consider the child's wishes. In this
regard Barron J interviewed two children, boys of nine and five years of age, in
N.A.D. v. T.D. (1985), as a result of which he identified a reluctance on their part
to have anything to do with their mother. In *M.W. v. D.W.* (1975), a bitter custody
dispute between the estranged parents of two young boys, the wife applied to
have her husband committed to prison for contempt of court, on the basis that
he had enticed the children away from her in defiance of a previous order
granting her custody. Kenny J interviewed two boys, aged 12 and 15, to assist
him in deciding the case. Both boys were very definite in expressing their desire
to live with the father and said that they would return to him no matter what the

Court decreed. They claimed that their mother had physically ill-treated them. Custody was awarded to the father.

Custody Disputes Between Parents and Outsiders

The Welfare Principle

The welfare principle, as set out in section 3 of the 1964 Act and enunciated by the Courts, also applies to disputes between parents and outsiders. However, it is clear from decided cases that it is only in exceptional circumstances that outsiders will be preferred to parents. This stems from the fact that both parents and child have constitutional rights which will override any statutory provision to the contrary. However, as constitutional rights in general are not absolute, a court can deprive the parents of custody where the welfare of the child so dictates. Section 14 of the 1964 Act enables a parent to apply to the Court for the production of his child who is in the custody of another. The Court may refuse to enforce the parental right to custody where a parent has abandoned or deserted the child. Section 16 provides that where a parent has abandoned or deserted a child or allowed that child to be brought up by another person (including a school or institution) at that person's expense, the Court shall not make an order that the child be delivered to the parent unless it is satisfied that the parent is a fit person to have custody. A third party cannot avail of the procedures contained in the 1964 Act to obtain custody of a child against its parents, but instead must have the child made a ward of court and ask for care and control.

The marital status of the parents of a child at the centre of a custody dispute between parents and outsiders may have an important bearing on how the Court resolves such a dispute. It is clear from a long line of cases that have addressed the issue that the parents of a marital child will only be deprived of custody in circumstances amounting to abandonment of parental duty. Even before the enactment of the Constitution, the Courts were reluctant to deprive married parents of the custody of their child except in the most extreme circumstances. This reluctance on the part of the Courts is evident from the judgment of Fitzgibbon LJ in *In Re O'Hara, an infant*, (1900), where he stated that 'misconduct, or unmindfulness of parental duty, or inability to provide for the welfare of the child, must be shown before the natural right can be displaced'. In that case, a widowed mother in domestic service and living in poor circumstances, surrendered her young daughter to a fairly well-off couple. Having acquired a modest home on remarriage, she was granted custody of her child on the basis that a mother forced to part with custody of her child in such circumstances could not be deemed to have abandoned the child. In *The State (Kavanagh) v. O'Sullivan* (1933) the Supreme Court held that a father, living in cramped conditions and with little money, who was forced to part with the custody of his three children when his wife was hospitalised for mental illness following the birth of the children, could not be deemed to have lost his 'natural right' by abandonment.

In cases decided since the enactment of the Constitution, greater emphasis has been placed on Articles 41 and 42, and the parental rights enunciated in those articles. It was established by the decision of the Supreme Court in *G. v. An Bord Uchtála* (1980) that parents of a child born to them in wedlock have a constitutional right to custody of the child under Articles 41 and 42. The natural parents of a child who subsequently marry one another automatically legitimate the child under the provisions of the Legitimacy Act 1931 so that the father, mother and child constitute a family within the meaning of Articles 41 and 42. The problems that can arise where the mother places the child for adoption prior to her marriage to the natural father were addressed *In Re J., an Infant* (1966) and in *K.C. v. An Bord Uchtála* (1985) (also known as *K.C. and A.C. v. An Bord Uchtála*).

The 'Compelling Reasons' Test

The decision of the Supreme court in *K.C. v. An Bord Uchtála* established the constitutional presumption that the welfare of both marital and legitimated children is to be found within the family referred to in Articles 41 and 42 of the Constitution, and that this presumption can only be rebutted where there are 'compelling reasons' why a child should be removed from the custody of its parents who are married to one another. The facts of *K.C.* show that the mother placed her child for adoption but later withdrew her consent, as a result of which the prospective adopters applied to the Court for an order under section 3 of the Adoption Act 1974 dispensing with the mother's consent to the making of an adoption order, and an order granting them custody of the child. About a month after the institution of the proceedings, the mother married the natural father, thereby legitimating the child. The High Court held that the child so legitimated and its natural parents constituted a family for the purposes of Articles 41 and 42. As the natural father had not consented to the adoption of the child, the prospective adopters were not entitled in law to an order under section 3 of the 1974 Act. However, on the question of custody, Lynch J held that the welfare of the child required that she be left with the prospective adopters, as the child had been with them for about two years and had become bonded to them. Any order returning the child to her natural parents would cause immediate suffering and possible long term serious harm to her. The natural parents appealed this decision.

In allowing the appeal of the natural parents, the Supreme Court carried out a major review of the law in this complex area. In his judgment, Finlay CJ said that section 3 of the Guardianship of Infants Act 1964 must be construed to mean that there is a constitutional presumption that the welfare of the child, which is defined in section 2 of the 1964 Act in terms identical to those contained in Article 42.1, is to be found within the family, unless the Court is satisfied on the evidence that 'there are compelling reasons why this cannot be achieved' or 'that the evidence establishes an exceptional case where the parents have failed to provide education for the child and continue to fail to provide education for the child for moral or physical reasons'.

The Supreme Court in *K.C.* did not give any examples of the type of conduct that amounts to 'compelling reasons'. Accordingly, reference must be made to the principles that have been developed by the Supreme Court in interpreting section 3 of the Adoption Act 1988, which permits the adoption of a marital child where the parents 'for physical or moral reasons, have failed in their duty towards the child' and such failure amounts to 'an abandonment on the part of the parents of all parental rights'. For an example of conduct that amounted to abandonment of parental duty, reference is made to the decision in *Southern Health Board v. An Bord Uchtála* (1995). The High Court held that parents who had persistently physically abused their child were guilty of conduct that amounted to an abandonment of parental rights. The Court granted an order under section 3 of the 1988 Act authorising the Adoption Board to make an adoption order in respect of the child. Reference is also made to the case of *Southern Health Board v. An Bord Uchtála* (1999), where the Supreme Court held that the word 'abandon' in section 3 of the 1988 Act had a wider legal meaning than parents simply physically deserting a child. In delivering the judgment of the Court, Denham J stated that the word 'abandon' could be used where parents by their actions failed 'in their duty so as to enable a court to deem that their failure constituted an abandonment of parental rights'. For a more detailed consideration of both of these cases, see Chapter 13.

Disputes as to custody between the mother of a non-marital child and a third party arise in the context of the mother seeking to regain custody of her child after placing it for adoption, and an application by the prospective adopters to dispense with the mother's consent under section 3 of the Adoption Act 1974. The extensive body of case law on disputes between the natural mother and the prospective adopters is considered in detail in Chapter 13.

Variation and Discharge of Custody Orders

There is no finality in the making of a custody order. Section 12 of the 1964 Act enables the Court to vary or discharge any previously-made order. The party deprived of custody can at any time in the future ask to have the original order varied or discharged on the basis of changed circumstances or new evidence of such matters as parental unsuitability. For example, the case of *M.W. v. D.W.* (1975) originally came before the High Court in 1972, when the Court gave custody of two boys, then aged 9 and 12, to their father. The evidence showed that the father could provide a stable home for the boys, whereas the mother, who had left the family home, was unable to convince the Court that she could properly care for them. The case came before the High Court again in 1974, when the Court accepted evidence of the husband's adultery adduced by the wife, and varied the original order by granting custody to her. This decision was confirmed by the Supreme Court on appeal. In 1975, the wife commenced proceedings in the High Court to have the husband committed to prison for contempt of court, alleging that the husband had enticed the children away from her in defiance of the 1974 order. Having heard the expressed preference of the two boys, by this time aged 12 and 14, to remain with their father, and accepting their allegations of ill-treatment by the mother, the Court gave custody to the father. In *C. v. B.* (1996) Denham J, in delivering the judgment of the Supreme Court in a case involving custody and unlawful removal of a child from the State under the Child Abduction and Enforcement of Custody Orders Act 1991, stated: ' the decision relating to custody of a child, especially a baby as in this case, is never final but evolves with the child, retaining in changing times the fundamental concept of the welfare of the child'.

Safeguarding the Interests of Children

A major feature of the Children Act 1997 (which inserts a new Part IV, sections 19 to 30, into the Guardianship of Infants Act 1964) is that it places emphasis on alternative dispute resolution procedures, namely counselling and mediation, in disputes as to custody of or access to children. Section 20 of the 1964 Act places an obligation on the solicitor acting for an applicant in proceedings under the Act concerning the welfare of the child to discuss with the applicant the possibility of the applicant engaging in counselling, mediation or effecting a deed or agreement in respect of custody or access. Prior to the institution of proceedings, the solicitor for the applicant must certify compliance with the section to the Court. The certificate signed by the solicitor must indicate that he has provided the names and addresses of persons qualified to give counselling or mediation. If the necessary certificate does not accompany the documents instituting the proceedings, the Court may adjourn the proceedings for such period as it considers reasonable to enable the solicitor fulfil these obligations.

Where proceedings for judicial separation or divorce are accompanied by proceedings under the 1964 Act, the solicitor acting for the applicant will be deemed to have complied with section 20 provided he has complied with similar requirements in separation or divorce proceedings. Under section 21 of the 1964 Act, there are similar provisions in relation to the solicitor acting for the respondent. Section 22 of the 1964 Act empowers the Court to adjourn proceedings for the purpose of enabling the parties to reach agreement in respect of the matters in dispute, with or without the assistance of a third party. Section 23 provides that oral or written communications between the parties and a third party in seeking agreement are not admissible in evidence.

Other provisions of the 1964 Act (as inserted by section 11 of the 1997 Act) which are designed to safeguard the interests of children include a facility to enable agreements relating to custody and access to be made a rule of court (section 24); the requirement that in certain circumstances the wishes of the child be taken into consideration in proceedings relating to his welfare (section 25); the power of the District Court to order social reports in proceedings under the Act (section 26) and the provision that a child to whom proceedings under the Act relate need not be brought before the Court for the hearing unless the Court so directs (section 27).

The role of the guardian *ad litem* has been extended by section 28 of the 1964 Act (as inserted by section 11 of the 1997 Act) to proceedings involving custody and access disputes, contested applications by natural fathers for guardianship and applications by relatives and those *in loco parentis* for access to children. The section empowers the Court to appoint a guardian *ad litem* where it is satisfied that it is in the child's best interests to do so. In making its decision, the Court must take into account the age and understanding of the child, social worker reports affecting the welfare of the child, the welfare of the child, the wishes of the child and any submissions made to the Court by the parties to the proceedings or any other person to whom they relate. Provision is also made for the guardian *ad litem* to be legally represented if the gravity of the issues involved so requires.

Evidence of Children

Part III of the Children Act 1997 updates the law on the giving of evidence by children. Section 21 facilitates the taking of evidence from a child by providing that children may give evidence through live television link in proceedings concerning their welfare. Section 22 allows for the giving of evidence by television link through an intermediary, having regard to the age or mental condition of the child. Section 23 provides for the admission of certain hearsay evidence where the child is unable to give evidence by reason of age, or the giving of oral evidence by the child, either in person or by television link, would not be in the best interests of the child. In any civil proceedings, the Court is empowered by section 28 to hear the evidence of a child under the age of 14 years otherwise than on oath or affirmation. However, the Court must first be satisfied that the child is capable of giving an intelligible account of events which are relevant to the proceedings. In the course of her judgment in *Re M.K., S.K. and W.K.* (1999), Denham J said that there are 'special concerns which must be addressed' in relation to children's evidence, and that in cases involving alleged child sexual abuse against a close relative, such as a father, 'there are often added difficulties'. The learned judge added that 'the nature of the allegation, the age of the child, and in this case the issues of disability, place a particularly heavy burden on the courts to achieve justice'.

The Protection of Children in International Situations

The Protection of Children (Hague Convention) Bill 1998 will, when enacted, give the force of law in the State to the 1996 Hague Convention on Jurisdiction,

Applicable Law, Recognition, Enforcement and Co-operation in Respect of Parental Responsibility and Measures for the Protection of Children. The purpose of the Convention is to improve the protection of children in international situations by avoiding conflicts between contracting States in respect of jurisdiction, applicable law, recognition and enforcement of measures for the protection of children. The Convention recognises the importance of international co-operation for the protection of children and, taking into account the United Nations Convention on the Rights of the Child 1989, confirms that the best interests of the child are to be a primary consideration.

The objects of the Convention, as set out in Article 1, are:

(a) to determine the State whose authorities have jurisdiction to take measures directed to the protection of the person or property of the child;
(b) to determine which law is to be applied by such authorities in exercising their jurisdiction;
(c) to determine the law applicable to parental responsibility;
(d) to provide for the recognition and enforcement of such measures of protection in all contracting States;
(e) to establish such co-operation between the authorities of the contracting States as may be necessary in order to achieve the purposes of the Convention.

The term 'parental responsibility' is defined in Article 1.2 as including parental authority, or any analogous relationship of authority determining the rights, powers and responsibilities of parents, guardians or other legal representatives in relation to the person or the property of the child. Article 2 provides that the Convention applies to children from the moment of birth until the age of 18 years.

Chapter II of the Convention deals with jurisdiction. Article 5 provides that jurisdiction in proceedings relating to the protection of the person or property of the child is vested in the contracting State where the child is habitually resident. By way of exception to Article 5, Article 8 states that jurisdiction may be taken over a child habitually resident in another contracting State if a court considers that would be in the child's best interests, and the appropriate court in the other contracting State agrees or has requested it to take jurisdiction. Article 10 provides that a court in a contracting State dealing with an application for divorce, legal separation or annulment may, subject to certain conditions, exercise jurisdiction over a child habitually resident in another contracting State. The conditions referred to in Article 10 are that (a) at least one of the child's parents habitually resides in the State in question; (b) one of the parents has parental responsibility for the child, although not necessarily the parent who habitually resides in the State in question; (c) each parent and any other person having parental responsibility for the child has accepted the Court's jurisdiction;

and (d) the exercise of such jurisdiction is in the best interests of the child. In all cases of urgency, Article 11 permits the contracting State in whose territory the child, or property belonging to the child, is present, to have jurisdiction to take any necessary measures of protection.

Chapter III of the Convention deals with the applicable law. Article 15 provides that, in exercising their jurisdiction under the provisions of Chapter II, the contracting States shall apply their own law. In exceptional cases, the Contracting States may apply the law of another State with which the situation has a substantial connection. Article 17 states that the exercise of parental responsibility is governed by the law of the State of the child's habitual residence. Article 19 provides for the protection of a third party who in good faith enters into a transaction with another person who is entitled to act as the child's legal representative under the law of the State where the transaction is concluded.

Chapter IV of the Convention deals with recognition and enforcement. Article 23 provides that the measures taken in one contracting State shall be recognised by operation of law in all other contracting States. Recognition may be refused in certain circumstances, including (a) if the measure was taken without jurisdiction; (b) if the measure was taken without the child or the person having parental responsibility having been given the opportunity to be heard; (c) if such recognition is manifestly contrary to the public policy of the requested State, taking into account the best interests of the child. Article 26 provides that measures taken and enforceable in one contracting State shall be enforceable in other contracting States. A declaration of enforceability may only be refused for one of the reasons set out in Article 23.

Chapter V of the Convention provides for co-operation between contracting States. Article 29 requires each contracting State to designate a Central Authority to co-operate with Central Authorities in other contracting States. Article 30 sets out the functions of a Central Authority, and these include facilitating agreed solutions for the protection of a child's person or property in cases to which the Convention applies. Another important function of a Central Authority is, on the request of a competent authority in another contracting State, to provide assistance in discovering the whereabouts of a child who may be present in its territory and in need of protection.

United Nations Convention on the Rights of the Child

Since Ireland ratified the Convention in September 1992, any new legislation affecting the welfare of children must take account of the general and substantive principles set out in the Convention. For example, section 11 of the Children Act 1997, (inserting a new section 25 in the Guardianship of Infants Act 1964), requires the Court to take the wishes of a child into consideration in deciding the welfare of the child, in effect giving statutory expression to one of the general principles of the Convention that children have the right to be heard (Article 12).

Also, under Article 21 of the Convention, States Parties are required when legislating for adoption to ensure that the best interests of the child shall be the paramount consideration. See Chapter 13. The Constitution Review Group Report 1996 also makes reference to certain articles of the Convention. See Chapter 1.

The Convention is a charter of human rights enjoyed by the child, which include civil and political rights as well as economic, social and cultural rights. Many of these rights have been identified by the Courts as unenumerated rights under the Constitution. A child is defined as a person under 18, unless national laws specify an earlier age of majority. The Convention sets minimum legal standards for the protection of children's rights, and where individual States Parties set higher standards than those set out in the Convention, the higher standard always applies. The general principles of the Convention provide that States Parties shall ensure each child enjoys full rights without discrimination, that the best interests of the child shall be a primary consideration, that every child has an inherent right to life and that children have the right to be heard. States Parties have an obligation to implement the Convention by promoting the rights of the child through administrative, legislative, judicial and other measures.

The substantive provisions of the Convention include: a) civil rights and freedoms, including the right of a child to a name and nationality (Article 7), the right to freedom of expression (Article 13), the right to freedom of thought, conscience and religion (Article 14), the right to freedom of association (Article 15) and the right to have his or her privacy protected (Article 16). Capital punishment and life imprisonment are prohibited and no child shall be subjected to cruel, inhuman or degrading treatment or punishment (Article 37(a)); b) family environment and parental guidance (Article 5); c) basic health and welfare (Article 6); d) education, leisure and recreation (Articles 28 and 29); e) special protection measures in situations of armed conflict (Article 38), conflict with the law (Article 40), exploitation (Article 39) and membership of a minority or indigenous group (Article 30).

Further Reading

Shatter, *Family Law* 4th. Ed. Dublin: Butterworths 1997.

Binchy, *A Casebook on Irish Family Law.* Abingdon: Professional Books 1984.

O'Reilly, 'Custody Disputes in the Irish Republic: The Uncertain Search for the Child's Welfare'? (1977) 12 Ir Jur (n.s.) 37.

Council for Social Welfare, 'The Rights of the Child: Irish Perspectives on the U.N. Convention'. Dublin 1990.

United Nations Convention on the Rights of the Child: First National Report of Ireland (Department of Foreign Affairs, Dublin 1996).

CHAPTER FIFTEEN

CHILD ABDUCTION

Child abduction usually occurs where a marriage has broken down and the parents are in dispute about custody of the children. It involves one parent taking a child out of the country of its habitual residence without the consent of the other parent or in defiance of a custody order. Long before child abduction became the huge problem that it is today, and prior to the enactment of the Child Abduction and Enforcement of Custody Orders Act 1991, the Courts in Ireland and the United Kingdom set themselves against these unilateral movements of children across international frontiers. The Courts took the view that the removal of children from their country of habitual residence by one of the parents, who happens to have connections with another country, is a practice that should not be tolerated, unless such removal could be justified. In dealing with applications for the return of children to their country of habitual residence following their abduction, the Courts applied the well-established comity of courts doctrine, to the effect that a court in one jurisdiction should recognise and enforce an order made by a court in another jurisdiction, provided the order was not incompatible with the fundamental principles of law in the enforcing jurisdiction.

The Comity of Courts Doctrine

In *Northampton County Council v. A.B.F. and M.B.F.* (1982) the High Court refused to return a marital child to the care of a local authority in England on the grounds that to do so would infringe the fundamental rights of the child under the Constitution. In delivering the judgment of the Court, Hamilton J stated that in normal circumstances he would have returned the child to the care of the local authority on the basis of the comity of courts doctrine. However, the return of the child would result in its adoption without the consent of its lawful father, a situation which was not permissible under Irish adoption law at that time. On the other hand, in *Kent County Council v. C.S.* (1984) the High Court ordered that a child who had been brought to Ireland by the father in defiance of a court order be returned to England. Prior to the child's removal by the father, it had been placed in the care of the County Council by court order. The Court had further ordered that the child should not be removed from the jurisdiction of England and Wales. The Court refused a full hearing on the merits, being satisfied that the County Council did not intend placing the child for adoption. Accordingly, there was no question of the father being denied his fundamental rights under Articles

41 and 42 of the Constitution. In delivering judgment, Finlay P stated that the appropriate forum to determine the future welfare of the child was a court in the country in which it was born and intended to be brought up.

The resolve of the Courts in this jurisdiction to deal with the issue of child abduction by applying the comity of courts doctrine was again evident in the Supreme Court decision in *Saunders v. Mid Western Health Board* (1989). Three infants, who were wards of court and in the care of Hampshire County Council by consent order, were brought to Ireland by their parents. At the request of the County Council, the Mid Western Health Board caused the District Court to issue a warrant authorising the Gardaí to locate the children and, if there was evidence of ill treatment or an offence having being committed against them, to take them to a place of safety. The children were handed over to the health board without any enquiry as to their welfare being conducted. The parents made a complaint to the High Court under Article 40.4.2. of the Constitution that the children were being unlawfully detained by the health board. On the same day, the County Council applied to the Court for the return of the children. The Court acknowledged that the children's detention was not authorised by the District Court warrant. However, the health board was acting at the request and with the authority of the County Council into whose care the children had been committed by final orders of an English court. The children had been unlawfully removed from the care of the County Council in breach of a consent order. Having regard to the degree of comity which exists between the Courts in the relevant jurisdictions, the High Court ordered that the children be returned to the County Council on foot of valid English orders. On appeal Finlay CJ, in upholding the decision of the High Court, stated:

> As a general principle, subject to exceptions in the interests of justice, the comity of the Courts and the question of the welfare of the children requires or demands that disputes and matters affecting their custody and upbringing when they fall to be determined by the Courts, should be determined by the Court of the jurisdiction in which they ordinarily reside and in which they were intended to be brought up.

Regulatory Framework

International law

In 1980, the Hague Conference on Private International Law, recognising the ever-increasing problem posed by the abduction of children across international frontiers, and in an effort to curb the practice and provide for the prompt return of children to their country of residence, adopted the Convention on the Civil Aspects of International Child Abduction. In the same year at Luxembourg, the Council of Europe adopted the European Convention on Recognition and Enforcement of Decisions Concerning Custody of Children and on Restoration of Custody of Children. The Hague Convention has world-wide application, whereas the Luxembourg Convention only applies as between members of the Council of Europe. The purpose of the Hague Convention, which has world-wide application, is to resolve the problem of child abduction by providing for the immediate return of the child. The Luxembourg Convention, which applies to Europe only, is directed to the recognition and enforcement of custody decisions made in other jurisdictions.

Statutory Regulation

Both Conventions were given the force of law in Ireland by the Child Abduction and Enforcement of Custody Orders Act 1991, which came into effect on the 1 October 1991. The principal features of the 1991 Act are as follows:

(1) It designates the High Court as the 'judicial or administrative authority' having jurisdiction to hear and determine applications under both Conventions.

(2) It provides for the setting up of a Central Authority to process applications to return a child removed to the State and applications to secure the return of a child removed from the State.

(3) It requires the Central Authority, on a request made to it by another Central Authority, to furnish information in relation to the social background of a child under the terms of Article 7(d) of the Hague Convention and to make enquiries under Article 15.1.b. of the Luxembourg Convention.

(4) It enables the Court to declare that a removal or retention was wrongful under the Hague Convention or that a removal was unlawful under the Luxembourg Convention.

(5) It sets out the circumstances in which the Court may refuse an application for recognition or enforcement of a custody decision in the State under the Luxembourg Convention.

(6) It empowers the Court to order any person who, it has reason to believe, may have relevant information as to the whereabouts of a child to disclose it to the Court.

(7) It confers extensive powers on a member of the Garda Síochána to detain a child who he reasonably suspects is about to be or is being removed from the State in breach of court orders in relation to custody, access or wardship, and specifies how a child so detained is to be dealt with.

The 1991 Act, in so far as it gives effect to the Hague Convention, successfully withstood a constitutional challenge in *Wadda v. Ireland* (1994). In that case the wife, an Irish citizen, resided with her husband, a Moroccan citizen, and child in the United Kingdom. As a result of marital difficulties, the wife removed the child to Ireland and instituted proceedings to be appointed sole guardian of the child and for custody of the child under the Guardianship of Infants Act 1964. The husband applied for an order returning the child to the United Kingdom under the 1991 Act. The proceedings under the 1964 Act were stayed pending the outcome of the claim under the 1991 Act. The High Court held that the husband was entitled to an order returning the child to the United Kingdom, but put a stay on the order to enable the wife to seek a declaration that the relevant provisions of the 1991 Act were inconsistent with the Constitution, in that they failed to protect the rights of the child by depriving her of an adjudication by an Irish court and failed to protect the rights of the family as the primary and natural unit of society. The Court rejected the wife's claim and held that the personal rights of children under Article 40.3.1. of the Constitution are fully protected and vindicated by Article 20 of the Hague Convention, which enables a court to refuse to return a child where this would not be permitted by the fundamental principles of the law of the State. The Court further held that the Hague Convention did not violate Articles 41 and 42 of the Constitution, as Articles 13 and 20 entitle the Court to refuse to return children where the constitutional rights of parents and children are endangered.

Part II of the 1991 Act gives effect to the Hague Convention, while Part III gives effect to the Luxembourg Convention. The Court having jurisdiction as 'the judicial or administrative authority' for the purposes of both conventions is the High Court — sections 7 and 23 respectively. Sections 8 and 22 provide for the setting up of a Central Authority to discharge the functions of a Central Authority under both Conventions.

Where an application is addressed to the Central Authority under the Hague Convention in respect of a child removed to the State, the Central Authority must take the appropriate action to secure the return of the child — section 9. Where a child has been removed from the State to another contracting State, a person having an interest in the child may apply to the Central Authority to take the appropriate action to secure the return of the child — section 10. Nothing in Part II of the Act shall prevent a person making a direct application to the Court in respect of the breach of rights of custody of, or breach of rights of access to, a child removed from the State — section 11.

Any application for recognition and enforcement of a custody decision in the State under the Luxembourg Convention may be addressed to the Central Authority in the State, and the Central Authority, if satisfied that the application is in order, shall take action or cause action to be taken under the Convention to secure the recognition or enforcement of the decision — section 24. However, an application may be made direct to the Court under the Luxembourg Convention for recognition and enforcement — section 25.

Interim powers are conferred on the Court where an application has been made or is about to be made to it under the Hague Convention or the Luxembourg Convention respectively. The Court can, either of its own motion or on an application made to it *ex parte*, give such directions as it thinks fit for the purpose of securing the welfare of the child concerned, or preventing prejudice to interested persons or changes in the circumstances relevant to the determination of the application — sections 12 and 26.

Where a person involved in proceedings before the Court under the Hague Convention in respect of a child removed to the State, knows that proceedings are already pending before another Court in relation to the custody of the child, that person shall give notice to the other Court accordingly. The other Court, on receipt of such notice, and on notifying the parties to the proceedings, shall stay all further proceedings and notify the Court of the stay — section 13. Similarly, where a person involved in proceedings before the Court under the Luxembourg Convention for the recognition or enforcement of a decision relating to custody made in another contracting State, knows that an application relating to custody is pending in or before any court in the State and such proceedings were commenced before the proceedings, that person shall give notice to the Court accordingly, and the Court may stay all further proceedings until the other proceedings have been determined. Where the custody proceedings in the Court in the State were commenced after the proceedings before the Court under the Luxembourg Convention, that Court shall stay all further proceedings until the proceedings under the Luxembourg Convention have been determined — section 27.

Where the Central Authority is requested by another Central Authority to provide information in relation to the social background of a child under the terms of Article 7(d) of the Hague Convention, the Central Authority may request a report from a probation and welfare officer or a health board in respect of the child. The Central Authority may also request any court which is in possession of a report relating to the child to furnish a copy of such report. Any such request must be complied with — section 14. Section 30 makes similar provision in relation to reports for the purposes of the Luxembourg Convention.

The Court, on the application of any person appearing to have an interest in the matter, can make a declaration that the removal of a child from, or his retention outside the State, was wrongful within the meaning of Article 3 of the Hague Convention. Where the Central Authority is requested by a person who appears to have an interest in the matter or by the Central Authority in another State on his behalf, the Central Authority shall assist such person or Central Authority in making an application under the section — section 15. Sections 16 and 33 deal with the provision of documents relating to custody by courts in the

State to persons wishing to make application under the Hague and Luxembourg Conventions respectively in another contracting State.

Applications for recognition and enforcement of custody decisions are to be made to the Central Authority in the State. Where the Central Authority in the State is satisfied that the Luxembourg Convention applies to the application, it shall take action or cause action to be taken to secure the recognition or enforcement of the decision — section 24. Section 28 sets out the grounds on which an application for recognition and enforcement of a decision relating to custody may be refused under the Luxembourg Convention. A detailed analysis of the appropriate articles of the Convention is contained below.

A decision relating to custody in respect of which an enforcement order has been made for the purposes of the Luxembourg Convention shall have the same force and effect as if it were a judgment of the High Court — section 29. A person who has obtained a decision relating to custody in a contracting State may submit an application for recognition or enforcement of that decision to the Central Authority in any other contracting State — section 32, giving effect to Article 4 of the Luxembourg Convention.

Where a decision in the State of origin relating to custody is varied or revoked in that State, any person having an interest in the matter may apply to the Court for an order varying or revoking the Court's order of recognition or enforcement of that decision. On any such application coming before it, the Court may discharge or vary the order of recognition or enforcement as the case may be — section 31.

Under the terms of section 34, where a court in the State makes a decision in relation to the custody of a child who has been removed from the State, that Court may declare the removal to be unlawful for the purposes of Article 12 of the Luxembourg Convention. The interpretation of section 34 and Article 12 was the subject of a Supreme Court decision in *C. v. B.* (1996), which is considered in more detail later. Section 36 enables the Court to order any person whom it has reason to believe may have relevant information as to the whereabouts of a child to disclose that information to the Court. A failure to comply with an order of the Court under section 36 amounts to contempt of court.

The Hague Convention

The Hague Convention applies to children under the age of sixteen and who are habitually resident in a contracting State before the breach of rights of custody or access. The objects of the Hague Convention as set out in Article 1 are:

(a) to secure the prompt return of children wrongfully removed to or retained in any contracting State; and
(b) to ensure that rights of custody and of access under the law of one contracting State are effectively respected in the other contracting States.

The underlying policy of the Hague Convention was succinctly summarised by Waite J in the English case of *P. v. P. (Minors) (Child Abduction)* (1992) (cited with approval by Keane J in *Wadda v. Ireland*) as follows:

> The whole jurisdiction under the Convention is, by its nature and purpose, peremptory. Its underlying assumption is that the courts of all its signatory countries are equally capable of ensuring a fair hearing to the parties and a skilled and humane evaluation of the issues of child welfare involved. Its underlying purpose is to ensure stability for children, by putting a brisk end to the efforts of parents to have their children's future decided where they want and when they want, by removing them from their country of residence to another jurisdiction chosen arbitrarily by the absconding parent.

In deciding that Spain was the proper forum to determine the issues of custody and access, Denham J, delivering the judgment of the Supreme Court in *P. v. B.* (1995) said that 'the spirit of the Convention is to protect children from the harmful effects of wrongful removal or retention from and to return them promptly to, the country of their habitual residence'.

The application of the Hague Convention has proved to be a fertile source of litigation both here and in the United Kingdom. The central provisions of the Convention are to be found in Articles 3, 12, 13 and 20, and it is these Articles that have given rise to the bulk of the litigation in both jurisdictions.

Article 3

The removal or retention of a child is to be considered wrongful where:

(a) it is in breach of rights of custody attributed to a person, an institution or any other body, either jointly or alone, under the law of the State in which the child was habitually resident immediately before the removal or retention; and

(b) at the time of the removal or retention those rights were actually exercised, either jointly or alone, or would have been so exercised but for the removal or retention.

The rights of custody mentioned in sub-paragraph (a) above, may arise in particular by operation of law or by reason of a judicial or administrative decision, or by reason of an agreement having legal effect under the law of the State.

Habitually Resident

The term 'habitually resident' is not defined in the Hague Convention. The Law Reform Commission, in their report on Domicile and Habitual Residence as Connecting Factors in the Conflict of Laws (L.R.C. 1983) (Dec 83), recommended that a person's habitual residence should be determined having regard to the centre of his personal, social and economic interests. The Supreme Court had to determine the issue of a child's habitual residence in *C.K. v. C.K.* (1993). Denham J referred to the English case of *V. v. B. (A Minor) (Abduction)* (1991) which equates 'habitual residence' with 'ordinary residence`, and said that even if the test is not similar to 'ordinary residence', it appeared to her on the facts of the case that the children were ordinarily and habitually resident in Australia. They had been there by agreement since 1989 until their removal on the 30 September 1992. It was originally planned that the parties would stay until 1996. The children were settled in primary school, in a home which the parties had purchased. The learned judge had no doubt that they were habitually resident in New South Wales, Australia.

In *Z.S-A. v. S.T.* (1996) the High Court held that the child was not habitually resident in England at the time of its removal to Ireland. Laffoy J was guided by the principles enunciated by Brandon LJ in *C. v. S.* (1990), to the effect that the expression 'habitually resident' 'is not to be treated as a term of art with some special meaning', but is to be understood 'according to the ordinary and natural meaning of the two words which it contains'. It is a question of fact to be decided by reference to all the circumstances of any particular case. Brandon LJ went on to point out that there is a significant difference between a person ceasing to be habitually resident in one country and his subsequently becoming habitually resident in another country. He went on to say that:

> A person may cease to be habitually resident in country 'A' in a single day if he or she leaves with a settled intention not to return to it but to take up long term residence in country 'B' instead. Such a person cannot, however, become habitually resident in country 'B' in a single day. An appreciable period of time and a settled intention will be necessary to enable him or her to become so. During that appreciable period of time the person will have ceased to be habitually resident in country 'A' but not yet have become habitually resident in country 'B'.

That the 'habitual residence' of a child is not governed by the same rigid rules of dependency as applied under the law of domicile is clear from the decision *In re C.M.* (1999). The case involved a claim by the unmarried Irish mother of a three year old girl who had lived all her life in Spain, but as an Irish citizen, to have the child's future decided by the Irish courts. In deciding that the Spanish courts should decide the child's future, Mc Guinness J rejected the mother's contention that the 'habitual residence' of a child born to an unmarried woman was that of its mother and followed that of the mother if she took up residence in another country.

Rights of Custody

Rights of custody are defined by Article 5 of the Hague Convention as including rights relating to the care of the child, and, in particular, the right to determine the child's place of residence. The person seeking the return of the child must establish that he exercised rights of custody at the time of the removal or retention. The case law clearly indicates that, except in rare cases, the issue of custody should be determined in the jurisdiction of the child's habitual residence (see *A.S. v. P.S.* (1998)). The meaning of the phrase 'rights of custody' has been considered by the Courts in Ireland and the United Kingdom. In the English case of *Re B (a Minor) (Abduction)* (1994) Waite J said:

> The phrase had to be construed in the widest possible sense so as to give effect to the objective of the Hague Convention which was to spare children who were already suffering the effects of a breakdown of their parents relationship further disruption.

Even where the phrase is given its widest possible meaning, a court is still faced with difficulties in deciding whether rights of custody exist and were being exercised at the time of the removal or retention. The Supreme Court was urged to give a novel meaning to the term 'rights of custody' in *H.I. v. M.G.* (1999), where it was submitted that the term included inchoate rights of custody. The plaintiff, an Egyptian national and US citizen, and the defendant, a British citizen, went through a ceremony of marriage according to the Islamic rite in New York in 1991. The marriage was not recognised either in New York or the USA. A son was born of the union. The defendant acknowledged the plaintiff as the natural father of the child. The child, a US citizen, lived with his parents in New York for the first five and a half years of his life. The defendant left the plaintiff, taking the child with her, at the end of 1996. She brought the child to Ireland in February 1997. Prior to her departure from the USA, the defendant instituted proceedings in New York seeking custody of the child in which she named the plaintiff as the putative father. The plaintiff also instituted proceedings seeking visitation rights. On 26 February, the New York Court made an order for the production of the child in Court on 26 March 1997.

The plaintiff instituted proceedings in the High Court whereby he sought the return of the child to New York under article 12 of the Hague Convention. The High Court had to decide as a preliminary issue whether the plaintiff had any cause of action under the Convention. The Court found that the plaintiff had not established that, at the date of the removal, he had any established rights of custody under New York law. Under New York law, the mother of a non-marital child had sole rights of custody of the child until such time as paternity was established by court order or a paternity agreement was approved by the Court. Accordingly, the plaintiff did not have rights of custody by operation of law or by court order, as required by Article 3 of the Convention. However, the fact that both parties had acknowledged paternity of the child by the proceedings before the New York Court was significant. It was also significant that the defendant had conceded in evidence that the establishment of paternity by the plaintiff would be a mere formality. In the circumstances, the Court concluded that approval would have been given to the paternity agreement by the New York Court had the defendant not removed the child from the jurisdiction of the State of New York. Although the plaintiff did not have a legal right of custody, he still had rights under the Convention, namely, the inchoate right to have the paternity agreement approved under the law of the requesting State, thereby establishing a *prima facie* right to custody. The High Court held that the removal was in breach of the rights of custody of the plaintiff within the meaning of Article 3. On appeal, the Supreme Court rejected the finding of the trial judge, and held that the term 'rights of custody' did not embrace inchoate rights of custody.

Article 12

> Where a child has been wrongfully removed or retained in terms of Article 3 and, at the date of the commencement of the proceedings before the judicial or administrative authority of the contracting State where the child is, a period of less than one year has elapsed from the date of the wrongful removal or retention, the authority concerned shall order the return of the child forthwith.

> The judicial or administrative authority, even where the proceedings have been commenced after the expiration of the period of one year referred to in the preceding paragraph, shall also order the return of the child, unless it is demonstrated that the child is now settled in its new environment.

> Where the judicial or administrative authority in the requested State has reason to believe that the child has been taken to another State, it may stay the proceedings or dismiss the application for the return of the child.

The purport and effect of Article 12 is to ensure the prompt return of the child, where there has been a finding of wrongful removal or retention under Article 3. Where less than a year has elapsed from the date of removal or retention, the child should be returned forthwith. Even where more than a year has elapsed, the Court must still order the return of the child, unless it is shown that the child is now settled in its new environment. Accordingly, the powers contained in Article 12 are both mandatory and discretionary, depending on the amount of time that has elapsed since the date of removal or retention.

In *M.D.P. v. S.M.B.* (1998) the High Court held that the onus of proving that 'the child is now settled in its new environment' under Article 12 is on the person resisting the return of the child to the country of its habitual residence. In the course of her judgment, Laffoy J reviewed English and American cases which indicate that children should be returned to the country of their habitual residence unless the person resisting their return can establish a degree of settlement which is more than mere adjustment to surroundings. The word 'now' refers to the date of the commencement of the proceedings, and not the date of the hearing. The word 'settled' involves a physical element of relating to, being established in, a community and an environment, and an emotional element denoting security and stability. The 'new environment' must encompass place, home, school, people, friends. The learned judge concluded that the evidence adduced by the mother did not go much further than indicating mere adjustment to surroundings by the child. It did not indicate the element of permanence which the word 'settled' connotes.

Delay

Delay in prosecuting a claim under the Hague Convention is not of itself a defence. In *M.D.P. v. S.M.B.* Laffoy J said that it was well-settled in this jurisdiction that applications under the Convention must be initiated and processed with due expedition. However, the Convention did not prescribe a time limit within which applications must be commenced. She rejected the submission by counsel for the defendant that delay should be treated as a 'stand alone' defence. While accepting that delay is a component of other defences available under the Convention (for example, the discretionary limb of Article 12 and acquiescence under Article 13), the learned judge emphasised that delay, on its own, cannot be determinative. On appeal, the Supreme Court reversed the decision of Laffoy J who had ordered that the child be returned to Spain. In deciding that the child could remain in Ireland with her mother, Denham J said that the Supreme Court was basing its decision largely on the fact that there had been long and inappropriate delay, amounting to acquiescence, on the part of the father in commencing proceedings against the mother in the Irish Courts.

Since the objective of the Hague Convention, as set out in the Preamble, is to ensure the 'prompt return' of abducted children to the country of their habitual residence, the Supreme Court was critical of unreasonable delay in two recent cases. In *A.S. v. P.S.* (1998) Denham J pointed out that the proceedings had commenced in October 1996 and only concluded in March 1998, and remarked: 'It is entirely unsatisfactory to have a delay such as exists in this case. It defeats in part the purpose of the Hague Convention. Parties and professionals in these cases have a duty to proceed with expedition'. In *K. v. K.* (1998) Denham J again stressed that 'it is necessary to ensure that these summary proceedings proceed urgently. Only such a process will meet the Convention and protect the children'.

Removal and Retention — Mutually Exclusive Concepts

A person seeking the return of a child to the jurisdiction of its habitual residence under Article 12 of the Hague Convention must base a claim on either the 'wrongful removal' or 'wrongful retention' of the child. In *Z.S-A. v. S.T.* (1996) Laffoy J endorsed the finding of Brandon LJ in *Re H. and Anor. (Minors)* (1991), to the effect that removal and retention are mutually exclusive concepts. He reasoned that retention is not a continuing state of affairs but an event occurring on a specific occasion. Removal occurs when a child is taken from the State of its habitual residence across the frontier of that State, whereas retention occurs where a child, which has previously been for a limited period of time outside the State of its habitual residence, is not returned to that State on the expiry of such limited period. He felt that his interpretation of the Convention was strongly supported by the fact that, throughout the Convention, removal and retention are linked by the word 'or' rather than the word 'and', which indicates that each is intended to be a real alternative to the other. The facts of *Z.S-A. v. S.T.* show that the defendant took the children from England to Ireland with the consent of the plaintiff, following the breakdown of the parties' marriage. The plaintiff subsequently visited and stayed for a holiday with the defendant and children in Ireland, at the end of which period he made it clear to the defendant that he did not wish the children to continue to reside in Ireland. The plaintiff claimed the return of one of the children under Article 12, alleging that the child had been wrongfully removed to and retained in Ireland. Laffoy J held that, on the basis of the reasoning of Brandon LJ, there was no evidence that the child was wrongfully removed from England by the defendant, and treated the plaintiff's claim for the return of the child under Article 12 as being based on the wrongful retention of the child. On the basis that retention under the Convention is an event occurring on a specific occasion, the plaintiff's claim as formulated did not offend this concept of retention.

Article 13

> Notwithstanding the provisions of the preceding Article, the judicial or administrative authority of the requested State is not bound to order the return of the child if the person, institution or other body which opposes its return establishes that-
> (a) the person, institution or other body having the care of the person of the child was not actually exercising the custody rights at the time of removal or retention, or had consented to or subsequently acquiesced in the removal or retention;

or

(b) there is a grave risk that his return would expose the child to physical or psychological harm or otherwise place the child in an intolerable situation.

The judicial or administrative authority may also refuse to order the return of the child if it finds that the child objects to being returned and has attained an age and degree of maturity at which it is appropriate to take account of its views.

In considering the circumstances referred to in this Article, the judicial and administrative authorities shall take into account the information relating to the social background of the child provided by the Central Authority or other competent authority of the child's habitual residence.

The Preamble to the Hague Convention stresses that 'the interests of children are of paramount importance in matters relating to their custody'. It cannot be in the best interests of children to abduct them across State borders. It is for this reason that the mandatory nature of the Convention dictates that, except in rare cases, children's best interests are to be determined by Courts of the jurisdiction of their habitual residence. The rare cases where a Court may refuse to order the return of a child abducted across an international frontier are contained in Articles 13 and 20 of the Convention.

Under the terms of Article 13, the Court in the requested State 'is not bound to order the return of the child' in the exceptional cases outlined in the article. In effect, the Court is permitted, but not required, to refuse to order the return of the child in those circumstances. In delivering his judgment in *B.B. v. J.B.* (1998) Keane J pointed out that the exceptions allowed by Article 13 are permissive, not mandatory. The learned judge referred to Article 18 of the Convention which allows a Court of the requested State to order that the child be returned, even where the person opposing the application establishes that the case comes within one of those exceptions. Article 13(a) empowers the Court in the requested State to refuse to order the return of a child if the person opposing the return can establish that the person seeking the return 'was not actually exercising the custody rights at the time of removal or retention'. The meaning of the phrase 'custody rights', and the question whether those rights were actually being exercised at the time of removal or retention, has already been considered earlier in the chapter when discussing the effect of Article 3. It is a defence to an application for the return of a child to the country of its habitual residence if the person resisting the return can establish that the person seeking the return 'had consented to or subsequently acquiesced in the removal or retention' (Article 13(a)).

Consent

The law on consent was the subject of a comprehensive review by the Supreme Court in *B.B. v. J.B.* (1998). The child the subject of the proceedings was born in England in 1994 to an Irish father and English mother. Following the breakdown of the marriage, the mother left the child in the father's custody on the condition that she could have access to the child where possible. The father returned to Ireland with the child in 1996. Having considered the evidence, which included a document signed by the mother in the nature of a custody agreement and a letter written by her to the father, the trial judge concluded that there was no wrongful removal and refused the mother's application for the return of the child to England. The mother appealed to the Supreme Court on the basis that the trial judge erred in holding that there was no wrongful removal of the child and in holding that the mother had consented to the removal. The mother also contended that even if the removal had been with consent, the trial judge erred in not exercising a discretion as to whether the child should be returned to England. The Supreme Court upheld the finding of the trial judge on the matter of consent, but allowed the appeal on the ground that the trial judge erred in not exercising his discretion. The following principles emerge from the decision of the Court:

(1) The removal of a child from the place of its habitual residence constitutes a *prima facie* breach of the custody rights of the parent who continues to reside in that place.
(2) The burden of proving that there was consent to the removal falls on the person who alleges that there was consent.
(3) Where there has been consent to the removal under the terms of Article 13, there is no obligation on the Court to order the return of the child.
(4) Even where there has been consent to the removal or retention of the child, the Court retains a discretion under Article 13 as to whether to return the child. This discretion is not limited by Articles 3 or 12.

In *M.D. v. A.T.D.* (1998) the High Court had to consider the situation where a mother refuses to return with her child to the country of habitual residence on foot of an order made under Article 12 of the Hague Convention. O'Sullivan J found that the father had consented to the mother taking their son to Ireland, but, in reliance on the decision of the Supreme Court in *B.B. v. J.B.*, exercised his discretion to order the return of the child to the place of his habitual residence in England. The evidence revealed a history of physical violence between the parties, and that the father had been 'verbally abusive in a racist way' to his wife's daughter, whom the couple had adopted. The daughter, who was almost sixteen years of age at the date of the application, had accompanied the mother when she took the son to Ireland initially. The daughter was not prepared to return to

England in any circumstances, and the mother would not leave her, even if the Court ordered the return of her four and a half year old son to England. O'Sullivan J, having been invited by counsel for the father to adopt the approach of the Court of Appeal in *Re C (A Minor)(Abduction)* (1989), considered the weight to be attached to the refusal by a mother to return with a young child in the context of the Hague Convention, and said that it seemed to him 'that a Court should be astute not to permit an abducting parent to set the Convention at naught by refusing to travel with a returning child'. Having considered the threat to the welfare of the son of returning him to England, the learned judge said that a returning order would not expose the child to a grave risk of psychological harm in the terms of Article 13(b) of the Convention, and in exercising his discretion, considered 'that the balance favours the making of a returning order'.

Acquiescence

The meaning to be attributed to the term acquiescence for the purposes of Article 13 of the Convention has been considered in a number of Supreme Court cases, most notably *P. v. B.* (1995), *K. v. K.* (1998) and *A.S. v. P.S.* (1998). In *P. v. B.* Denham J said that acquiescence for the purposes of Article 13 meant acceptance of the removal or retention of the child. It is a matter to be decided on the circumstances of each case. She cited with approval the following passage from the judgment of Waite J in *W. v. W. (Abduction: Acquiescence)* (1993):

> Acquiescence means acceptance. It may be active arising from express words or conduct, or passive arising by inference from silence or inactivity. It must be real in the sense that the parent must be informed of his or her general right of objection, but precise knowledge of legal rights and remedies and specifically the remedy under the Hague Convention is not necessary. It must be ascertained on a survey of all relevant circumstances, viewed objectively in the round. It is in every case a question of degree to be answered by considering whether the parent has conducted himself in a way that would be inconsistent with him later seeking a summary order for the child's return.

The facts of *P. v. B.* show that the mother brought the child from Spain, the country of its habitual residence, to Ireland without notifying the father. On learning that the mother had taken the child to Ireland, the father acceded to the mother's request to give her some time to consider the situation, believing that in due course she would return to Spain. In all the circumstances of the case and applying the correct test to the evidence, the Court held that there was no acquiescence by the father.

In *K. v. K.* the mother took two children from Scotland, the place of their habitual residence, to Ireland without the father's consent. The parties' relationship was turbulent and the mother alleged that the father had been abusive towards her in the presence of the children. The Court held that the removal was wrongful. The mother resisted the children's return to Scotland on the basis of the father's acquiescence. As evidence of the father's acquiescence, she referred to letters written by him containing expressions of regret for his conduct towards her. In these letters, he expressed his love for his wife and children and indicated that he would not go to court. The mother also referred to his application to the District Court in Ireland for custody, his delay in starting the proceedings, his application for a divorce in Scotland and his request for a transfer to Ireland in his job. The Court was not satisfied that the letters, the general tone of which was to seek reconciliation, and his actions, evidenced acquiescence by the father. In her judgment, Denham J took the opportunity of reviewing the law on acquiescence, and expressed her agreement with recent English and American cases on the concept of acquiescence, which emphasise the necessity to ensure a common international approach to the interpretation of the Hague Convention. She stated as follows:

> Consequently, rather than adopt a formalistic approach, I am satisfied that the matter of interpreting the term 'acquiescence' under the Hague Convention should be approached on a strongly factual basis with a common sense interpretation of the term applied. There should not be an analysis by way of applying principles of national law.

The High Court considered the defence of acquiescence in *M.D.P. v. S.M.B.* (1998), the first case in Ireland involving a second abduction. The first abduction was the subject of proceedings in *P. v. B.* (1995), when the Supreme Court ordered that, subject to fulfilment of certain undertakings given by the father, the child should be returned to Spain. The mother duly returned to Spain with the child for the Spanish Court to determine the issues of custody and access. While the case was pending before the Spanish Court, and in defiance of an order of the Court that the child should not leave Spain, the mother took the child to Ireland in October 1996. The father did not initiate proceedings under the Hague Convention for the return of the child until May 1998. Having reviewed the law on Article 13(b), Laffoy J held that despite the inordinate delay in bringing the proceedings, the mother had not established that the conduct of the father unequivocally showed that he had led the mother to believe that he was not asserting or going to assert his right to invoke the Hague Convention. The fact that the mother continued to pursue her allegations of sexual abuse of the child against the father in the criminal courts in Spain, and that almost immediately on her return she instructed her solicitor in Ireland and set about assembling the evidence to defend a claim for the return of the child, indicated that she was under no misapprehension as to the father's likely action. On appeal, the

Supreme Court overruled the decision of Laffoy J. In deciding that the child could remain in Ireland with her mother, Denham J held that the delay on the father's part in commencing proceedings in Ireland under the1991 Act was long and inappropriate and amounted to acquiescence.

Grave Risk of Physical or Psychological Harm

The so-called grave risk defence arises under Article 13(b) of the Hague Convention. To successfully invoke this defence, the person opposing the return of the child must satisfy the Court that 'there is a grave risk that his or her return would expose the child to physical or psychological harm or otherwise place the child in an intolerable situation'. There is a considerable body of case law on the topic in Ireland and in other signatory States of the Convention, which shows a consistent approach in applying Article 13(b). Laffoy J described the defence in *M.D.P. v. S.M.B.* (1998) as follows:

> It is recognised as a rare exception to the fundamental principle that a child who has been wrongfully removed or retained should be returned to the State of his habitual residence. It has been recognised that the defence may only succeed in very exceptional circumstances.

The Supreme Court had the opportunity to consider the *grave risk* defence for the first time in *C.K. v. C.K.* (1993). Following the breakdown of the parties' marriage, the father took the two children to Ireland from Australia, the place of their habitual residence. The mother had formed a relationship with another man, G.W., and she told the father she intended to divorce him. The father was upset at the proposed divorce and concerned at the children living in the house with their mother and G.W. as a 'live-in-lover'. In opposing the mother's application for the return of the children to Australia, the father submitted that the return of the children would expose them to grave risk, in that the presence of G.W. in the house with the mother would be morally and/or psychologically bad for the children. On the basis of an undertaking given by the mother that G.W. would not live with her or the children on their return to Australia pending the completion of the custody proceedings, the Court held that there was no evidence that the children would be subjected to physical or psychological harm if they were returned to Australia. The test to be applied, according to Denham J, is whether there is grave risk that the return of the children would expose them to physical or psychological harm or otherwise place them in an intolerable situation. The test must be read as a whole. Not only must the risk be a weighty one, it must be one of substantial, and not trivial, psychological harm.

In *K. v. K.* (1998) the mother pleaded the grave risk defence. She alleged that the father was violent to her and harassed her in front of the children. The High Court found no evidence of a grave risk of physical or psychological harm to the children or that they would be placed in an intolerable situation if returned to

Scotland. The Supreme Court dismissed the mother's appeal. The facts established by the mother did not show that the children would suffer grave risk from the father. The Court was satisfied that he was a loving parent. The conflict in the family was between the parents. As the divorce application of the father was pending in Scotland and the habitual residence of the children was Scottish, the issues of custody and access and all other family issues should be determined in that jurisdiction. In her judgment Denham J stated:

> The grave risk or intolerable situation envisaged may arise because of the relationship, or lack of it, between parents. If the conflict can be abated and undertakings and circumstances created to protect the children prior to the Court Orders in the requesting country then the policy of the Convention to return children to the Country of their habitual residence will be met. Also, the particular children affected by the Convention in a case will have their interest protected.

Even where there is evidence of a grave risk of harm to the child, the Court still retains a discretion to order the return of the child to the country of its habitual residence. This is in keeping with the underlying philosophy of the Hague Convention and the heavy burden of proof required to meet Article 13(b). The Court considering the application for the return of the child is entitled to consider whether the risk of harm can be reduced or eliminated by undertakings or by reliance on court procedures in the requesting State.

Undertakings

Undertakings have been sought and given in cases in Ireland and other contracting States. The following passage from the judgment of Denham J in *P. v. B.* (1995) sets out the law in relation to undertakings:

> I am satisfied that undertakings may be given by a party to proceedings under the 1991 Act and accepted by the court. They are entirely consistent with the 1991 Act and the Hague Convention, they are for the welfare of the child during the transition from one jurisdiction to another. Undertakings may be of particular significance to very young children.

In *A.S. v. P.S.* (1998) there was evidence before the Court that the father had sexually abused one of the children. The mother resisted the return of the two children to England by pleading the grave risk defence. The Supreme Court held that the trial judge erred in law in determining that there was a grave risk without considering the option of the children living in the family home with the mother, in the absence of the father, pending custody hearings. The grave risk was the presence of the father in the family home, and not the family home itself or the

English jurisdiction. The Court ordered the return of the children to England on foot of undertakings by the father, one of them being to vacate the family home to enable the mother and children to live there pending and during the custody hearing. In *K. v. K.* (1998) Denham J cited with approval the following passage from the judgment of La Forest of the Canadian Supreme Court in *Thompson v. Thompson* (1994):

> Through the use of undertakings, the requirement of Article 12 of the Convention that 'the authority concerned shall order the return of the child forthwith' can be complied with, the wrongful actions of the removing party are not condoned, the long-term best interests of the child are left for a determination by the court of the child's habitual residence, and any short-term harm to the child is ameliorated.

The use and effectiveness of undertakings depends on there being procedures for their recognition and enforcement in the Courts of the country to which the child is being returned. While *P. v. B.* (1995) is clear authority for the acceptance of undertakings, that case does not deal with the question of their enforcement by the foreign court. In *L.P. v. M.N.P.* (1998) McGuinness J had to rely on English decisions where the question of the reciprocal enforcement of undertakings was considered. The learned judge cited an extract from the judgment of Waite LJ in *Re M (Abduction Non-Convention Country)* (1995) to the effect that judges in one country are entitled and bound to assume that Courts in another country will take the same serious view of a failure to honour undertakings given to a court (of any jurisdiction). However, this dictum of Waite LJ does not address the problem that the common law concept of undertakings may not be part of the particular legal codes of the States of mainland Europe. *L.P. v. M.N.P.* involved an application to the Court by the father, an Italian citizen, for an order for the return of his daughter to Italy, the country of the child's habitual residence. The mother resisted the application by pleading the grave risk defence. At the request of the Court, the Central Authority in Ireland, in accordance with the terms of Article 7 of the Hague Convention, sought information from the Central Authority in Italy on the recognition and enforcement of undertakings in that country. However, the information forthcoming from the Italian Central Authority did not clarify the matter to a degree that would have enabled McGuinness J to consider the matter further. She stated that this problem will have to be resolved by communication and discussion between Central Authorities in the respective States that are signatories to the Hague Convention.

Article 13 of the Convention also allows the Court to 'refuse to order the return of the child if it finds that the child objects to being returned and has attained an age and degree of maturity at which it is appropriate to take account of its views'. In *C.K. v. C.K.* (1993) the father of the children requested the Court to hear the eldest child, who was almost eight years old, arguing that he was a bright mature child. Denham J spoke to the boy in chambers and found him to be intelligent, articulate and sensitive. She was satisfied as a result of her interview that while the boy would be happy to live in Ireland with his father, he would be equally happy to live in Australia with his mother. The High Court concluded in *L.P. v. M.N.P.* that a child's own view should only be taken into account where the Court was satisfied of the child's maturity, intelligence and ability to understand matters. As the child the subject of the proceedings in that case was very young (six years old at the commencement of the proceedings), the Court felt there was nothing to be gained in interviewing her.

Article 20

> The return of the child under the provisions of Article 12 may be refused if this would not be permitted by the fundamental principles of the requested State relating to the protection of human rights and fundamental freedoms.

Under the provisions of Article 20 of the Convention, the Court can refuse to return a child to the country of its habitual residence where its return would be contrary to the guarantees relating to the protection of human rights contained in the Constitution. The Supreme Court held in *C.K. v. C.K.* (1993) that Article 20 did not require, on the facts of the case, that there should be an inquiry into the welfare of the children under the Guardianship of Infants Act 1964 in addition to the jurisdiction set out in the 1991 Act. Article 12 requires the Court to order the return of the children unless it would be in breach of Articles 13 or 20 to do so. There was no evidence before the Court that a return of the children to Australia would be in breach of their constitutional rights. In *L.P. v. M.N.P.* (1998) the mother resisted the return of the child to Italy in reliance on Articles 13 and 20 of the Convention. She argued that on her return the child would be placed in the custody of her grandparents on foot of an interim custody order of the Italian Court. In the course of the hearing, Mc Guinness J was concerned that the return of the child would remove her from the custody of her mother for an indefinite and lengthy period without the possibility of appeal, in breach of the constitutional rights of the child as a 'fundamental principle of the State'. However, on the last day of the trial the learned judge was informed that the Italian Court had varied its interim custody order and had granted custody to the mother. This allayed any fears that the judge had that an order returning the child might be in breach of Article 20.

The Luxembourg Convention

The preamble to the Luxembourg Convention of the Council of Europe acknowledges that the welfare of children can be better protected if decisions concerning the custody of a child are widely recognised and enforced. The Convention has put in place a mechanism whereby the custody of children, which has been arbitrarily interrupted by their improper removal across an international frontier, can be promptly restored. The purpose of the Luxembourg Convention is to provide a mechanism for the recognition and enforcement of foreign custody orders, without the need for a court in the State addressed to consider the substantive issues involved. In *A.S. v. E.H. and M.H.* (1996) Budd J put the matter rather succinctly when he stated: 'The Luxembourg Convention sets its face against the foreign decision being reviewed as to its substance'.

The main provisions of the Luxembourg Convention can be summarised as follows:

(1) The Convention enables a person who has obtained a decision relating to custody of or access to a child under the age of sixteen years in one contracting State to have that decision recognised and enforced in another contracting State.
(2) Applications for recognition and enforcement are made through the Central Authority in the State addressed.
(3) The original decision relating to the child may not be reviewed by the Court to whom the application for recognition and enforcement is made.
(4) However, the Convention makes provision for the refusal of recognition and enforcement where the proceedings are defective, the decision is incompatible with a decision which has already been recognised, or the child has insufficient connection with the State in which the decision was made.
(5) Recognition may also be refused where the decision is manifestly incompatible with fundamental principles relating to the family and children in the State addressed, or where by reason of a change in circumstances, including the passage of time, it is manifestly no longer in accordance with the child's welfare.
(6) However, if the improper removal of the child occurred less than six months before the application for recognition and enforcement of the decision, return is virtually mandated by the Convention.

Decisions Relating to Custody

A decision relating to custody is defined in Article 1 of the Convention as 'a decision of an authority in so far as it relates to the care of the person of the child, including the right to decide on the place of his residence, or to the right of access to him'. An 'improper removal' for the purposes of Article 1 means the removal of a child across an international frontier in breach of a decision relating to his custody, and also includes:

(i) the failure to return a child across an international frontier at the end of a period of the exercise of the right of access to this child or at the end of any other temporary stay in a territory other than that where the custody is exercised;

(ii) a removal which is subsequently declared unlawful within the meaning of Article 12.

Restoration of Custody

Article 8 requires the Central Authority of the State addressed to take the necessary steps forthwith to restore the custody of a child, where the child and his parents had as their sole nationality the nationality of the State of origin and the child's habitual residence was in that State, and the request is made within six months of the improper removal. Where the request is made within six months of the improper removal, the recognition and enforcement of a decision relating to custody cannot be refused unless a reservation has been made by the contracting State addressed pursuant to Article 17. Ireland has in fact entered a reservation in section 28 of the 1991 Act, to enable an application for recognition and enforcement of a decision relating to custody to be refused on any of the grounds specified in paragraphs (a) to (d) of Article 10.1 as follows:

(a) where the effects of a decision are manifestly incompatible with the fundamental principles of the law of the State addressed;
(b) where, as a result of a change in circumstances, including the passage of time, it is no longer in accordance with the child's welfare. (In this case, Article 15 requires that the child's wishes be ascertained, unless this is impracticable having regard to the child's age and understanding);
(c) where the child has close links with the State addressed; or
(d) where there exists a conflicting decision given in the State addressed or in a third State which is enforceable in the State addressed.

It was contended by the mother in *R.J. v. M.R.* (1994) that an order returning a non-marital child to England, so that the father could exercise a right of access to the child, would be manifestly incompatible with the fundamental principles of Irish law, and contrary to the welfare of the child. The Supreme Court, taking into account the improved position of the natural father of a non-marital child under Irish law since the enactment of the Status of Children Act 1987, and the fact that in this case the father was not seeking custody, rejected the mother's contention and ordered the return of the child to England. Before doing so, however, the Court put safeguards in place to ensure compliance with its order.

Absence of Close Links with State of Origin

Where the close links of the child and his parents with the State of origin do not exist, but where the request to restore the custody of the child is made within six months of the improper removal, Article 9 allows the refusal of the request where the decision was given in the absence of the defendant or his legal representative, and (a) the defendant was not given sufficient notice of the proceedings to arrange a defence and this was not due to him concealing his whereabouts, or (b) the authority giving the decision did not have the necessary jurisdiction based on habitual residence. In *S.D. v. R.S.* (1996) the High Court refused to order the return of two children to England who had been brought to Ireland by the mother. The mother had only been given two days notice of the proceedings before the English court, which declared that the removal from the English jurisdiction was unlawful pursuant to the Luxembourg Convention. Costello P held that there had been no proper service of the proceedings on the mother under the terms of the Convention, as the father had been aware of the mother's whereabouts and had not given her adequate time to arrange legal representation or attend the proceedings.

The importance of strict compliance with the provisions of the 1991 Act and the Luxembourg Convention is evident from the decision of the High Court in *P.M. v. V.M. (orse V.B. or V.McK.)* (1997), where Kinlen J felt himself bound by the decision of Costello P in *S.D. v. R.S.*. In holding that the proceedings were not in accordance with the Luxembourg Convention, Kinlen J said:

> It is not a concern of this Court as to decide which is the most suitable household or who is the most suitable person to look after this unfortunate child who is, or was, suffering from symptoms of heroin withdrawal on his birth. This Court is only concerned with whether the strict requirements of the Abduction Convention are in reality complied with.

Incompatibility of Custody Decisions

Article 9 also permits refusal where the decision is incompatible with a custody decision which became enforceable in Ireland before the removal of the child, unless the child was habitually resident in the requesting State for one year prior to the removal. Where a request for recognition and enforcement is not made within six months of the improper removal, the grounds of refusal set out in Articles 9 and 10 may be invoked, without the need for a contracting State to enter a reservation invoking those grounds.

No Decision on Custody at Time of Removal

Article 12 deals with cases where there has been no court decision on custody at the time of improper removal. In effect, the Article provides that where there is no enforceable decision as to the custody of a child in a contracting State at the time of his improper removal, the provisions of the Luxembourg Convention shall apply to any subsequent decision relating to the custody of the child and declaring his removal unlawful given in a contracting State at the request of an interested person. In *C. v. B.* (1996) the Supreme Court held that, for the purposes of section 34 of the 1991 Act and Article 12, a court only had jurisdiction to declare that a child had been unlawfully removed from the State in circumstances where that Court had already made a decision in relation to the custody of that child. The District Court had made a decision granting custody to the father subsequent to the mother removing the child to England. The father subsequently obtained an order from the High Court declaring that the child had been unlawfully removed from the State. The Supreme Court ruled that, in the circumstances of the case, the High Court had no jurisdiction to grant the declaration in question.

In resisting the return of a child to England in the case of *A.S. v. E.H. and M.H.* (1996), the defendants relied on the decision in *C. v. B.* It is interesting to note that Budd J was prepared to rely on the comity of courts doctrine to order the child's return where there were procedural defects in the plaintiff's application which would preclude the Court relying on the Luxembourg Convention. Budd J cited with approval the judgment of Finlay CJ in *Saunders v. Mid-Western Health Board* (1989) as authority for the Court's taking cognisance of the comity of courts doctrine. The approach of Budd J was perfectly in accord with Article 19, which provides as follows:

> This Convention shall not exclude the possibility of relying on any other international instrument in force between the State of origin and the State addressed or on any other law of the State addressed not derived from an international agreement for the purpose of obtaining recognition or enforcement of a decision.

Procedure on Request for Recognition or Enforcement

Article 13 lays down the procedure to be followed when a request is made for recognition or enforcement of a decision relating to custody in another contracting State. It provides that the request must be accompanied by the following documents: a) a document authorising the Central Authority in the State addressed to act for the applicant; b) an authenticated copy of the decision; c) where a decision was given in the absence of the defendant or his legal representative, proof that the defendant was duly served with the proceedings; d) a document which establishes that, in accordance with the law of the State of origin, the decision is enforceable; e) if possible, a statement indicating the whereabouts of the child in the State addressed; f) proposals as to how the custody of the child should be restored. In refusing the return of two children to England in *S.D. v. R.S.* (1996), Costello P held, *inter alia*, that the plaintiff had not satisfied the Court through the production of documentary evidence, as he was required to do under Article 13.1.c., that the defendant had been duly served with the originating summons or any other document prior to the decision for which recognition and enforcement was sought. Non-compliance with the requirements of Article 13 was again in issue in *P.M. v. V.M. (orse V.B. or V.McK.)* (1998) where the Supreme Court, in upholding the decision of Kinlen J in the High Court, refused to order the return of the child to England. The Court held that the request for recognition or enforcement of the English Court's decision was not accompanied by a document which established that the defendant was served with the document that instituted the proceedings or an equivalent document.

Preventing Abduction
Section 11 of the Guardianship of Infants Act 1964
A parent who suspects the possibility of abduction, perhaps because of the other parent's threats or connections with another country, should obtain an order under section 11 of the Guardianship of Infants Act 1964 prohibiting the other parent removing the child from the jurisdiction without the prior approval of the Court. Where there is an order in force under section 11 of the 1964 Act, the parent in whose favour the order was made may register an objection to the issue of a passport for the child. Where the child already has an Irish passport (or is included on a parent's), the Court may require its surrender.

Powers of Garda Síochána
Section 37 of the 1991 Act confers extensive powers on a member of the Garda Síochána to detain a child who he reasonably suspects is about to be, or is being removed, from the State in breach of a custody or access order, an order in relation to the care of the child, an order made under the Hague Convention for the return of the child, or an order under the Luxembourg Convention for recognition or enforcement of a decision relating to custody. The child may also be detained under this section while proceedings for one of the above orders are pending, or an application for one of those orders is about to be made. Where a child is detained under section 37(f) the 1991 Act, a member of the Garda Síochána shall as soon as possible (a) return the child to the person granted custody, unless the member has reasonable grounds for believing that such person will act in breach of the order made, or (b) where the child has been in the care of a health board, return the child to that board, or (c) in a case other than one under (a) or (b) above, or where the member is of the belief referred to in (a) above, deliver the child into the care of the health board for the area in which the child is for the time being.

Role of Health Board
Where a member of the Garda Síochána delivers a child into the care of a health board under section 37, a parent or a person acting in *loco parentis* must be informed as soon as possible. Where the child is the subject of proceedings under the Hague or Luxembourg Conventions, the Central Authority in the State must

be informed. Where a child is delivered into the care of a health board, the board shall arrange suitable care and accommodation for the child, which may include placing the child in foster care or residential care, pending the making of an application to the District Court. An application must be made by the health board to the District Court within three days of the child's delivery into its care for directions as to the child's release from such care or otherwise in relation to the child's care. The District Court may make such order as it thinks appropriate as to the custody of, or access to, the child, without prejudice to any other proceedings that are pending in relation to the child.

Child Abduction as an Offence

Sections 16 and 17 of the Non-Fatal Offences Against the Person Act 1997 create new criminal offences in the case of child abduction. Under section 16, in the case of a child under the age of sixteen years, it is an offence for anyone who is a parent, a guardian or a person to whom custody of the child has been granted by a court to take, send or keep the child out of the State in defiance of a court order or without the consent of each person who is a parent or guardian or to whom custody has been granted, unless the leave of the Court is obtained. Section 16 does not apply to a parent who is not a guardian of the child. It is a defence under section 16 where the accused has been unable to communicate with the requisite persons, having taken all reasonable steps to do so, but believes that they would all consent if they were aware of all the relevant circumstances. It is also a defence for the accused to show that he had no intention of depriving others having rights of guardianship or custody in relation to the child of those rights.

Section 17 of the 1997 Act makes it an offence for any person, other than a person to whom section 16 applies, without lawful authority or reasonable excuse to intentionally take or detain a child under sixteen years of age from the lawful control of any person having lawful control of the child. It is a defence for the accused to have honestly believed that the child had attained the age of sixteen years. The penalty for a breach of either sections 16 or 17 is a fine not exceeding £1,500 or imprisonment for up to twelve months, or both, on summary conviction, or, on conviction on indictment, a fine or imprisonment for up to seven years, or both.

Further Reading

Shatter, *Family Law* 4th. Ed. Dublin: Butterworths 1997.
Binchy, *Irish Conflict of Laws*. Dublin: Butterworths 1988.
Law Reform Commission, Report on the Hague Convention on the Civil Aspects of International Child Abduction and Some Related Matters (LRC 12 - 1985).

CHAPTER SIXTEEN

PROTECTION OF CHILDREN — HEALTH BOARD INTERVENTION AND WARDSHIP

From time to time, the State is forced to intervene between a child and its parents or guardian for the purpose of removing the child from the home for its protection, or to provide some form of intermediate protection by way of supervision. The protection is usually achieved by means of intervention by a health board in the life of a child. Such health board intervention is now regulated by the Child Care Act 1991.

The primary purpose of the Child Care Act is to provide for the care and protection of children at risk. A statutory obligation is placed on health boards to promote the welfare of children who are not receiving adequate care and protection. In *F.N. v. Minister for Education* (1995) Geoghegan J stated that the 1991 Act provided a statutory scheme for dealing with many children in need of care, in that it gave health boards the powers of a parent in certain cases. However, the Act did not permit any kind of civil containment or detention by the health boards. Where neither the parents nor the health board could deal with the very special needs of a child who was in urgent need of special treatment, attention and education, with an element of containment or detention necessary for the treatment to be effective, there was a constitutional obligation on the State under Article 42.5 of the Constitution to cater for those needs in order to vindicate the constitutional rights of the child. In reaching his decision Geoghegan J cited with approval the cases of *G. v. An Bord Uchtála* (1980); *In Re Article 26 and the Adoption (No. 2) Bill 1987* (1989), and *M.F. v. Superintendent Ballymun Garda Station* (1990).

In *D.B. v. Minister for Justice* (1999) Kelly J, in endorsing the decision of Geoghegan J in *F.N. v. Minister for Education*, described the applicant as 'one of an increasing number of young people coming before the Court who, for their own welfare, required to be cared for by the Eastern Health Board in a secure environment from which they cannot readily escape'. Noting that no secure unit of accommodation had been put in place in the three years or so since the need for such accommodation was first identified by Geoghegan J, Kelly J expressed his dismay that 'inter-departmental wrangles over demarcation lines' should have been allowed to delay the provision of secure accommodation for young people such as the applicant. He described the situation that existed as 'a scandal'. As no undertaking was forthcoming from the Minister for Health and Children as to when secure accommodation would be available, the Court granted a mandatory injunction against the Minister compelling him to proceed to establish a high support facility at Portrane by a specified date. Kelly J expressed his regret that this course had to be adopted, but felt that such a course was the only way that the Court could fulfil its obligation under the Constitution to safeguard the welfare of minors such as the applicant.

A child is defined in section 2 of the Act as a person under the age of 18 years other than a person who is or was married. As a result, the age up to which health boards are obliged to promote the welfare of children and, where necessary, take them into care, has been raised from 16 to 18 years.

Duty of Health Board to Promote Welfare of Children

Section 3 of the 1991 Act imposes a duty upon every health board to promote the welfare of children in its area who are not receiving adequate care and protection. In this regard, a health board must take positive steps to identify children who are at risk. Section 3(2) places great emphasis on the importance of giving priority to the welfare of the child by providing as follows:

In the performance of this function, a health board shall —

(a) take such steps as it considers requisite to identify children who are not receiving adequate care and protection and co-ordinate information from all relevant sources relating to children in its area;

(b) having regard to the rights and duties of parents, whether under the Constitution or otherwise -

(i) regard the welfare of the child as the first and paramount consideration, and

(ii) in so far as is practicable, give due consideration having regard to his age and understanding, to the wishes of the child, and

(c) have regard to the principle that it is generally in the best interests of a child to be brought up in his own family.

The wording of section 3(2) appears to recognise the fact that in giving paramountcy to the welfare of the child, a health board may interfere with the rights of the family under Articles 41 and 42 of the Constitution. In an effort to avoid a potential conflict of interests, a health board is obliged, in the exercise of its function, to have regard to the rights and duties of parents, the child's own wishes and the fact that a child's own needs are best met by remaining within the family. In making the assumption that a child's needs are best met by remaining within the family unit, section 3 is merely acknowledging the importance placed on the marital family by the Constitution. Potentially, this might cause some difficulty for a court faced with the decision of separating a child from its parents, and this is dealt with later when considering the role of the Court under section 24.

Bearing in mind the emphasis that the Act places on children remaining within the family unit where possible, section 3(3) requires a health board to provide child care and family support services, and for such purposes a health board may provide and maintain premises and make such other provision as it considers necessary or desirable. This measure is designed to promote the welfare of children in vulnerable and marginalised families, thereby minimising the instances in which a child may have to be taken into care by a health board.

Report as to Adequacy of Services

For the purpose of complying with its requirement under section 3(3) of the 1991 Act, a health board is obliged under section 8 to prepare an annual report on the adequacy of the child care and family support services available in its area. In preparing a report, a health board shall have regard to children who are not receiving adequate care and protection and, in particular, those children whose parents are dead or missing or whose parents have deserted or abandoned them; children who are homeless; children who are at risk of being neglected or ill-treated; children whose parents are unable to care for them due to ill-health or for any other reason. Notice of the preparation of the report must be given to any child care advisory committee established in accordance with section 7 and any other bodies whose purposes include the provision of child care and family support services. In preparing its report, a health board must have regard to the views or information supplied by such committee or bodies. A copy of the report must be submitted to the Minister for Health.

Voluntary Care

Section 4 of the 1991 Act is meant to facilitate the taking of children into care on a voluntary basis, i.e. with the consent of a parent or person acting *in loco parentis*. The section is designed to cater for orphans and abandoned children, and children whose parents agree to them being taken into care because they are unable to care for them because of illness or family problems. A health board is obliged to take into care a child in its area who appears to require care and protection that he is unlikely to receive unless taken into care. A health board cannot take a child into care under section 4 against the wishes of his parents or a person acting *in loco parentis*. This is so even if the child is in danger. In such an eventuality, the health board should avail of the emergency provisions available under the Act.

Once a child has been taken into voluntary care, the health board must maintain the child in its care for as long as his welfare requires it and while he remains a child for the purposes of the Act. Where a child has been taken into voluntary care because he appears to be lost or deserted or abandoned, the health board must endeavour to reunite him with his parents, where this appears to be in the best interests of the child.

The underlying intention of section 4 is to provide a simple means of ensuring short-term care of children in temporary difficulties. Despite this fact a child may be in voluntary care for a long period. Problems may arise where a parent wishes to reclaim his child in circumstances which the health board consider to be against the best interests of the child. Clearly, it is incumbent on the health board in such a situation to apply to the Court for an emergency care order under section 13, followed by an application for either a care order (section 18),or a supervision order (section 19).

Homeless Children

Section 5 of the 1991 Act imposes on health boards a duty to provide suitable accommodation for homeless children who are not received into care. Where it appears to a health board that a child in its area is homeless, the board shall enquire into the child's circumstances. If, as a result of such enquiry, the board is satisfied that there is no accommodation available which the child can occupy, then, unless the child is received into care of the board under the provisions of the Act, the board shall take such steps as are reasonable to make suitable accommodation available to him.

The High Court decided in *P.S. (a minor suing by his next friend and mother P.S.) v. The Eastern Health Board* (1994) that a health board must comply with the requirement in section 3 of promoting the welfare of the child in discharging its duty under section 5. In declaring that the building in which the applicant resided on an emergency basis was no longer suitable accommodation, Geoghegan J made use of sections 3 and 5 to set out the type of accommodation that must be provided by the respondent to a homeless boy such as the applicant. The case involved a fourteen year old boy who had lived away from home for many years. His accommodation during that time included different homes, hostels and garda stations. He lived rough on the streets when expelled from homes or thrown out of hostels for anti social behaviour, which included violence and the use of drugs. The Gardaí contacted the health board after he had spent about 35 nights living rough on the streets. He was eventually accommodated in a house in Rathmines, where he resided at the time of the application. Evidence from a social worker established that the building was not a fit place for the applicant to remain, while an architect stated that the building was not fit for human habitation

Provision of Adoption Services

Section 6 of the 1991 Act requires each health board to provide or ensure the provision in its area of a service for the adoption of children in accordance with adoption legislation. A health board may take a child into care with a view to his adoption. However, the child may not be taken into care or maintained with a view to adoption against the wishes of a parent or person acting *in loco parentis*.

Removal of Child to Safety by Member of Garda Síochána

Section 12 of the 1991 Act enables a member of the Garda Síochána, without warrant, to remove a child to safety where the garda has reasonable cause to believe that the child has been or is being assaulted, ill-treated, neglected or sexually abused. There must be an immediate and serious risk to the health or welfare of the child and it would not be sufficient to wait for the health board to apply for an emergency care order under section 13. For the purpose of removing the child to safety, the garda may be accompanied by other persons (for example, a social worker) and may, without warrant, enter any house or other place (if need be by force) and remove the child to safety.

A child who is removed by a garda to safety must be delivered up to the health board as soon as possible so that the board can apply for an emergency care order. The health board must, unless it returns the child to his parent or person acting *in loco parentis*, apply for an emergency care order at the next sitting of the District Court held in the same District Court district. Where the next sitting of the District Court in the same district is not due to be held within three days of the delivery up of the child to the health board, an application may be made to any judge of the District Court under section 13(4)(b). It is lawful for a health board to retain custody of a child pending the hearing of an application for an emergency care order.

Emergency Care Orders

Section 13 of the 1991 Act provides that, on the application of a health board, a judge of the District Court may make an emergency care order where there is reasonable cause to believe that (a) there is an immediate and serious risk to the health or welfare of a child which necessitates his being placed in the care of a health board or, (b) there is likely to be such a risk if the child is removed from the place where he is for the time being. An emergency care order places the child in the care of a health board for up to eight days. One can only assume that this limited period of duration was imposed with a view to safeguarding the right of parents not to have their children removed from their custody for longer than is necessary. At the same time, the limited period of duration of an emergency care order may not afford a health board sufficient time to assess the difficulties in the family. If the health board wishes to pursue care proceedings it has the option of applying for an interim care order under section 17.

For the purpose of executing an emergency care order, a judge of the District Court may issue a warrant to a member of the Garda Síochána authorising him to enter (if need be by force) any premises where a child is and to deliver the child into the custody of a health board. The garda may be accompanied by other members of the force and such other persons as may be necessary.

An emergency care order shall be made by the judge of the District Court where the child resides, or is for the time being. Where a judge is not immediately available, an order may be made by any judge of the District Court. An application for an emergency care order may be made *ex parte* and elsewhere than at a public sitting of the District Court where the urgency of the matter so requires. An appeal from an emergency care order shall not stay the operation of the order. An emergency care order enables a judge of his own motion, or on application by any person, to give directions (a) as to whether a child's whereabouts should be disclosed, (b) as to access arrangements (if any) and the conditions to apply, and (c) as to medical or psychiatric examination, treatment or assessment of the child.

Where a child is received into care by a health board from a member of the Garda Síochána under section 12 or as a result of an emergency care order under section 13, the board is required by section 14, as soon as possible, to inform or cause to be informed a parent having custody of him or a person acting *in loco parentis* that this has happened, unless the parent or person is missing or cannot be found. There is no need to inform the parent or person acting *in loco parentis* of the placing of the child in the custody of a health board under section 13 if the parent or person is given a copy of the emergency care order or is present in court on the making of the order. Section 15 obliges a health board to provide or make arrangements with the registered proprietors of residential centres or other suitable persons for the provision of suitable accommodation for the care of children in emergencies.

Care Proceedings

Section 16 of the 1991 Act places a duty on a health board to apply for a care order or a supervision order, as it thinks fit, where it appears to the board that a child in its area requires care or protection which he is unlikely to receive unless a court makes such an order in respect of him.

Interim Care Orders

Section 17 of the 1991 Act enables the Court, on the application of a health board, to make an interim care order placing a child in the care of the board pending an application for a care order under section 18. An interim care order may be made whether or not an emergency care order is in force. Usually, the purpose of an interim care order is to cover the interim period between the expiry of an emergency care order and the determination of an application for a care order. Before making an interim care order, the Court must be satisfied (a) that an application for a care order has been or is about to be made, (b) that there is reasonable cause to believe that any of the grounds for the making of a care order under section 18(1) exists or has existed and, (c) that the protection of the health or welfare of the child requires him to be placed or maintained in the care of a health board pending the determination of the application for a care order.

The effect of an interim care order is that the child must be placed or maintained in the care of a health board for a period not exceeding eight days, or where the health board and the parent having custody of the child or person acting *in loco parentis* consent, for a period exceeding eight days. An extension or extensions of such period may be granted, on the application of any of the parties, where the Court is satisfied that the grounds for an interim care order continue to exist. An extension in excess of eight days can only be granted with the consent of a parent or person acting *in loco parentis*. An application for an interim care order or an extension thereof, can only be made on notice to a parent or person acting *in loco parentis*, except where the Court, in the interests of justice or the welfare of the child, directs otherwise. This enables parents to oppose the making of an interim care order.

Where an interim care order is made following an emergency care order, the Court may order that any directions in force under section 13(7) shall continue, subject to any variations made by the Court. Where no such directions are in force, or where an application for an interim care order is not an interim measure following on from an emergency care order, the Court may give directions in accordance with section 13(7). The directions that may be given include the withholding of the location of the child, arrangements as to access, and the medical or psychiatric examination, treatment or assessment of the child.

Care Orders

A care order commits a child into the care of a health board. It can only be made in favour of a health board. The legal effect of a care order is that a health board obtains parental authority for the child so long as the care order lasts. However, it is clear from the judgment of McCracken J in *Eastern Health Board v. McDonnell* (1999), which is dealt with in more detail later, that sections 24 and 47 of the 1991 Act give ultimate responsibility for the child to the District Court. The practical effect of a care order is that the child will be placed in residential care or with foster parents or relatives.

Section 18 of the 1991 Act enables the Court, on the application of a health board, to make a care order provided it is satisfied that:

(a) the child has been or is being assaulted, ill-treated, neglected or sexually abused, or

(b) the child's health, development or welfare is being unavoidably impaired or neglected, or

(c) the child's health, development or welfare is likely to be avoidably impaired or neglected, and that the child requires care or protection which he is unlikely to receive unless he is placed in the care of a health board.

i.e.

As a result of this latter provision, the Court may not make a care order merely because one of the conditions for the making of a such an order exists. In addition, the Court must be satisfied that the child requires care or protection which he is unlikely to receive unless he is taken into care.

A care order commits the child to the care of a health board until he reaches the age of 18 years or for such a shorter period as the Court may determine. Where the order applies for a shorter period, the Court may, of its own motion or on the application of any person, extend the operation of the order where it is satisfied that the grounds for the making of a care order continue to exist. A care order gives a health board parental control over the child to do what is reasonable for the purpose of safeguarding or promoting the child's health, development or welfare. In particular, a health board can decide the type of care to be provided for the child under section 36, consent to any necessary medical or psychiatric examination, treatment or assessment with respect to the child and, consent to the issue of a passport to enable the child to travel abroad for a limited period.

Where, on an application for a care order, the Court is satisfied that it is not necessary or appropriate to make a care order, and it is desirable that the child be visited periodically in his home by or on behalf of the health board, the Court may make a supervision order under section 19. This provision could be utilised by the Court where it is satisfied that one of the conditions exists for the making of a care order, but that it is not necessary to make such an order for the child's care and protection. As a measure of interim relief pending the hearing of an application for a care order, the Court, of its own motion or on the application of any person, may give directions as to the care and custody of the child or may make a supervision order in respect of the child. Any such direction or supervision order shall cease to have effect on the determination of the application for a care order. When making a care order, the Court may also order the parents to contribute money to the health board for the maintenance of the child. Such an order may be varied or discharged on application to the Court by the parent required to contribute.

Supervision Orders

This is an order placing a child under the supervision of a health board. A supervision order does not confer responsibility for the child on the health board, and the child cannot be removed from his home. The health board merely has the right to have the child visited regularly to monitor his welfare and to give advice to parents as to the care of the child. Section 19 of the 1991 Act provides for the making of a supervision order on grounds identical to those for a care order under section 18. However, the standard of proof is not as stringent in that the Court may make a supervision order where it is 'satisfied that there are reasonable grounds for believing' that the conditions exist, whereas the Court cannot make a care order unless it 'is satisfied' that the conditions do exist.

The effect of a supervision order is to authorise the health board to have the child visited as often as it considers necessary for the purpose of satisfying itself as to the welfare of the child, and giving any necessary advice to parents or a person acting *in loco parentis* as to the care of the child. A parent or person acting *in loco parentis* who is not satisfied with the manner in which a health board is carrying out a supervision order may apply to the Court for directions in relation to the supervision of the child. The Court may give such directions as it considers appropriate and the health board must comply.

The Court may, on the application of a health board, either at the time of making a supervision order or at any time during the currency of the order, give directions as to the care of the child, which may require the parents to bring the child for medical or psychiatric examination, treatment or assessment at a hospital, clinic or other place specified by the Court. A supervision order remains in force for up to twelve months, but shall cease to have effect when a child reaches 18 years. A health board can apply for a further supervision order on or before the expiration of a supervision order. Failure to comply with the terms of a supervision order is punishable on summary conviction by a fine not exceeding £500 and/or a term of imprisonment not exceeding six months.

Child Care and Related Proceedings

Where a court is dealing with any proceedings under the Guardianship of Infants Act 1964, the Judicial Separation and Family Law Reform Act 1989 or any other proceedings for the delivery or return of a child, and it considers that it may be appropriate for a care order or supervision order to be made, section 20 of the 1991 Act enables the Court to adjourn the proceedings and direct the health board for the area to undertake an investigation into the child's circumstances. In carrying out an investigation into the child's circumstances the health board must consider whether it should (a) apply for a care order or supervision order, (b) provide services or assistance for the child or his family or, (c) take any other action with respect to the child. Where, following an investigation, the health board decides not to apply for an order or provide services or assistance or take any other action, it must inform the Court of its reasons for so doing. However, there is nothing the Court can do to reverse the health board's decision.

Appeal, Variation and Discharge of Orders

Section 21 of the 1991 Act provides that an appeal from an interim care order, a care order or a supervision order shall only stay the operation of the order where the Court that made the order or the appeal court so determines. Section 22 enables the Court, of its own motion or on the application of any person, to vary or discharge an order or any condition or direction attaching thereto. In the case of a care order, the Court can discharge the order and replace it by a supervision order.

Invalid Care Orders

Section 23 of the 1991 Act is designed to ensure that, where it subsequently transpires that a care order when originally made was invalid, the child can be kept in care pending the making of a new order authorising the care. Where the Court finds or declares that a care order is for any reason invalid, the Court, of its own motion or on the application of any person, may refuse to order the delivery or return of the child to a parent or any other person, if it is of the opinion that this would not be in the best interests of the child.

Where the Court refuses to order the delivery or return of the child, it may:

(a) make a care order as if it were the Court to which the application for a care order had been made under section 18,
(b) make an order remitting the matter to a judge of the District Court in a district where the child resides or is for the time being or was residing when the invalid order was made or applied for,
(c) direct that a care order made under paragraph (a) be deemed to have been made by a judge of the District Court in a district specified by the Court, or
(d) where it makes an order under paragraph (b), make a temporary care order under paragraph (a) pending the making of an order by the Court to which the matter or question has been remitted.

The Welfare Principle

Section 24 of the 1991 Act requires the Court to regard the welfare of the child as the first and paramount consideration in any proceedings relating to the care and protection of a child. However, in considering the child's best interests, the Court must have regard to the rights and duties of parents, whether under the Constitution or otherwise, and the wishes of the child, having regard to his age and understanding. This is in keeping with the underlying philosophy of the Act that a child's interests are best served by remaining within the family unit, and that State intervention is only justified where it is necessary to remove the child from the family for his care and protection. It also coincides with the policy of child protection agencies of taking into care only those children who have been abused or neglected.

Before making a decision which will have the effect of removing the child from the family unit, the Court must be satisfied that the child's personal rights under Article 40.3 are vindicated, while at the same time having due regard to its natural and imprescriptible rights under Articles 41 and 42. This was the formula devised by the Supreme Court in *Re Article 26 and the Adoption (No. 2) Bill 1987* (1989) based on the wording of Article 42.5 which provides that:

> In exceptional cases, where the parents for physical or moral reasons fail in their duty towards their children, the State as guardian of the common

good, by appropriate means shall endeavour to supply the place of parents, but always with due regard for the natural and imprescriptible rights of the child.

The principle established in the *State (D. & D.) v. Groarke and Others* (1990) that a court must be satisfied that there are 'compelling reasons' before giving custody of a child to a person other than its parents, reinforces the view that the needs of a child are best met by remaining within the family. The case also emphasises the fact that the Court, in having regard to 'the rights and duties of parents', must ensure that any enquiry, as to whether it is in the best interests of a child that he be removed from the custody of a parent, is conducted in accordance with natural justice and fair procedures. This requires that a parent accused of sexually abusing a child be given full details of the allegations against him and any supporting evidence prior to the Court hearing.

The need to conduct an enquiry into allegations of child sexual abuse against a parent in accordance with fair procedures and principles of natural justice was again emphasised by the Supreme Court in *Re M.K., S.K. and W.K.* (1999). The case involved an appeal by the parents of three children who had been made wards of court by the High Court on the application of the Eastern Health Board. The High Court had accepted the hearsay evidence of a speech therapist and social worker to whom one of the children had complained that she had been persistently sexually abused by the father. Costello P held that a court, in exercising its discretion to admit hearsay evidence in wardship proceedings, must be satisfied of the necessity to do so. The President stated that the necessity might arise where the child is not old enough to give sworn testimony in court or where the giving of evidence in court would be traumatic and against the welfare of the child. The Supreme Court confirmed the finding of Costello P that hearsay evidence is admissible in wardship proceedings. However, the Supreme Court held that the President of the High Court had failed to carry out an appropriate enquiry as to whether it was necessary to adduce hearsay evidence. In delivering the judgment of the Court, Denham J stated:

> I am satisfied that the process whereby hearsay evidence was admitted in this case was not in accordance with fair procedures to either the mother, the father or indeed the children given their constitutional rights. The very difficult problems created when there are allegations of child sexual abuse of children in the home and the concern for the welfare of the children require fair procedures in Court to vindicate the constitutional rights of all the parties and the children.

The decision of the Supreme Court in *Southern Health Board v. C.H.* (1996) applies the principles of wardship proceedings in relation to the admissibility of hearsay evidence to proceedings under the 1991 Act. In that case, the Court was concerned with the admissibility of the expert evidence of a social worker, backed up by video recordings of his interviews with the child, in relation to allegations that the father had sexually abused his six year old daughter. O'Flaherty J described the proceedings as in the nature of an enquiry as to what is best to be done for the child in the particular circumstances pertaining. He stated that the Court is entrusted with the child's welfare and must undertake an investigation of what is in the best interests of the child, whether to be placed with the father or the Board. He also stated that the rights of the father must be safeguarded, as far as practicable, consistent with discharging the primary obligation of considering the best interests of the child. The Court held that hearsay evidence should be allowed in an enquiry as to the child's welfare where the child is incapable of giving oral evidence in court, or where the trauma she might suffer would make it undesirable that she should come to give evidence.

Section 24 obliges the Court to take the child's wishes into account where he is of an age to understand the nature of the proceedings and the effect an order of the Court may have on him. It is significant that section 25 of the Children Act 1997 also requires the Court to consider the wishes of the child in any proceedings in which the welfare of a child is in question. Whereas there was no such statutory obligation to consider the wishes of the child in custody matters under the Guardianship of Infants Act 1964, the Courts did in fact consider the wishes of a child in applications brought under section 11 of that Act. In *M.W. v. D.W.* (1975) Kenny J was unable to decide a custody dispute between parents on the basis of their evidence alone, and decided to interview the two children of the marriage, boys aged 12 and 15. The boys expressed their desire to live with the father. They alleged that the mother had physically ill-treated them and stated that they would return to the father no matter what the Court decided. The Court awarded custody to the father. Barron J interviewed two children, boys aged 9 and 5, in *N.A.D. v. T.D.* (1985), as a result of which he concluded that their mother's desertion 'has produced a natural reluctance on the part of her children to have anything to do with her'.

Parental responsibility and the rights of a child may be in conflict on occasion. Where this is the case, the Courts must resolve the conflict by giving paramountcy to the welfare of the child. In the English case of *Gillick v. West Norfolk Area Health Authority and Another* (1986) Scarman LJ stated that 'parental rights yield to the right of the child to make his own decision when he reaches a sufficient understanding and intelligence to be capable of making up his own mind on the matter.' In that case, the House of Lords acknowledged that in some circumstances, in the absence of parental consent to medical treatment, a child had the right to decide whether or not she should have contraceptive advice and treatment. Ultimately, it should be stressed that the Court, having considered the rights of parents and the child's wishes, must adjudicate on the application before it in a particular case by promoting the welfare of the child.

The respective roles of the District Court and health boards in caring for children under the 1991 Act were considered in *Eastern Health Board v. McDonnell* (1999). The High Court held that the District Court is entitled to impose some form of control or conditions in regard to the care of a child, which restrict the operation of the health board, after a child care order under section 18 of the 1991 Act has been granted. The Court held that it was the function of the Courts and not of local authorities or health boards to ensure that constitutional rights given to an individual were upheld. In delivering the judgment of the Court, McCracken J referred to two specific provisions of the 1991 Act, namely sections 24 and 47, which satisfied him that the District Judge was entitled to give directions regarding the care of the two children in question. Section 24 clearly provides that the Court shall have regard to the welfare of the child as the first and paramount consideration. This obligation on the Court in dealing with proceedings under the Act cannot be passed on or delegated to a health board. McCracken J described section 47 is an all-embracing and wide-ranging provision which is intended to entrust the ultimate care of a child who comes within the Act in the hands of the District Court. Section 47 enables the District Court, of its own motion or on the application of any person, to give directions on any matter pertaining to the welfare of the child. Unlike section 24, this is not limited to cases where there are proceedings before the Court, but rather to situations where the child is already in the care of a health board. The learned judge went on to state that section 47 is intended to give the overall control of children in care to the District Court. However, the District Court should only interfere in the day to day decisions of a health board when matters that might adversely affect the welfare of a child are brought to its attention.

The Court's Powers

For the purpose of discharging its duty in relation to the care and protection of children who are at risk under section 24 of the 1991 Act, the following powers are conferred on the Court:

(1) to make a child a party to all or part of care proceedings and, where it is deemed fit, to appoint a solicitor to represent a child. Where a solicitor is appointed, the costs and expenses incurred shall be paid by the health board unless the Court otherwise orders — section 25.

(2) to appoint a guardian *ad litem* for the child where the child is not already a party to the proceedings. The costs of the appointment shall be borne by the health board unless, on the application of the board, the Court orders any other party to the proceedings to bear them. The appointment of a guardian *ad litem* shall lapse where the child is made a party to the proceedings — section 26.

(3) to obtain a report from such person as it may nominate on any question

affecting the welfare of the child. In deciding whether or not to request a report, the Court shall have regard to the wishes of the parties before the Court but shall not be bound by such wishes. A copy of the report must be made available to the parties or their legal representatives. The person making the report may be called as a witness. The costs of the report shall be borne by such party or parties as the Court may order — section 27.

(4) To conduct the proceedings without the presence of the child. Section 30 makes it clear that it shall not be necessary to bring the child before the Court, or for him to be present for all or any part of the hearing unless the Court, of its own motion or at the request of any of the parties, is satisfied that it is necessary for the proper disposal of the case. However, the Court must accede to a request by the child to be present for any part or all of the proceedings unless the Court considers that, having regard to the age of the child or the nature of the proceedings, it would not be in the child's best interests to accede to the request.

Section 30 would appear to acknowledge the fact that it is not desirable to put a very young child through the trauma and distress that is generally associated with a court appearance. This is particularly so where a case involves severe physical or sexual abuse. However, where the Court considers that a child is of an age when he is capable of understanding the issues involved and the implications that an order of the Court might have for him, he must be brought before the Court so that his wishes can be ascertained in accordance with section 24.

Jurisdiction of the Court

The District Court and the Circuit Court on appeal have jurisdiction to hear and determine proceedings under the 1991 Act — section 28. Proceedings may be dealt with by the District Court for the district where the child resides or is for the time being. Section 29 states that proceedings involving the care and welfare of a child shall be held otherwise than in public, and that the provisions of sections 33(1), 33(2) and 45 of the Judicial Separation and Family Law Reform Act 1989 shall apply to care proceedings under the 1991 Act. In effect, this means that not only must proceedings be held in private, but also that they be as informal as possible, without wigs or gowns being worn by judges or barristers. Section 29 also requires the District Court, and the Circuit Court on appeal, to sit at a different place or at different times or on different days from those at or which ordinary sittings of the Court are held.

The publication or broadcast of any matter that would be likely to identify the child who is the subject of care proceedings is prohibited by section 31. However, where the Court is satisfied that it would be appropriate to do so in the interests of the child, it may dispense with the prohibition on publication or broadcast to such extent as may be specified. Any person or body corporate found to be in breach of the ban on publication or broadcast may be fined up to £1,000 and/or imprisoned for up to 12 months on summary conviction. The terms 'broadcast' and 'written publication' are defined in the section.

The Court has power to presume or declare the age of a child after making due enquiry as to his age — section 32. Any such presumption or declaration shall establish the true age of the child until the contrary is proved. Section 33 provides for the making of rules of court as to the service of documents and the furnishing of information and documents by the parties in care proceedings. Section 34 makes it an offence for any person having custody of a child to fail or refuse to deliver up the child on foot of an order of the Court to do so. A copy of the order must have been shown to the person in question. A person shall be deemed to have been shown a copy of the order if he was present in court when the order was made. A fine of up to £500 and/or imprisonment for up to 6 months is the penalty prescribed for a breach of the section. The Court is empowered to issue a warrant for the purpose of enforcing an interim care order or a care order — Section 35. The warrant authorises a member of the Garda Síochána, accompanied by other members of the force or other persons as may be necessary, to enter (if need be by force) any premises where the child is, or where there are reasonable grounds to believe that the child is, and to deliver the child into the custody of the health board.

The Provision of Care by Health Boards

Whatever the reason for a child coming into the care of a health board and whichever the legal route by which he comes into care, section 36 of the 1991 Act requires the board to provide care for him in whichever of the following ways it considers to be in the child's best interests:

(a) by placing him with a foster parent, defined as a non-relative, or
(b) by placing him in residential care, defined as a centre registered under the Act as a children's residential centre, a residential home run by a health board or a school or other place of residence. (Where necessary, a child may be sent to a hospital or any institution which provides nursing or care for children suffering from physical or mental disability), or
(c) by placing a child eligible for adoption under adoption legislation with a suitable person with a view to adoption, or
(d) by making such other suitable arrangements (which may include placing the child with a relative) as the health board thinks proper.

Residential Care

To facilitate the accommodation and maintenance of a child by placing him in residential care, section 38 of the 1991 Act requires a health board to make arrangements with the registered proprietors of children's residential centres, or with other suitable persons, to ensure the provision of an adequate number of residential places for children in its care. A health board may itself, with the approval of the Minister, provide and maintain residential centres for children. The Minister must make regulations as regards the conduct of homes or other premises provided by health boards. These regulations may prescribe requirements as to the maintenance, care and welfare of children while being maintained in centres; the numbers, qualifications and availability of staff at centres; the design and maintenance of centres; the quality of the accommodation provided in centres; the food provided in centres; the records to be kept in centres. The relevant regulations are the Child Care (Standards in Children's Residential Centres) Regulations 1996.

Section 40 requires the Minister to make regulations governing the placement of children in residential care by a health board under section 36. The relevant regulations are the Child Care (Placement of Children in Residential Care) Regulations 1995. The Regulations cover the conditions for placement, the form of the contract between the health board and the persons providing residential care, and the supervision and visiting of children in residential care.

Foster Care

The Minister is obliged by Section 39 of the 1991 Act to make regulations governing the placement of children in foster care, which may fix the conditions under which children may be placed with foster parents, prescribe the form of contract between the health board and foster parents, and provide for the supervision and visitation by the health board of children in foster care. The relevant regulations are the Child Care (Placement of Children in Foster Care) Regulations 1995. Before placing a child with foster parents, a health board must investigate both the child's circumstances and his new home to ensure that the foster parents are fit and proper persons to look after children, and that they are capable of meeting the child's needs. This is intended to achieve the aim of 'matching' the child concerned to his new family as far as possible, thus, in theory at least, minimising the risk of future breakdown in the placement. As regards the religious upbringing of a child in foster care, the wishes of the child's guardian should, where possible, be respected.

Once a child has been placed with foster parents, the health board must supervise the placement and visit the child to ensure his continued welfare. The frequency of visits set out in the 1995 Regulations should be regarded as the minimum requirement. The child's welfare may dictate more frequent visits. The supervision and visitation requirements, in addition to ensuring the child's welfare, will also benefit foster parents by enabling them to receive advice and practical help from the social worker supervising the placement. Where a child is adopted by his foster parents, section 44 provides that a health board may continue to contribute to the maintenance of the child as if he continued to be in foster care. Where a child is adopted, any care order in force in respect of him ceases to have effect.

Placement with Relatives

The Minister is obliged by section 41 of the 1991 Act to make regulations in relation to the placement of children with relatives. The regulations may fix the conditions under which children may be placed with relatives, prescribe the form of contract between the health board and relatives, and provide for supervision and visitation by the health board of children placed with relatives. The relevant regulations are the Child Care (Placement of Children with Relatives) Regulations 1995. A relative is defined in the Regulations as 'the spouse of a relative of that child and a person who has acted in *loco parentis*.' The duties of relatives are prescribed. Generally, relatives are required to take all reasonable steps to promote the child's health, development and welfare. Specifically, relatives must permit visitation, maintain confidentiality, seek medical care for the child, co-operate in facilitating access by parents, notify a change in residence, and arrange for the care of the child in their absence.

Before placing a child with relatives, a health board must assess both the circumstances of the child and the suitability of the relatives. Once a child has been placed with relatives, the health board must supervise the placement and arrange for the child to be visited by a social worker in accordance with the 1996 Regulations.

Duty of Health Board to Facilitate Reasonable Access

A health board is obliged to facilitate reasonable access to a child in care by his parents, any person acting *in loco parentis*, or any other person who, in the opinion of the board, has a *bona fide* interest in the child. Such access may include allowing the child to live temporarily with any such person — section 37 of the 1991 Act. Any person who is dissatisfied with the access arrangements may apply to the Court for such order as it thinks proper regarding access to the child by that person. The Court may vary or discharge the access order on the application of any person. On the application of a health board, the Court may make an order authorising the board to refuse to allow a named person access to the child, or vary or discharge that order on the application of any person. The Court can order that access be refused if it considers it necessary to do so in order to safeguard or promote a child's welfare. Where a child is in voluntary care under section 4 of the 1991 Act, access cannot be denied to a parent or person acting *in loco parentis*.

Provision for Review of Cases by Health Board

Health boards are required to review the case of each child in care in accordance with regulations to be made by the Minister — section 42 of the 1991 Act. The Regulations may make provision as to the manner in which cases are reviewed, the frequency of reviews, and the requirement that a health board consider whether it would be in the best interests of the child to be given into the custody of his parents. The Regulations governing the review of cases of children in care are the Child Care (Placement of Children in Residential Care) Regulations 1995, the Child Care (Placement of Children in Foster Care) Regulations 1995 and the Child Care (Placement of Children with Relatives) Regulations 1995.

Removal of Child from Custody of Person with whom Placed

Section 43 of the 1991 Act enables a health board, in accordance with Regulations made by the Minister, to remove a child in its care from the custody of any person with whom he has been placed under section 36. The various regulations governing the placement of children in care, already referred to, require a health board to notify the person who has custody of the child of its intention to remove the child and to afford such person the opportunity of making representations. Where the health board decides to proceed with the removal, it must inform the relevant person of its decision and the reasons for it. The health board must request that the child be delivered up at a particular time and place. Refusal or neglect to hand over the child enables the health board to apply for an order directing the hand over. Where the Court orders that the child be delivered up to the health board, a copy of the order must be shown to the person required to deliver up the child. A person shall be deemed to have been shown a copy of the order where he was in court when it was made. Should such person not comply with the order he is liable to a fine not exceeding £500 and/or imprisonment of up to 6 months. He may also be held to be in contempt of court. The removal of a child from care under this section terminates the contract between the health board and the relevant person.

Assistance for Child on Leaving Care

Where a child leaves care, section 45 of the 1991 Act enables a health board to provide assistance for him until he reaches the age of 21 years, provided the board is satisfied that he needs assistance. Any such assistance may be continued beyond the age of 21 to enable a person complete a course of education. The assistance can take the form of visiting the child and supporting him with education, training and accommodation requirements. The health board may contribute towards the cost of accommodation and pay the fees or costs involved in training.

Recovery of Children Unlawfully Removed from Care

Where a child is removed from the custody of a health board or any person acting on behalf of a health board without lawful authority, section 46 of the 1991 Act enables the board to seek the assistance of the Garda Síochána to recover the child.

Where the Court is satisfied by an information on oath that a named person can produce the child, it may order such person to deliver up the child into the custody of a health board. Where the person having actual custody of the child, on being shown a copy of the order and having been required to hand over the child, refuses to do so, he is liable on summary conviction to a fine not exceeding £500 and/or imprisonment for up to 6 months. He may also be held to be in contempt of court. A person present in court when an order is made is deemed to have been shown a copy of the order. An application for an order to hand over a child may be made *ex parte* and otherwise than at a public sitting of the Court, where the urgency of the matter so requires.

The Court may issue a warrant authorising a member of the Garda Síochána, accompanied by other members of the force and such other persons as may be necessary, to enter any premises (if need be by force) to recover a child in respect of whom an order under this section has been made. A warrant may be issued elsewhere than at a public sitting of the Court where the matter is urgent.

Children's Residential Centres

A 'children's residential centre' is defined in section 59 as any home or other institution for the residential care of children in the care of health boards or other children who are not receiving adequate care and protection, excluding institutions that are owned or maintained by the State or a health board, institutions that provide for the care and maintenance of children who are ill or physically or mentally handicapped and mental hospitals.

Prohibition of Unregistered Centres

Section 60 of the 1991 Act provides that it shall not be lawful for any person to carry on a children's residential centre unless the centre is registered and the person is the registered proprietor thereof. A person shall not be in charge of a centre unless it is registered.

Registration of Centres

Section 61 of the 1991 Act provides for the registration by health boards of children's residential centres. Each health board must establish and maintain a register of such centres in its area. The contents of the register are prescribed. The register shall be open for public inspection free of charge at all reasonable times. A health board may register or refuse to register any centre and may remove a centre from the register. Registration lasts for three years.

The circumstances in which a health board may refuse registration or remove a centre from the register are set out. They include non-compliance by the centre with the Child Care (Standards in Children's Residential Centres) Regulations 1996, the unsuitability of the applicant as a person convicted of an offence, failure to furnish information requested by the board, and the contravention of a condition imposed by the board. The refusal to register must be notified to the applicant for registration, who shall have the right to make representations and appeal to the District Court. A health board may, on registration or thereafter, attach conditions to the operation of the centre, attach different conditions in the case of different centres, and amend or revoke any condition. Provision is also made for the form an application for registration must take, and the renewal of registration for centres. It is an offence to contravene a condition attaching to a registration.

By virtue of section 62 of the 1991 Act, an appeal lies to the District Court against the decision of a health board to refuse to register a centre, to remove a centre from the register, to attach conditions to registration, or to amend or revoke a condition. An appeal must be brought within 21 days of the notification by the health board of its decision. The Court may confirm the decision of the health board, or direct the board to register or restore registration of the centre, or direct the withdrawal of a condition or the amendment or revocation of a condition. The decision of the District Court on a question of fact is final.

The Minister is required by section 63 of the 1991 Act to make regulations ensuring proper standards in children's residential centres, including adequate and suitable accommodation, food and care for children and the proper conduct of centres. The Child Care (Placement of Children in Residential Care) Regulations 1995 oblige health boards to ensure that centres comply with the regulations and the Child Care (Standards in Children's Residential Centres) Regulations 1996 impose specific obligations on the registered proprietor and person in charge of a centre.

Section 65 of the 1991 Act requires the registered proprietor of a children's residential centre to give 6 months notice in writing to the health board for the area of his intention to cease to carry on the centre. A health board may accept shorter notice if it thinks fit. At the expiration of 6 months from the date of the notice (unless the notice is withdrawn or the period of registration has expired) the centre shall cease to be registered. A person guilty of an offence under Part VIII of the Act shall be liable on summary conviction to a fine not exceeding £1,000 or to imprisonment for a period not exceeding 12 months or to both.

Wardship

The jurisdiction regarding wards of court, which is now exercised by the President of the High Court, is an ancient jurisdiction deriving from the Sovereign as *parens patriae*, that is, the protector of his subjects, such as children and persons of unsound mind, who were incapable of looking after their persons or property. In *Re M.,S. and W., Infants* (1996) Costello P described the wardship jurisdiction as follows:

> In exercising jurisdiction in wardship proceedings, a judge is exercising a special jurisdiction. It originated in the doctrine that infants are to be treated as specifically under the protection of the sovereign who, as *parens patriae*, had charge of persons not capable of looking after themselves.

In exercising its wardship jurisdiction, the Court must regard the welfare of the child as the first and paramount consideration. In conducting a wide ranging review of English and other authorities on wardship in *Re M.,S., and W., Infants,* Costello P pointed out that even though an inquiry in wardship matters was a judicial one, it was not to be regarded as an ordinary action between parties. Accordingly, the rules of natural justice are not rigorously adhered to in wardship proceedings, lest they hinder the Court in its task of ensuring that the welfare of the child prevails. For example, wardship proceedings are held *in camera*, the presiding judge might see the ward and parents separately and the rules as to the admission of hearsay evidence may be relaxed. In the course of her judgment in *Re M.K., S.K. and W.K.* (1999) (an appeal from the decision of Costello P in *Re M.,S. and W., Infants*) Denham J, in describing the wardship jurisdiction, stated:

> The Judge is placed in the position of a good parent who must decide prudently on issues relating to the welfare of the child. The kernel of the jurisdiction is the welfare of the child. This ancient jurisdiction places the Court in a particular position of responsibility. It must conduct an inquiry as to what, in all the circumstances, is in the best interests of the child.

Historically, the wardship jurisdiction was used to protect the property of orphans and other persons who were incapable of looking after themselves. Nowadays, although the protection of a ward's property is still one of the purposes of the wardship jurisdiction, a typical ward of court is no longer an orphan whose property needs protection, but a child of a broken home, or a child who is out of control, or a child who needs protection from abuse. Wardship lasts until a child attains its majority at the age of 18 — see Age of Majority Act 1985. Any person can issue wardship proceedings in relation to a child, provided he has a legitimate reason for doing so. Order 65 of the Rules of the Superior Courts 1962 provides that proceedings to make a minor a ward of court shall be commenced by originating summons supported by a grounding affidavit which shall include, *inter alia*, particulars of proposals as to care, maintenance, residence and education of the ward.

Wardship vests custody of the child in the Court for so long as the child remains a ward. The Court then delegates care and control of the ward to an individual or body who take responsibility for the ward's day-to-day upbringing.

Major decisions affecting the ward's welfare, such as education, consent to adoption, consent to surgery, etc. are taken by the Court. Interference with a ward involving disobedience of an order of the Court amounts to contempt of court. The ward is similarly liable if he disobeys Court orders.

The scope of the wardship jurisdiction is unlimited and a child can be made a ward of court in any situation where his or her welfare is in issue. For example, prior to the enactment of the Children Act 1997, (see Chapter 14) relatives of a child, such as grandparents, who had no other means of obtaining access to the child, had to avail of the wardship jurisdiction. The wardship jurisdiction was extensively used in an effort to prevent child kidnapping prior to the enactment of the Child Abduction and Enforcement of Custody Orders Act 1991 (see Chapter 15). As was pointed out in Chapter 14, outsiders seeking to obtain custody of a child, or endeavouring to retain custody of a child already in their possession, against the wishes of parents must usually apply to have the child made a ward of court, so that the question of the child's welfare can be decided.

Frequently, the wardship jurisdiction is invoked where it is necessary to protect a child at risk and a health board considers its powers under the Child Care Act 1991 are inadequate, e.g. where a parent of a child in voluntary care under section 4 wishes to take the child back against the wishes of the board. In the *Southern Health Board v. C.H.* (1996) the Supreme Court likened the proceedings in issue in that case to proceedings in which a court exercises its wardship jurisdiction. The Court was entrusted with responsibility for the child's welfare and that was the first and paramount consideration. The case involved an application by a widowed father under section 11 of the Guardianship of Infants Act 1964 to regain custody of his daughter from the board. The father had consented to the child being taken into voluntary care some time previously. The board resisted the application on the grounds that there were allegations that the father had sexually abused the child. Similarly, in *Re M.,S. and W., Infants* (1996) the High Court made three children wards of court on the application of the Eastern Health Board on the grounds that one of the children had been sexually abused by their father. The evidence of abuse was hearsay, in that the abused child had reported it to a speech therapist. Costello P stated that the hearsay rule has never been strictly applied in wardship proceedings. In exercising this jurisdiction the Courts have always acted in the interests of the child's welfare. On appeal, the Supreme Court (*Re M.K., S.K. and W.K.* (1999)) confirmed that hearsay evidence is admissible in wardship proceedings. It is interesting to note that section 23 of the Children Act 1997 gives the Court discretion to admit hearsay evidence in civil cases where the child is too young to give evidence or where the Court is of the view that the giving of oral evidence by a child is contrary to the welfare of the child. The Court can also refuse to admit such evidence where there is a risk of it resulting in unfairness to any of the parties to the proceedings.

The wardship jurisdiction has been invoked by persons with an interest in the child who consider that the guidance and protection of the Court is required. Two English cases provide good examples. In *Re D.* (1976) a mother had given her consent to the sterilisation of her eleven year old mentally handicapped daughter. An educational psychologist had the girl made a ward of court, and the Court ordered that the operation should not take place. In *Re X. (A Minor)(Wardship: Jurisdiction)* (1975) a girl's stepfather made her a ward of court and sought an injunction to prevent the publication of a book which alleged that her deceased father had been a sex pervert who engaged in sordid and degrading conduct. The stepfather claimed that there was a risk of psychological injury to the girl should she learn of the book's references to her father. The Court refused to grant the injunction as it would be too restrictive in the particular circumstances of the case, but made it clear that it could grant such an injunction in an appropriate case.

Further Reading

Shatter, *Family Law* 4th. Ed. Dublin: Butterworths 1997.

Ward, *The Child Care Act 1991*. (Annotated Legislation). Dublin: Round Hall Sweet & Maxwell 1997.

Ferguson & Kenny, *On Behalf of the Child*. Dublin: A & A Farmar 1995.

North Western Health Board, 'Child Care Act 1991'. Conference Papers, Donegal 1993.

O'Halloran & Gilligan, 'A Comparative Review of New Legislation in Northern Ireland and the Republic of Ireland: The Children (N.I.) Order 1995 and The Child Care Act 1991'. Southern Health & Social Services Board 1996.

Durcan, 'Recent Cases on Hearsay Evidence in Civil Child Sexual Abuse Proceedings'. (1996) 14 ILT 284.

Gilligan, 'Irish Child Care Services: Policy, Practice and Provision' (Dublin: IPA, 1991).

Task Force on Child Care Services: Final Report (Dublin: Stationery Office, 1980).

'Children First: National Guidelines for the Protection and Welfare of Children' (Dublin: Stationery Office, September 1999)

CHAPTER SEVENTEEN

THE COURTS ADMINISTERING FAMILY LAW — STRUCTURE AND JURISDICTION

The District Court

The District Court is a court of limited jurisdiction. It possesses original jurisdiction only. Proceedings are relatively informal and are devoid of the usual trappings of wigs and gowns. Because of the summary nature of District Court proceedings, there is an automatic right of appeal to the Circuit Court. A District Judge, of his own motion, or at the request of either of the parties to the proceedings, may state a case on a point of law for determination by the High Court. The District Court, as presently constituted, has the following jurisdiction in family law matters:

Guardianship and Custody

Under sections 5 and 13 of the Guardianship of Infants Act 1964, as amended by the Courts Act 1981, the District Court can make orders as to guardianship, custody and access. The District Court is empowered to exercise jurisdiction under the new Part IV of the 1964 Act (as inserted by section 11 of the Children Act 1997).

Maintenance

Section 23 of the Family Law (Maintenance of Spouses and Children) Act 1976, as amended by the Courts Acts 1981 and 1991 and the Family Law Act 1995, confers on the District Court the power to make orders by way of periodical payments of up to £200 per week in favour of a spouse and £60 per week in favour of a dependent child. The Court can also make a lump sum order of up to £5,000. Under section 5 of the Guardianship of Infants Act 1964, as amended by the Courts Acts 1981 and 1991, the Court can award maintenance for the support of a child up to £60 per week and a lump sum of £5000. The District Court can now make a maintenance agreement (other than a separation agreement) a rule of court — section 15 of the Children Act 1997.

The Family Home

Sections 9 and 10 of the Family Home Protection Act 1976, as amended by section 54 of the Family Law Act 1995, enable the District Court to make orders for the disposal of household chattels whose value does not exceed £5000.

Domestic Violence

The Domestic Violence Act 1996, as amended by the Family Law (Miscellaneous Provisions) Act 1997, confers on the District Court the power to make a safety order for up to five years (section 2), a barring order for up to three years (section 3), an interim barring order (section 4) and a protection order (section 5).

Child Care

The District Court alone exercises original jurisdiction under the Child Care Act 1991, as amended by the Children Act 1997.

The Circuit Court

Section 38 of the Family Law Act 1995 provides that when the Circuit Court is exercising jurisdiction in family law matters it is known as the Circuit Family Court. The Circuit Family Court sits at a different place or at different times to ordinary sittings of the Circuit Court. Proceedings are as informal as is practicable and consistent with the administration of justice. Neither judges nor lawyers wear wigs or gowns. An appeal lies from a decision of the Circuit Court to the High Court and a case may be stated to the Supreme Court on a point of law. Recent legislation in the area of family law has greatly extended the scope of the jurisdiction of the Circuit Court.

Guardianship and Custody

The Circuit Family Court exercises jurisdiction concurrently with the District Court to make orders as to custody, guardianship and access.

Maintenance

The Circuit Family Court has an unlimited jurisdiction to make orders by way of periodical or lump sum maintenance under the Family Law (Maintenance of Spouses and Children) Act 1976, as amended, and section 11 of the Guardianship of Infants Act 1964, as amended.

The Family Home

The Circuit Family Court exercises jurisdiction concurrently with the High Court to make orders under sections 4, 5 and 9 of the Family Home Protection Act 1976. In any proceedings under the 1976 Act where the rateable valuation of any property involved exceeds £200, the Court, at the request of any party having an interest in the proceedings, must transfer the proceedings to the High Court.

Domestic Violence

Section 1 of the Domestic Violence Act 1996 confers on the Circuit Family Court, jurisdiction to make safety orders, barring orders, interim barring orders or protection orders for an unlimited period.

Matrimonial Property

The Circuit Family Court exercises jurisdiction concurrently with the High Court to make orders under section 36 of the Family Law Act 1995 in relation to property disputes between spouses.

Nullity

Under section 39 of the Family Law Act 1995 the Circuit Family Court can, concurrently with the High Court, grant nullity decrees.

Judicial Separation and Divorce

Concurrently with the High Court, the Circuit Family Court can grant decrees of judicial separation under section 31(2) of the Judicial Separation and Family Law Reform Act 1989 and decrees of divorce under Article 41.3.2 of the Constitution and section 38(1) of the Family Law (Divorce) Act 1996. The Circuit Court can also make preliminary and ancillary orders, as set out in the Family Law Act 1995 and the Family Law (Divorce) Act 1996, on granting decrees of judicial separation and divorce.

Succession

Under section 6 of the Succession Act 1965, the Circuit Family Court exercises jurisdiction in succession proceedings concurrently with the High Court. Where the rateable valuation of any property of the deceased exceeds £200, the Circuit Family Court can only deal with proceedings under the Act if the parties so consent.

The Partition Acts 1868 and 1876

The Circuit Family Court can, concurrently with the High Court, order the partition of property.

Disputes between Engaged Couples

Section 8 of the Family Law Act 1981, as amended by section 13 of the Courts Act 1991, gives the Circuit Family Court jurisdiction, concurrently with the High Court, to resolve disputes between engaged couples whose engagements have broken down.

Wardship

The Circuit Family Court has jurisdiction concurrently with the High Court in wardship matters. Where property of the minor involved in the wardship proceedings exceeds £200, the High Court alone has jurisdiction.

Declarations as to Marital Status

Under section 38 of the Family Law Act 1995 the Circuit Family Court exercises jurisdiction concurrently with the High Court to make declarations as to marital status under Part IV of the Act.

Declarations as to Parentage

Section 33 of the Status of Children Act 1987 confers exclusive jurisdiction on the Circuit Family Court to make declarations as to parentage under Part VI of the Act.

Appellate Jurisdiction

By virtue of section 84 of the Courts of Justice Act 1924, either party to the proceedings may appeal a decision of the District Court to the Circuit Family Court, which conducts a full re-hearing of the case.

The High Court

The matrimonial jurisdiction formerly exercised by the ecclesiastical courts is now exercised by the High Court by virtue of the Courts Act 1961. Under section 33 of the Judicial Separation and Family Law Act 1989, as amended by section 38 of the Family Law Act 1995, family law proceedings before the High Court shall be as informal as is practicable and consistent with the administration of justice. In addition to exercising an original and appellate jurisdiction, the High Court exercises an extensive consultative and supervisory jurisdiction. Its consultative jurisdiction extends to dealing with cases stated from the District Court and hearing challenges as to the constitutionality of legislation. In exercising its supervisory jurisdiction, the High Court can grant the state side orders of *Certiorari*, *Mandamus* and *Prohibition*. An order of *certiorari* has the effect of quashing a decision of an inferior court or tribunal which has acted in excess of jurisdiction. An order of *mandamus* compels a person or body to carry out a legal duty. An order of *prohibition* prevents a court or other body or person exercising a power that it does not possess. The High Court exercises jurisdiction concurrently with the Circuit Court in the following matters:

The Family Home

The High Court can hear disputes between spouses in relation to the family home under the Family Home Protection Act 1976.

Matrimonial Property

The High Court can resolve disputes between spouses as to the ownership of matrimonial property under section 36 of the Family Law Act 1995.

Nullity

The High Court, as successor to the old ecclesiastical courts, can grant decrees of nullity.

Judicial Separation and Divorce

The High Court grants decrees of judicial separation and divorce and also makes preliminary and ancillary orders under the Family Law Act 1995 and the Family Law (Divorce) Act 1996.

Succession

The High Court has extensive jurisdiction in proceedings under the Succession Act 1965.

Partition Acts 1868 and 1876

The High Court can make orders for sale in lieu of partition of jointly-owned property.

Disputes between Engaged Couples

Under the Family Law Act 1981, as amended, the High Court can resolve disputes between engaged couples whose engagements have terminated.

Wardship

The High Court has inherited the ancient *parens patriae* jurisdiction formerly exercised by the Sovereign in wardship proceedings.

Declarations as to Marital Status

The High Court has full original jurisdiction to make declarations as to marital status under Part IV of the Family Law Act 1995.

The High Court exercises exclusive jurisdiction in the following matters:

Adoption
under the Adoption Acts 1952 - 1998.

Child Abduction
under the Child Abduction and Enforcement of Custody Orders Act 1991.

Habeas corpus

in matters concerning the custody and welfare of children under Article 40.4 of the Constitution.

Guardianship and Maintenance

The jurisdiction previously exercised by the High Court concurrently with the District Court and Circuit Court under section 5 of the Guardianship of Infants Act 1964 and section 23 of the Family Law (Maintenance of Spouses and Children) Act 1976 appeared to have been curtailed or removed by the Courts Act 1981, which purported to confer jurisdiction for guardianship and custody matters exclusively on the District Court and the Circuit Court. However, two decisions of the High Court, namely *R. v. R.* (1984) and *O'R. v. O'R.* (1985), seem to suggest that any legislative curtailment of the original jurisdiction of the High Court might fall foul of the Constitution. Unfortunately, there is some confusion in the matter as a result of the Supreme Court decision in *Tormey v. Ireland and the Attorney General* (1985) (which did not specifically address the issue of the High Court's jurisdiction under the Acts of 1964 and 1976), to the effect that the Oireachtas has power under Article 34.3.4 of the Constitution to confer exclusive jurisdiction in particular matters on the District Court and Circuit Court.

Appellate Jurisdiction

An appeal lies to the High Court from a decision of the Circuit Court. The High Court conducts a full re-hearing of the case — section 39 of the Courts of Justice Act 1936. The High Court also hears appeals by way of case stated from the District Court on points of law. The determination of the High Court on the point of law in issue is transmitted to the District Judge who referred the matter in the first instance. The District Judge decides the case by applying the law as interpreted by the High Court.

The Supreme Court

The Supreme Court does not have original jurisdiction in family law matters. As part of its appellate jurisdiction, it hears appeals from the High Court. The Supreme Court considers appeals on the basis of a transcript of the evidence heard in the High Court, and as a general rule it will only hear oral evidence in exceptional cases. In proceedings under the Child Abduction and Enforcement of Custody Orders Act 1991, the Supreme Court occasionally hears the testimony of children. The Supreme Court also hears appeals by way of case stated from the Circuit Court.

Legal Aid

The Scheme of Civil Legal Aid and Advice was established in 1980 on a non-statutory basis following the Pringle Report on Civil Legal Aid and Advice 1977 and the decision of the European Court of Human Rights in *Airey v. Ireland* (1979), which found Ireland to be in breach of Article 6 (fair procedures) and Article 8 (respect for family life) of the European Convention on Human Rights, by not providing free legal aid in family law matters. The scheme was administered by the Legal Aid Board in Law Centres situated throughout the country. The scheme was finally placed on a statutory footing by the Legal Aid Act 1995. The scheme is means-tested and income from all sources, including social welfare payments, is taken into account. A merits test also applies in each case, in that an applicant for legal aid has to satisfy the Board that he has reasonable grounds for taking or defending the case, that he has a reasonable chance of success and that the proceedings are the most satisfactory method of achieving the result sought. In proceedings concerning the welfare of a child, the last mentioned condition does not apply. In addition to supplying legal advice, the Law Centres provide a successful applicant with representation by a solicitor and, where necessary, a barrister.

The general rule is that an applicant can only receive legal aid in having a case dealt with by the lowest court having jurisdiction in the matter in question. However, where an unaided litigant has chosen a higher forum, the applicant may receive aid. The scheme does not cover conveyancing matters or disputes concerning rights and interests in or over land in general. However, property disputes between spouses under section 36 of the Family Law Act 1995 are included, as are proceedings under the Family Home Protection Act 1976 and the Family Law Act 1981. The scheme does not apply to proceedings where an element of foreign law is involved. However, legal aid is available in proceedings under the Child Abduction and Enforcement of Custody Orders Act 1991. See, for example, *M.D. v. A.T.D.* (1998), where the father, an English citizen, was granted legal aid towards the cost of seeking the return of his child who had been brought to Ireland by the mother.

Reform of Family Courts Structure

Because of the ever-increasing volume of cases coming before the Courts administering family law and the outmoded facilities and procedures available to judges and family law practitioners, the urgent need for reform has been officially recognised. A number of significant reports in recent years have highlighted shortcomings in the system, and made very valuable suggestions for reform that would have the effect of transforming the whole area of the administration of family law. The Report of the Law Reform Commission on Family Courts 1996 made a number of very important recommendations, not least the setting up of regional family courts. The Report of the Task Force on Violence Against Women, April 1997 made a number of recommendations in relation to the administration of family law, the most significant being (a) the setting up of regional family courts as recommended by the Law Reform Commission, (b) that the criteria for appointment of judges should include suitability for dealing with family law cases, (c) the provision of specialist training by suitably qualified persons for all those involved in the judicial process, including judges themselves, to improve their awareness and understanding of the complex issues involved in family law matters, and (d) the elimination as far as possible of delays in dealing with family law cases. Other important recommendations of the Task Force Report are dealt with in Chapter 11.

The Report of the Working Group on a Courts Commission, November 1998, which was chaired by Denham J of the Supreme Court, recommended that family law divisions should be set up in the High, Circuit and District Courts, with improved resources in staff and in ancillary services, and that this should be put into effect in the short term. In the longer term, there should be planned progress towards the establishment of regional family courts as recommended by the Law Reform Commission, with Information Desks, staffed by a Courts Assistance Officer, located in all large court venues.

In response to the Task Force on Violence Against Women Report, the Government set up the National Steering Committee on Violence Against Women. The latter body issued its first Interim Report in March 1999. In Chapter 6 of the Steering Committee Report entitled "The Law - Responses and Developments", it is stated that the recommendation of the Law Reform Commission that regional family courts be set up is "under active consideration" and that the recommendations of the Working Group on a Courts Commission referred to above are "under consideration". The Steering Committee Report points out that the principle of judicial independence enshrined in the Constitution "excludes any action by the Executive which could be interpreted as direct interference in the exercise of those functions including imposing a training or briefing programme on them". The Report also refers to the fact that the Minister for Justice, Equality and Law Reform has made funds available for judges, at all levels, to enable them attend information seminars and conferences both at home and abroad. Also, the Courts and Court Officers Act 1995 provides that any person applying for appointment as a judge must be prepared to undertake such courses of training or education as requested by the Chief Justice or the President of the Court to which that person may be appointed. The Report then goes on to state that it is intended to have a network of Family Law Courts throughout the country with separate family law suites. An Information Desk has been set up in the Four Courts in Dublin, and the situation with regard to other venues is under review.

Further Reading

Shatter, *Family Law* 4th Ed. Dublin: Butterworths 1997.

Duncan & Scully, *Marriage Breakdown in Ireland: Law and Practice*. Dublin: Butterworths (Ireland) 1990.

Law Reform Commission. Report on Family Courts (LRC 52 – 1996).

Report of Task Force on Violence Against Women. Dublin: Stationery Office, April 1997.

First Report of National Steering Committee on Violence Against Women. Dublin: Stationery Office, March 1999.

INDEX

Index

Index

Garda Siochana
  child abduction, powers in relation to, 226
  emergency care orders, powers under, 232–3
  removal of child to safety, powers as to, 232
gifts
  engaged couples, between, 14–15
  third parties, from, 15
  wedding gifts, 14
grave risk defence
  child abduction cases, 218–19
guardian *ad litem*
  custody and access disputes, role in, 198
  power of court to appoint, 240
guardianship of children, 183, 184–5
  constitutional position, 184
  court-appointed guardians, 187
  divorce situations and, 67
  Guardianship of Infants Act 1964, 184–5
    definition of 'infant', 184
  joint guardianship, 184
  jurisdiction of courts
    Circuit Court, 252
    District Court, 251
    High Court, 256
  non-marital child, 6, 183, 184
  parental rights and duties, 5, 183
    natural father's rights, 6–7
    natural mother's rights, 7
  separation agreement, clause in, 46
  testamentary guardians, 187

habeas corpus
  High Court jurisdiction, 256
habitual residence
  child, of, 209–10
Hague Conference on Private International Law (1980), 203
Hague Convention on Protection and Co-Operation in respect of Intercountry Adoptions (1993), 179–81
Hague Convention on the Civil Aspects of International Child Abduction (1980), 203, 207–21

Hague Convention on the Protection of Children in International Situations (1996), 198–200
health boards
  care and protection of children, role in, 228–47. *see* further Child care
  access, facilitation of, 244
  adoption services, provision of, 231–2
  assistance for child on leaving care, 245
  care orders, 233–7
  courts' powers and jurisdiction, 240–242
  duty to promote welfare of children, 229–30
  emergency care orders, 232–3
  facilitation of voluntary care, 230–231
  foster care, placement of children in, 243–4
  homeless children, duties towards, 231
  placement of child with relatives, 244
  provision of care, 242–4
  removal of child from custody of person with whom placed, 245
  report as to adequacy of services, 230
  residential care, 242–3, 246–7
  review of cases, 244–5
  supervision orders, 235–6
  unlawful removal of child from health board care, 245–6
  welfare principle, 237–40
  child abduction cases, role in, 226–7
  domestic violence, role in
    safety or barring orders, applications for, 144–5
High Court
  appellate jurisdiction, 256
  consultative jurisdiction, 254
  family law jurisdiction, 254–6
    exclusive jurisdiction, 255–6
  guardianship and maintenance, jurisdiction in relation to, 256
  judicial review, powers of, 254
  supervisory jurisdiction, 254
homeless children, 230, 231
homosexuality
  invalidation of marriage and, 35–6

Index

judicial separation *continued*
  jurisdiction of courts
    Circuit Court, 253
    High Court, 255
  mediation, 44, 63–4
  pension entitlements, preservation of, 89
  reconciliation, 63–4
  rescission of decree, application for, 50
  separation agreement bar to obtaining
    decree of, 44, 50–51
  succession rights and, 50
jurisdiction of courts
  international co-operation in protection
    of children (Hague Convention),
    198–200

Law Reform Commission
  Report on Family Courts 1996, 257
Law Society
  Law Reform Committee Report on
    Domestic Violence (1999), 141, 143,
    147
legal aid, 256–7
  means test, 257
  merits test, 257
Legal Aid Board, 257
legitimacy, 151–2
legitimation, 154–5, 195
  placement of child for adoption prior to,
    195–6
  re-registration of birth, 156
lex domicilii, 16
lex loci celebrationes, 17
life assurance
  financial compensation orders, 83
  separation agreement and, 47
limping marriage, 70
living apart. *see also* Desertion
  divorce, ground for, 67–8
  judicial separation, ground for, 59–60,
    60–61
lump sum orders, 78–9, 106
  variation or discharge of, 101
lump sum payment, 45
Luxembourg Convention (1980), 203–4,
  221–6

maintenance. *see also* Maintenance orders
  agreement not to apply for, 45
  annual review of maintenance payments,
    45
  default in making maintenance
    payments, 111–12
  husband's common law duty to maintain
    wife, 104
  jurisdiction of courts
    Circuit Court, 252
    District Court, 251
    High Court, 256
  law relating to, 104–6
  lump sum payment, 45, 106
  mutual duty to maintain, 104–5
  periodic payments, 45, 106
  separation agreement, clause in, 45–6
    court order and, 45
    rule of court, 45–6
  void agreements, 45
maintenance orders, 104–14
  assessment of maintenance, 106–9
    needs of the family, 106–8
    property, financial resources and
      responsibilities, 106
    second relationship, effect of, 108–9
    separation agreement, effect of, 109
    spousal misconduct, relevance of, 108
  criteria, 104
  dependent children, for, 105
  discharge or variation of, 110
  enforcement of, 111–12
    attachment of earnings order, 111–12
    distress orders, 112
    foreign orders, 112–17
    imprisonment, 112
  foreign orders
    recognition and enforcement of, 112–17
  payment method, 111
  periodic and lump sum payments, 106
maintenance pending suit orders, 78
  variation or discharge of, 101
mandamus, order of, 254
manic depression, 30, 35
marital breakdown. *see also* Divorce; Judicial
  separation; Separation agreement

272